Semantic Web Security:

A Privacy-enhanced Usage Control Model

Sławomir Grzonkowski

Semantic Web Security: A Privacy-enhanced Usage Control Model

Preface

The role of cryptography has been decisive for modern civilization as it is one of the most fundamental building blocks of reliable communication. This invention, in its original form, is credited to ancient Egyptians, who used a simple code of hieroglyphic substitutions to enable privileged individuals to protect and share their knowledge.

The same benefits were rediscovered later by Julius Caesar who was using ROT-3, an encryption scheme also based on the idea of subsisting characters. Such a simple cipher was one of the key elements in the successful execution of his famous strategy known as divide and conquer.

Ancient Celts who were living in the territories of present Ireland developed a sample solution for Caesar's tactics: their cryptic Ogham alphabet [MacNeill 1929; Carney 1975]. The goal was to become independent from the usage of Latin so the neighboring Romans could not understand it. This invention is the first documented usage of cryptography in Ireland and it resulted in both military and religious advantages. It is noteworthy that Vigenère cipher, an extended version of Caesar's encryption, was still in use by the Confederacy in the 19th century during the American Civil War.

In more recent history, information security had also crucial impact on the world in which we live today: the Enigma machine was an electro-mechanical cipher machine build by Nazi Germany to encrypt messages during World War II. However, its algorithms were broken by the members of the Polish Cipher Bureau and handed over to the Allies before the outbreak of war. Thus all communication that was sent by this machine was compromised. This fact had an undoubted influence on the World War II results.

Today's ecommerce solutions also rely on cryptography. One of the most successful algorithms was announced in 1978 by Rivest, Shamir and Adleman as RSA. It enabled public key infrastructure by providing a practical means to realize reliable asymmetric cryptography, which are still in use nowadays products. After the RSA patent had expired, the UK intelligence announced that its employee Clifford Cocks, a British mathematician, described an equivalent system in an internal document in 1973. Since this document was classified, this government agency did not publicly acknowledge Cocks' contribution for the duration of the RSA patent.

My adventure with security and cryptography began in early 2005, when Digital Enterprise Research Institute (DERI) and Gdansk University of Technology (GUT) began their cooperation. I was working in a small team of research interns to develop a distributed system for managing distributed user profiles. One of my tasks was to pay special attention to security aspects of this system. This work focused my research interests on security topics and after the conclusion of this original project it led me to undertake the PhD studies which form the core material of this book.

Sławomir Grzonkowski, Galway, Ireland, 2012

Acknowledgments

I would like to thank to my supervisor, Dr. Peter Corcoran, for his proactive guidance through academia and supervision of this thesis work, and also for spending many hours improving my thesis even if his tight schedule did not allow him to. I am especially thankful for taking me over after one year of my studies.

I am also thankful to Bill McDaniel for providing a very good environment for work within the e-learning cluster and later in the DAI stream. In particular I appreciate the fact that he let me investigate thoroughly the ideas I believed in.

I thank to Prof. Stefan Decker for giving me the opportunity of doing my Ph.D in DERI; and for his support and supervision at the early stage of my studies.

I am indebted to Dr. Brian Wall for seeing opportunity in my ideas and also for stimulating me to work hard on them.

I would like to thank other people who worked with me, especially to Wojciech Zaremba for his help on on the early ZKP prototype implementation; and to Łukasz Korczyński and Anna Dąbrowska for their great performance on the SeDiCi project.

I am also thankful to prof. Manfred Hauswirth for his constructive feedback on the final version of this thesis, and also for his help in formulating a well structured documentation of my research.

I would also like to express my gratitude to prof. Witold Abramowicz for agreeing to be my external examiner, his scientific support, and also for his time and energy in reviewing my thesis.

I thank to my peers, colleagues and mentors at DERI for many stimulating conversations about research ideas and also for their help in settling in Ireland.

My work also benefited from Enterprise Ireland due to its financial support under the grants no. *ILP/05/203* and REI1005.

I dedicate the highest thanks to my parents, Elżbieta and Kazimierz, without their help I could not possibly done this work. They kept motivating me, even in the most stressful moments.

Sławomir Grzonkowski, Galway, Ireland, 2010

Abstract

Recently we have observed a growing demand for secure technologies for e-commerce that do not put customers at risk of identity theft. We have also experienced the advent of Web 2.0 which has led to new business models and which has changed the way users interact with the Web. This thesis proposes a set of strategies and enhancements towards providing improved security and privacy in such new settings.

We introduce a novel concept: Fair Rights Management (FRM). It can be classified as a usage control solution. FRM enables a flexible way of managing digital content. There was a need to provide additional security extensions to keep such a flexible model applicable. Thus, in our approach we take advantage of trust obtained from social networks. This is also the reason why we created an efficient zero-knowledge proof protocol that is lightweight enough to be deployed within existing web-applications. The proposed protocol is also successfully integrated with Semantic Web architecture and associated components. It enables practical Web and mobile applications which employ trust-based transactions as part of their workflow. This core contribution overcomes various disadvantages of prior art and enables a range of new applications and potentially new business models.

We show that compared to existing Usage Control Models (UCON) (i) FRM is a step towards fair use in the digital world and we also argue that our approach is enforced by law; (ii) the participants of the proposed solution do not put their privacy at risk. Our research shows that existing infrastructure is sufficient to support ZKP-based solutions; and thus, it is feasible to offer the users enhanced privacy within existing deployed solutions.

Contents

Preface   i

Acknowledgments   iii

Abstract   v

Contents   vii

I   Prelude   1

1   Introduction   5

1.1   Motivation   5

1.2   Research Questions   7

1.3   Contribution   8

1.4   Reader's Guide   9

II   State of the Art   13

2   Management and Usage Control of Digital Media   17

2.1   Access Control   18

2.2   Trust Management   21

2.3   Digital Rights Management   23

2.4   Usage Control Models   29

2.5   Fair Use 31

2.6   Summary and Conclusion 34

3 Web Authentication   **37**

3.1   Vulnerabilities of Authentication Protocols 38

3.2   Web Authentication Solutions 41

3.3   Summary and Conclusion 48

4 Trust Issues in The Social Semantic Web   **51**

4.1   Social Networks 51

4.2   Friend-of-a-Friend Vocabulary 54

III   Core   **59**

5 Conceptual Model   **63**

5.1   Existing Usage Control Solutions 63

5.2   FRM Usage Control Model 64

5.3   Structure of Authorization Decision 66

5.4   Model Definitions 67

5.5   Summary 70

6 Zero Knowledge Proof Authentication   **71**

6.1   Zero Knowledge Proof Authentication 71

6.2   Approaches to ZKP 73

6.3   Protocol Compositions 76

6.4   Usability Considerations of using ZKP Protocols 78

7 Implementation   **79**

7.1   Conceptual Model Implementation 79

7.2   Trust Management and Access Control 82

7.3   Applied Rights Expression Model 83

7.4   Rights Management Vocabularies 86

7.5 Digital Watermarking 88

7.6 Authentication Service 90

7.7 Application Scenarios 97

8 Evaluation **103**

8.1 Usability of a Web-based ZKP implementation 103

8.2 Sequential Composition 105

8.3 Parallel Composition 106

8.4 Concurrent Composition 114

8.5 Other Protocol Threats 117

8.6 Open Questions of Graph Isomorphism 118

8.7 Summary and Conclusion 119

IV Conclusions **121**

9 Summary and Future Work **125**

9.1 Summary 125

9.2 Conclusions and Contributions 126

9.3 Future Work 128

V Appendices **129**

A FRM Implementation Design **133**

A.1 Object Discovery 133

A.2 Object Download 134

A.3 Member Item 134

A.4 Borrow Object 134

A.5 Buy Object 135

A.6 Digital Watermarking 136

A.7 Content Player 136

B RDF Examples of FRM Data Samples   139

C Sampled Data   141

   C.1 Parallel composition 141

   C.2 Concurrent composition 141

D Academic Contributions   145

   D.1 Principle Academic Contributions 145

   D.2 Supplemental Publications and Academic Contributions 152

   D.3 Volunteer Work & Contributions 152

Bibliography   155

List of Figures   173

List of Tables   175

Glossary   177

Index   179

Part I

Prelude

*"I, myself, have had many failures and I've learned
that if you are not failing a lot, you are probably
not being as creative as you could be
-you aren't stretching your
imagination."*

— John Warner Backus

Chapter **1**

Introduction

In this chapter we explain our motivations and goals. A short historical overview of e-commerce and information dissemination solutions is presented to provide a context for our research. A reader's guide and overview of the thesis structure are also provided.

1.1 Motivation

There are two primary motivations for the research presented in this thesis. The first is the growing demand for secure technologies for e-commerce that do not put customers at risk of identity theft. The second is the advent of Web 2.0 and the social semantic web. It has led to new business models and has changed the way that user's interact with the web.

1.1.1 E-commerce

Commerce is defined as the exchange of goods and services between parties, typically for money. Originally, such exchanges were made face to face. Thus there was a natural element of trust increased by the familiarity of the seller by the buyer [Gefen 2000]. In the today's world we rely more and more on e-commerce, which at its most basic, is simply commerce as usual but transacted using electronic communication methods such as the telephone or internet. We are no longer able to have face to face meetings with the sellers, but we still need to gain trust somehow because *"virtually every commercial transaction has within itself an element of trust, certainly any transaction conducted over a period of time"* [Arrow 1972]. Trust also increases quality of business relations, reduces the need for exhausting negotiations, and decreases risk [Fukuyama 1995]. Therefore if we give up trust that we can gain, it will have drastic and painful consequences on our actions [Gambetta 1988].

In e-commerce, which is conducted without the physical presence of the parties, the necessity of other forms of trust became immediately obvious. New technologies such as Social Semantic Web (see Section 1.1.2) enabled new ways of capturing trust. For example, they made us able to use web technologies to explicitly define and rank the persons we trust and take advantage of the specified preferences during e-commerce transactions (see Section 4.1.1).

In electronically mediated transactions it is far easier for eavesdroppers to access, copy, redirect, and subvert legitimate transactions. Another problem is identity theft. This was a cumbersome and manual process for many years, but the advent of electronic records, communications, and commerce has made identity theft far easier and far more prevalent [Schneier 2008].

Consequently, an emerging science and industry have grown up around the security and authentication issues associated with e-commerce. New methods of encrypting transactions, of authenticating participants, and of protecting the identities of participants have been developed and used in practical e-commerce applications. We note, however, that existing solutions rely on the computational difficulty of certain mathematical functions such as integer factorization [Rivest *et al.* 1978]. Such solutions can become obsolete overnight with the advent of quantum computer that will be able to solve such functions in a polynomial time [Shor 1997]. The advent of quantum computing suggests that not only algorithms, but also the underlying mathematical problems will become outdated. For instance, it will be possible to detect eavesdropping; and thus, offer better protection against man-in-the-middle (see Section 3.1.2) attacks [Wegman & Carter 1981].

The current explosion of commerce onto the web could not have happened without trustable, verifiable, and simple security processes built into the workflow of e-commerce. As we move from wired connections to the web, new techniques and workflows are needed to ensure that wireless e-commerce transactions, which are easier to intercept and subvert, are secure and protected. Therefore, we need reliable security models which can scale over time to meet these attempts to subvert them, otherwise e-commerce transactions cannot continue to grow in value and convenience.

1.1.2   Web 2.0 and Social Semantic Web

The cost of information decreases over the span of human history. Initially being able to broadcast information was a unique privilege of kings and emperors. The advent of books provided much wider access to information and greatly facilitated its dissemination for educated people. The cost of making copies was still high and the average person could not afford to posses many books. The crucial achievement for the man kind was the discovery of electricity. Firstly, radio made audio information easy to broadcast to the masses. Radio devices were affordable for many individuals; and it was also possible for a group of people to listen to it at the same time. Shortly afterwards, TV enabled broadcasting of "moving pictures" in addition to audio information, broadening the appeal and further facilitating a wider dissemination of information. Since the 20th century, broadcasting information to the masses became a part of everyday life, although the costs of such broadcast were still prohibitive for a single individual.

The era when only only organizations or privileged individuals were able to broadcast information ended in 1989 after Tim Berners-Lee's conceived the idea of the World Wide Web (WWW). His project delivered a system for sharing interlinked hypertext documents that contained text, images and, eventually, other types of media files. Initially the project was designed for scientific communities, but it quickly gained world-wide approval as a communication choice of the future. WWW enabled individuals to both broadcast and to receive information. The former required an individual to posses a web server and some knowledge about creating hypertext pages. The later, required some equipment such a computer.

Two decades of continuos web development have resulted in many new ways that people use the web. It has become much more interactive and collaborative than its original creators envisaged. Nowadays users do not need to own servers and broadcasting is much easier. For example, a free blog account is now enough for an individual to start disseminating information. Today's web permeates many aspects of everyday life and can be received on mobile devices in more and more sophisticated ways. As a consequence of all these new ways in which the web is used, nowadays it is often referred as Web 2.0 [Musser & O'Reilly 2006]. However, Web 2.0 is not a set of new specifications or extensions, but is rather a landmark to describe how we use the Web today.

The growing volume of information broadcasted has caused other problems: as individuals we are overloaded with information. Thus, the World Wide Web Consortium (W3C), an organization lead by Tim Berners-Lee, has proposed an improvement to the original idea: the Semantic Web [Berners-Lee & Fischetti 1999].

Unlike Web 2.0, Semantic Web was proposed as an extension to the original web. It has a layered architecture[1] with the trust component forming the top, overarching, layer of the stack. Thus, the full protocol stack must be built before true semantic web applications will be brought into main stream usage.

An important step towards trust is Social Semantic Web (S2W). It emphasizes the importance of user created semantics and also takes into account relationships between the users. There are many facets of S2W. In this thesis we mainly focus on trust gained through users' social networks. We consider its benefits that could be used in existing e-commerce solutions such as Digital Rights Management (DRM) as there is a need to make it more consumer-friendly.

1.2 Research Questions

In the following chapters of this thesis we will address and answer a number of research questions, which are briefly summarized in this section:

- **How to create a more user-friendly DRM that offers a similar level of security as existing solutions?** Existing Digital Rights Management (DRM) solutions are outdated and do not satisfy customers' needs [Samuelson 2003]. They do not offer real social sharing that could begin to introduce Fair Use to the digital world [DMM 2003]. Usage Control solutions (UCON) that are the next evolution step following DRM inherit the same deficiency.

- **What is necessary to enable better privacy in existing DRM/UCON solutions?** UCON does not provide support to protect a users' privacy as it has been studied only rarely in the context of usage control for digital information [Park & Sandhu 2004].

---

[1]http://www.w3.org/2000/Talks/1206-xml2k-tbl/slide10-0.html

- **How Semantic Web technologies can be used to improve security of web applications?** Semantic Web technologies [Berners-Lee & Fischetti 1999] such as Friend-of-a-Friend (FOAF) [Dan Brickley and Libby Miller 2005] could potentially address the deficiency of social sharing in the context of web solutions because FOAF was designed to define an open, decentralized technology for connecting social Web sites, and the people they describe. However, this is still unclear how it could be achieved because FOAF was not designed to provide secure authentication and authorization.

- **What is necessary to enable authentication protocols using Zero-Knowledge proofs on the web?** Zero-Knowledge Proof (ZKP) [Goldwasser *et al.* 1985] authentication protocols are known as the most secure way of proving users' identity. ZKP could be used together with FOAF to provide both social aspects of the web and high security. Although there are many theoretical foundations for ZKP, for instance [Goldreich *et al.* 1988; Feige *et al.* 1988; Bellare *et al.* 1990; Goldreich & Krawczyk 1990; Goldreich & Krawczyk 1996; Dwork *et al.* 2004], such protocols still have not been widely used within existing web solutions. The reason is that ZKP protocols rely on a public key infrastructure that requires users to posses digital certificates; however, the vast majority of users are accustomed to password-based approaches to digital security.

- **What is necessary to enable more secure authentication protocols that does not involve digital certificates?** Digital certificates, which are used for example within SSL/TLS [Dierks & Allen 1999] protocols, are the foundation of the today's e-commerce, but this approach still does not take advantage of their full potential to preserve users' privacy: the users' credentials are still sent to the authenticating servers. Thus enabling a lightweight ZKP for web application that would preserve the users' privacy is still a challenging task.

1.3 Contribution

The research conducted by the author focuses on the synergy between security, trust, privacy and Semantic Web technologies. In particular, this thesis makes the following contributions:

- **A practical ZKP solution.** Our main contribution (see also Section 9.2) is the implementation of a practical and working version of ZKP that is successfully integrated with the Semantic Web architecture and associated components and which enables practical Web and mobile applications employing trust-based transactions as part of their workflow.

- **New business models for e-commerce.** Our core contribution overcomes various disadvantages of the prior art and enables a range of new applications and potentially new business models.

- **Better security and privacy for existing authentication solutions.** Our research shows that the existing infrastructure is sufficient to support ZKP-based solutions; and thus, it is feasible to offer the users enhanced privacy within the already deployed solutions.

- **A new model for DRM.** We also develop an improved DRM that we designed to meet the need of using social networks. We call it Fair Rights Management (FRM). We show that when compared to existing UCON solutions, FRM represents a significant step towards enabling fair use for social networks and we also argue that our approach can support a practical realization of fair use for digital content which is in keeping with current interpretations of the law.

This thesis is partially composed of the author's publications published as refereed papers in the proceedings of several international peer-reviewed journals, conferences and workshops. The preliminary publications relevant for this research were published in [Grzonkowski *et al.* 2005] and [Kruk *et al.* 2006b]. Then, contributions on authentication and trust were published in [Grzonkowski & Corcoran 2009; Grzonkowski *et al.* 2009; Grzonkowski *et al.* 2008b]. Our research on Digital Rights Management and access control was published in [Grzonkowski *et al.* 2007; Grzonkowski & McDaniel 2008]. This thesis also contains novel work that has not been published elsewhere. This unpublished work describes the conceptual model in Chapter 5 and its implementation in Chapter 7. A complete list of peer-reviewed publications is in Appendix D.

1.4 Reader's Guide

The thesis is divided into five main parts as shown in Figure 1.1. That includes a number of appendices. Every chapter is preceded with a brief introductory paragraph which explains how the work presented in that section fits with in the overall structure of the thesis. These parts are organized as follows:

- Part I - Prelude

    - *Chapter 1: Introduction*. It presents the thesis goals and structure of the thesis.

- Part II - State of the Art

    - *Chapter 2: Management and Usage Control of Digital Media*. Section 2.1 explains the historical developments of *Matrix Access Control*. This section also presents basic principles of authentication and authorization. We focus on Role-Based Access Control (RBAC), which is relevant for the definitions introduced in Chapter 4. RBAC is also relevant for understanding the prototype implementation presented in Chapter 7. Then, we introduce fundamental concepts of Digital Rights Management (DRM), Trust Management and Usage Control Models that are closely related to our main hypothesis. These are described in detail in the later sections of the thesis.

      Section 2.3 presents DRM in a more detailed way. Firstly, we give an overview of the controversial Digital Millennium Copyright Act (DMCA). Then, we discuss typical DRM software architectures. In this context the concept of Rights Expression Languages (REL) is introduced. We further present DRM solutions that take advantage of Semantic Web infrastructure. Finally, we describe two important DRM concepts: Digital Watermarking and Trusted Computing.

      In Section 2.4 we present a typical architecture of a usage control solution. This architecture is relevant for understanding the improvements demonstrated in Chapters 5 and 7.

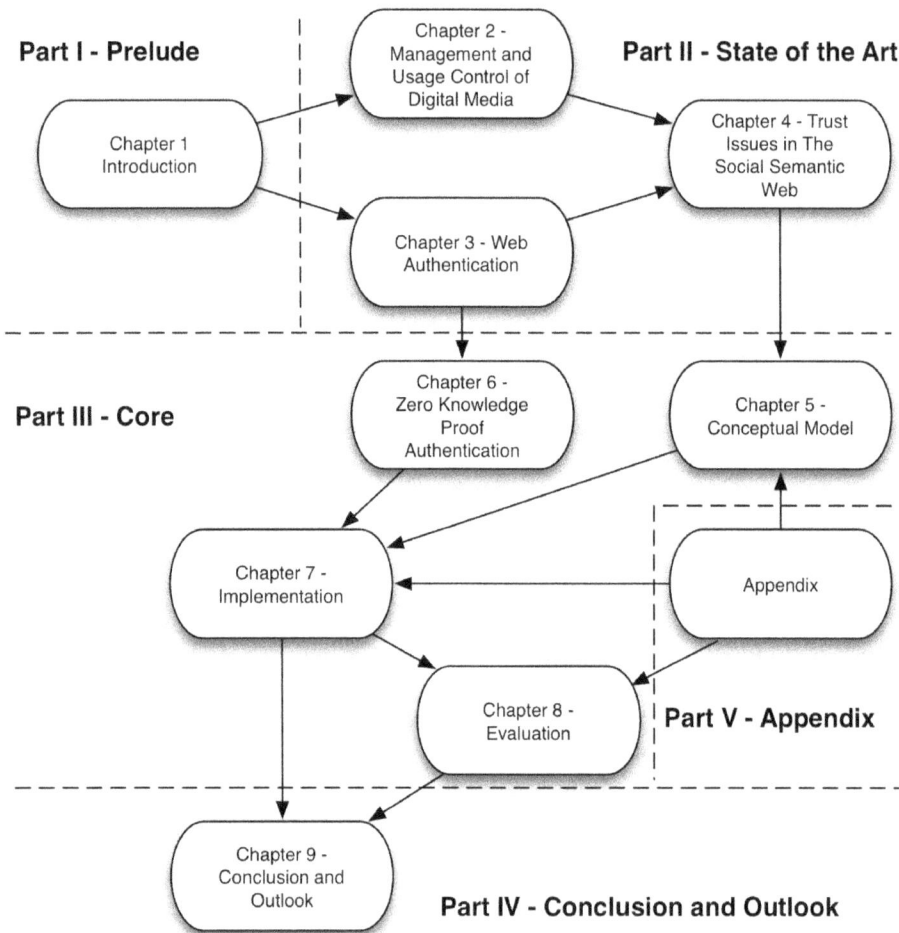

Figure 1.1: Thesis organization and relations between the chapters

Section 2.5 introduces basics of fair use. It describes how fair use is legislated in the U.S. and what are the implications for computer programs. It also describes how existing DRM solutions address the doctrine.

– *Chapter 3: Web Authentication*, presents the classical ways of authenticating users in web applications. In Section 3.1, we describe the main attacks to authentication protocols such as replay, interleaving, reflection, forced delay and chosen text attacks.

Section 3.2 introduces generic HTTP authentication solutions: Basic and Digest. Then, we present SSL/TLS that is widely used for e-commerce purposes. We also briefly describe the Kerberos protocol which forms the basis of a secure single sign-on solution. This idea, however, has not been widely deployed on the web. OpenID and OAuth whose concepts resemble those of the original Kerberos are becoming more popular as web authentication solutions and are also described. Here we discuss an authentication approach based on a browser plugin. Finally, we outline the most notable Password-based Authentication Key Exchange (PAKE) solutions that aim to provide secure communication using short and memorable passwords. The main security threats for such solutions are dictionary attacks and lack of resistance to a compromised server.

We conclude the chapter with a short comparison of the existing solutions and discuss their advantages and disadvantages.

– *Chapter 4: Trust Issues in The Social Semantic Web*, presents infrastructure elements that are used to develop the prototype described in Part III. In Section 4.1 we introduce Social Networks [Barnes 1954] that we use to represent relationships between people. Our presentation includes both practical examples and and theoretical definitions. The advent of online social networks has enabled new types of applications that work on top of these networks. Social networks, when combined with trust management, have created novel possibilities in the area of access control. They made authorization of strangers possible. They also provided a possibility of finding trusted users that are not directly connected. In Section 4.2, we present the Friend-of-a-Friend (FOAF) vocabulary which enables the exchange of social data on the web. We specifically focus on its applicability for trust management and authentication.

- Part III - Core

  – *Chapter 5: Conceptual Model*, describes the foundations and the conceptual model of Fair Rights Management (FRM), which is our contribution towards fair use in the digital world. To achieve this goal, we propose taking advantage of social networks and combining these with advanced techniques for negotiation of the terms of a transaction. We demonstrate our approach with a practical use case scenario (see Section 5.1). Next we explain how to apply and implement these proposed improvements into the framework of a more conventional DRM model. FRM introduces a model in which subjects are capable of specifying their own policies (see Section 5.2). Recursive rights delegation to trusted subjects is possible. Then, we demonstrate our improvements on the structure of authentication decisions (see Section 5.3). The model works in distributed environments ensuring that users' credentials and objects are kept secure. Finally, in Section 5.4 we define the necessary conceptual foundations to deliver and enable FRM.

  – *Chapter 6: Zero Knowledge Proof Authentication*, introduces the reader to the Zero Knowledge Proof (ZKP) authentication protocol, which is a secure method of claiming identity. In ZKP, the verifier is unable to learn anything from the authentication procedure and the prover is unable to repeat the procedure with another verifier. In Section 6.1, we describe the foundations of the ZKP idea. We also present a generic ZKP protocol. In Section 6.2, we present the mathematical background that is necessary to create a ZKP protocol. We discuss several approaches and we specifically focus on a class of solutions based on graph isomorphism. We describe various threats for such a protocol. Section 6.3 describes various approaches to composition of ZKP protocols. In Section 6.4, we discuss usability issues for a web deployment of ZKP.

  – *Chapter 7: Implementation*, presents our prototype implementation of Fair Rights Management (FRM) which is a semantic content distribution and usage control platform. The platform uses and extends the semantic web standards to satisfy existing usage control (UCON) requirements. Furthermore, FRM is developed towards the support of the most important fair use scenarios. It also provides a reliable identity management system, machine-readable digital licenses and protection means for the content that is being distributed.

In Section 7.1 we describe in detail how we implement the proposed conceptual model (see Chapter 5). Then, in Section 7.2 we present the applied trust management module. Further, in Section 7.3 we present the Rights Expression Language that we use. Section 7.4 describes the key classes and properties of the ontology model for FRM. Section 7.5 demonstrates our digital watermarking prototype implementation. The largest effort was, however, focused on developing our authentication service using Zero-Knowledge Proof protocol that is described in Section 7.6. Finally, in Section 7.7 we present several application scenarios for FRM and we analyze their threats.

– *Chapter 8: Evaluation*, describes the evaluation of our Zero-Knowledge Proof approach. We determine what are the requirements for a fast and secure implementation that enables practical realizations. In Section 8.1, we measure the number of necessary computations and data requirements across a number of the most popular web browser clients. We test the performance for four different families of web-browsers: Internet Explorer 8, Firefox 3.5, Safari 4, and Opera 9. We analyze stability and predictability of the ZKP algorithm. We also verify if the protocol satisfies the existing response-time standards. To complement our usability considerations, we measure the data overhead that is necessary to provide a successful implementation. We analyze three protocol compositions: sequential in Section 8.2; parallel in Section 8.3; and finally concurrent in Section 8.4. In Section 8.3.5, we use the obtained results to verify if existing browsers are fast enough to perform a secure authentication that is still transparent for end users. In Section 8.2, we analyze a scenario in which our ZKP implementation is sequential. We compare it with a parallel solution and we indicate differences. Then, in Section 8.5, we evaluate our approach against a number of security threats. We model an attack where a hacker is able to break the authentication procedure with a given confidence. We perform our analyses by performing a dictionary attack and also a naive brute-force attack. Finally, we investigate the number of ZKP challenge/authenticate cycles required to enable both a secure and usable solution.

• Part IV - Conclusion

    – *Chapter 9: Summary and Future Work*, sums up the thesis and analysis of the thesis contributions both major and minor.

• Part V - Appendix

    – *Appendix A: FRM Implementation Design* contains applied procedures for making online transactions.

    – *Appendix B: RDF Examples of FRM Data Samples* contains sample RDF data associated with presented diagrams.

    – *Appendix C: Sampled Data* contains results that we obtained conducting our evaluation for Chapter 8.

    – *Appendix D: Academic contributions* contains a list of publications and other academic contributions related to this studies.

Part II

State of the Art

*"To know that we know what we know, and to know
that we do not know what we do not know,
that is true knowledge."*

— Nicolaus Copernicus

16

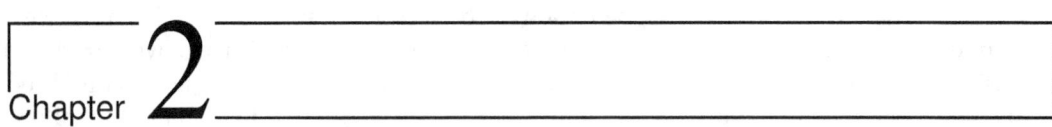

Chapter 2

Management and Usage Control of Digital Media*

The origins of current usage control solutions lie with Matrix Access Control, originally developed in the 1970s [Lampson 1971; Lampson 1974]. This approach and its subsequent historical evolution is described in Section 2.1. Here the basic principles of authentication and authorization are also outlined. We focus on Role-Based Access Control (RBAC), which is relevant for the definitions introduced in Chapter 4. RBAC is also relevant for understanding the prototype implementation presented in Chapter 7. Finally, the fundamental concepts of Digital Rights Management (DRM), Trust Management and Usage Control Models are introduced. These are closely related to the main hypothesis of this thesis and are described in detail in later sections.

Section 2.3 presents DRM in greater technical detail. Firstly, we describe the controversial Digital Millennium Copyright Act (DMCA). Then, we demonstrate typical DRM software architectures. We further describe Rights Expression Languages (REL) and present DRM solutions using the Semantic Web. Finally, we describe two important DRM components: Digital Watermarking and Trusted Computing.

In Section 2.4 we present a typical structure of a usage control solution. This structure is relevant for understanding the improvements demonstrated in Chapters 5 and 7.

Section 2.5 introduces basics of fair use. It describes how fair use is legislated in the U.S. and what are the implications. It also describes how existing DRM solutions implement fair use.

---

*This chapter is partially based on [Grzonkowski *et al.* 2007; Grzonkowski & McDaniel 2008; Grzonkowski *et al.* 2010]

2.1 Access Control

In this section we present basic principles of authentication and authorization. We further show the evolution of access control models, paying special attention to Role-based Access Control (RBAC) that is related to the notion introduced in Chapter 4. RBAC is also relevant to understand the prototype implementation presented in Chapter 7. Then, we introduce the basic concepts of Digital Rights Management, Trust Management and Usage Control Models that are fundamental to our main hypothesis. These are described in detail in the following sections.

2.1.1 Authorization and Authentication

Access control is an important aspect of computer security. It allows to permit or deny the use of a particular resource by a particular entity. It also defines the ways in which users can access system's resources. The first formal definitions of access control appeared in research papers of the early 1970s. The most fundamental concepts of access control are authorization and authentication. During the process of authentication, the user's claimed identity is confirmed. There are three main ways to confirm it [Schneier 2005]:

- *Something you know* - for example a password or PIN

- *Something you have* - for example an usb key or a swipe card

- *Something you are* - for example a retina pattern or a fingerprint

An authentication process was for a long time considered secure, if the user's identity was confirmed in at least two of three aforementioned ways. However, in the era of online financial transactions this is no longer considered a sufficient criterion for security [Schneier 2005]. Thus, there are efforts to improve the existing procedures such as [Brainard *et al.* 2006] who have proposed using using social networks, i.e., *somebody you know* as a fourth requirement for user authentication.

Since its introduction in the 1970s, access control gained a lot of attention and it has evolved through developments in trust management, digital rights management and usage control systems.

2.1.2 Access Control Models

The first widely-applied and formalized access control model was called Matrix Access Control [Lampson 1971; Lampson 1974]. In this model subjects initiate actions on objects. These actions can be permitted or denied depending on the access rights expressed in the authorization specification. This model is still widely used for describing resources in operating systems. Figure 2.1 depicts an example typical for Unix, in which subjects are given with read, write or execute permissions. For instance, *Alice* is given read and execute permissions to *File 1* that is own by *Bob*.

	File 1	File 2	File 3
Alice	rx	rwx	
Bob	rwx, owner		rwx, owner
Carol		rwx, owner	r

Figure 2.1: An example of access matrix model

Further research on this model resulted in other formal models and standards. Bell-Lapadula [Bell & Lapadula 1973] introduced extensions dedicated to the military needs. In 1983, the U.S. Department of Defense (DoD) proposed Discretionary Access Control (DAC) and Mandatory Access Control (MAC) models [Klein 1983]. However, claims that DAC was inappropriate for many commercial and civilian applications, resulted in the creation of Role-Based Access Control (RBAC). The main idea of RBAC (see Figure 2.2) was that the permissions should no longer be directly assigned to subjects (users), but rather to roles which are assigned to the subjects. The initial idea was extended with two important improvements: (i) subjects are also allowed having multiple sessions; (ii) roles can have constraints attached.

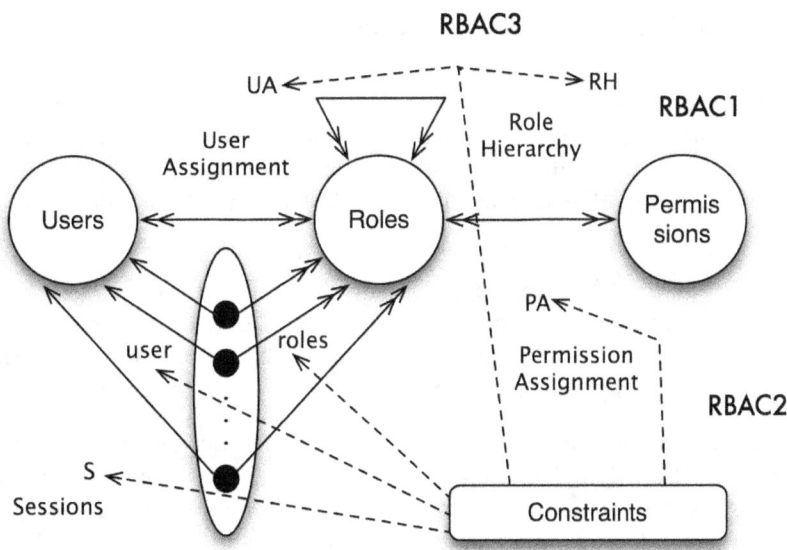

Figure 2.2: Role Based Access Control model [Sandhu *et al.* 1996]

[Ferraiolo & Kuhn 1992] proposed a formal definition of RBAC in 1992. Then, in 1996 [Sandhu *et al.* 1996] presented an RBAC framework consisting of four models. RBAC0 that specifies the minimum requirement for any implementation. RBAC1 that adds the concept of role hierarchies. Roles can inherit permissions from other roles. RBAC2 introduced constraints to the model. Both RBAC1 and RBAC2 include RBAC0 but they are incompatible with each other. The last model called RBAC3 merges properties of the all previous models: RBAC0, RBAC1, and RBAC2. The standardization of RBAC [Sandhu *et al.* 2000; Ferraiolo *et al.* 2001] began in 2000 and was finished in 2004.

After the success of RBAC, the main research stream was directed to adding contextual information to authorization decisions. [Nitsche *et al.* 1998] gave a high level description of a system using contextual information in medical workflows. [Bertino *et al.* 2001] proposed a language and algorithms to enforce constraints to ensure that tasks are performed within a given workflow and performed by predefined subjects and roles. [Ahn & Sandhu 2000] presented how to ensure security properties in RBAC using constraints. [Jajodia *et al.* 2001] presented an approach with contextual information that allowed for the specification of different access control policies that coexisted in the same system. [Covington *et al.* 2001] have extended RBAC with the notion of environment roles to provide context-aware applications. The roles were used to capture environment state. [Neumann & Strembeck 2003] presented xoRBAC: an integrated approach to engineer and enforce context constraints in RBAC environments. They demonstrated how to design and implement existing RBAC services to enable the enforcement of context constrains. The constraint evaluation component is the main element of xoRBAC. It checks if a set of actual sensor values match the corresponding context constraints and returns either true or false, depending on the result of the evaluation. Other significant efforts were focused on the support of teams, collaboration, permission delegation or providing temporal authorization.

2.1.3   Further Evolution of Access Control

The initial scope of access control has evolved from RBAC. This evolution went through Trust management and Digital Rights Management (DRM). The most recent trends are directed towards creating a usage control (UCON) framework [Zhang *et al.* 2008; Park & Sandhu 2004] that covers the aforementioned concepts. It provides a general purpose solution for protecting digital resources.

The concept of Trust Management was introduced by [Blaze *et al.* 1996] . Similarly to access control, trust management focuses on the control of access to server-side objects. This concept, however, relates authorization to a subject's capabilities and properties. Thus, opposite to access control, *trust management enables authorization of strangers.*

DRM extends the scope of access control to client-side devices. Again this has led to an evolution in the original concept of RBAC, as DRM is not only responsible for providing access control, but also for protecting the content after access is given to the user. Thus, it has to provide access control regardless the data location [Arnab & Hutchison 2007]. Other authors consider DRM as a special case of access control and delegation of rights [Adelsbach *et al.* 2005]. However, several differences were highlighted by these authors:

- Work in the context of access control usually does not consider operating systems, where rights may be distributed from a large number of a-priori unknown parties

- In access control systems verification of delegated resources is done by the reference monitor before granting a subject access to the resource in question

- Verification of delegated rights in their setting is much more involved than in standard applications of access control systems because verification of usage-rights involves similarity tests/proofs of digital works and authorship proofs

Another definition of DRM was proposed by [Rosenblatt & Dykstra 2003] who describe it as *"persistent access control of digital data"*.

2.2 Trust Management

The definition of trust used in this thesis is an attempt to merge the different perspectives of trust taken from the fields of computer science, psychology and sociology. These will now be discussed briefly. We also present examples how trust in computed in practical solutions. We shall provide our interpretation of what we mean by the term "trust" in the context of the current thesis in Chapter 4.

2.2.1 The Psychological Point of View

The Oxford English Dictionary [Simpson & Weiner 1971] defines trust as: *"Confidence in or reliance on some quality or attribute of a person or thing, or the truth of a statement"*. In fact, trust is often used interchangeably with related words like credibility, confidence or reliability. Trust is the basis for interpersonal interaction and also especially for cooperation within a social network (see Section 4.1). This leads to the question of how we can gain trust.

From the psychological point of view, the answer to this question originates from the theory of human attitudes. The theory specifies attitudes as "a person's inclination or tendency to evaluate in positive, neutral or negative ways other people, institutions, activities or even ideas", from [Eagly & Chaiken 1993].

In the process of forming an "attitude" there are three primary evaluative components [Eagly & Chaiken 1993]: (i) the cognitive component is connected with the opinion or belief segment; (ii) the affective component is related to emotions or a feeling segment; finally, there is (iii) the behavioral component which is responsible for the intention to behave in a certain way toward someone or something.

We could then ask how this theory operates in social networks. The affective component begins to operate when we are not able or we have no motivation to perform a rational and detailed analysis [Petty & Cacioppo 1986]. Such situations concern both the physical and virtual worlds. It often happens, when we cannot see the other person, that we have no time to perform such an evaluation or sometimes we are not skilled in the domain he/she represents.

If our motivation is slight and because the result of the aforementioned evaluation was low, there is a risk that the influence of the affective component will dominate the evaluation process. Thus, most people are prone to employ a "liking rule" [Cialdini 2001] especially when we reward others for being similar in appearance to us. It takes effect in statements like: *"He is OK"*, *"he is cheerful"*, but sometimes also: *"He is annoying"*, *"he makes me nervous"*, *"I do not like him"*. Of course, if we take into account only this component, our calculations are very subjective and often are dependent on our state of mind at that particular point in time. Although the emotional component seems to be negligible, research findings show that it is of major importance to the process of attitude formation for most people. One might say that we are ruled by the feelings of our hearts rather than the logic of our minds.

When the behavioral component is activated, the attitude is often perceived as the result of every interaction between two interested peers within a social network. If we behave in positive manner, we are more likely to identify our approach favorably. Similarly, negative experiences may lead to the conclusion that the other party is not likable and thus it is less trusted [Bem 1972]. Although the following examples seem to be paradoxical: *"I met him, so I like him"*, they are coherent with respect to cognitive dissonance theory [Festinger 1957]. We excuse our own behavior in this manner because humans wish to appear rational and consistent when doing things.

While utilizing the cognitive component, the user, who gives an opinion, assumes that the emotional relation is based on a rational and knowingly-established reputation about the other peer. If the central path of persuasion [Petty & Cacioppo 1986] is activated, then the attitude towards a virtual friend will be dependent on an analysis of concrete arguments such as reliability or objectivity.

If we take into account the aforementioned psychological aspects, it seems possible to design and implement a computer system that can evaluate the users of a social network (see Section 4.1). So far, most systems offer only one single summary value that evaluates a specified participant within a network.

The psychological model directs us towards a distributed evaluation of a user. Such an approach enables one to *minimize the subjectivity* of the estimation and puts obligations on the users to provide a more reliable and systematic personal evaluation of each other's participation on the network. In fact, this approach enables one to compare every evaluated person, and thus leads to a more consistent mechanism for evaluating people.

2.2.2 Trust in Computer Science

Unsurprisingly the concept of "trust" is also an important one within the context of computer systems. This has been the case since the early days of the 1960s and 1970s when users accessed a mainframe computer from remote terminals and logged in using usernames and passwords. In such an environment the principle was that only authorized users should have access to the mainframe. Later, during the 1980s and as computers became commoditized and the personal computer became commonplace the use of usernames and passwords was practically abandoned by the more popular operating systems. But when computer networking became ubiquitous during the 1990s the need for strict user authentication re-emerged.

There are three main areas of applying trust in computing: trusted systems, "web of trust", and trust metrics. Trusted systems, which are mainly related to security engineering, encompass areas such as risk management, surveillance, auditing, and communications. Extensive knowledge on security engineering has already been collected and analyzed by

Taipale [Yen *et al.* 2005] and has been researched in the Trusted Systems[1] project, which is a part of Global Information Society Project[2] lead by the World Policy Institute[3]. It investigates systems in which some conditional prediction about the behavior of people or objects within a system has been determined prior to authorizing access to system resources.

Then, the concept of "web of trust" is related to cryptography and focuses on technologies like PGP [Zimmermann 1995], OpenPGP-compatible [Callas *et al.* 2007] or public key infrastructure (PKI) [Gerck 2000]. They offer solutions, which require the trust endorsement of the PKI generated certificate authority (CA)-signed certificates.

The last and most popular concept is called a trust metric. It is also considered within the areas of psychology and sociology. The aim of it is to propose a measure of how a member of a group is trusted by other members. A comprehensive overview of such metrics has been prepared on the Internet community[4]; it presents a brief classification and provides many examples.

Existing metrics are diverse in many aspects. TrustMail [Golbeck *et al.* 2003] and FilmTrust [Golbeck & Hendler 2006] propose to take advantage of a Semantic Web-based social network, whereas other ideas also based on graph walking use different approaches such as subjective logic [Jøsang 1999].

Furthermore, an interesting model [Staab *et al.* 2004; Xiong & Liu 2002][5] was proposed in PeerTrust, which concerns a decentralized Peer-to-Peer electronic community. The important contribution of these authors is to build a trust model that considers only three factors: the amount of satisfaction established during peer interaction, the number of iterations between peers and a balance factor for trust.

The EigenTrust [Kamvar *et al.* 2003] algorithm resembles PageRank [Page *et al.* 1999] but has been used in the context of file-sharing systems. This method computes global trust for peers, where the value is based on the history of uploads. It enables the system to choose the peers with a history of reliable downloads. Therefore, malicious peers can be excluded from the network.

2.3 Digital Rights Management

This section presents Digital Rights Management (DRM). Firstly, we describe the controversial Digital Millennium Copyright Act (DMCA). Then, we describe some typical DRM software architectures. We further describe Rights Expression Languages (REL) and present a DRM solution integrated with the framework of the Semantic Web. Finally, we describe two important DRM components: Digital Watermarking and Trusted Computing. Those concepts are part of the prototype implementation and support the understanding of the material presented in Chapter 7.

---

[1]Trusted systems: http://trusted-systems.info/

[2]The Global Information Society Project: http://global-info-society.org/

[3]World Policy Institute: http://worldpolicy.org/

[4]TrustMetrics: http://moloko.itc.it/trustmetricswiki/moin.cgi/ PaperTrustMetricsSurvey

[5]PeerTrust Homepage: http://www-static.cc.gatech.edu/projects/disl/PeerTrust/

2.3.1 DRM and DMCA

Digital Rights Management (DRM) systems have been in existence since the early 1990s; their initial aim was to control the distribution of consumer media by protecting the content. Since 1998, all such systems are supported by the legal framework of the controversial Digital Millennium Copyright Act (DMCA) [DMCA 1998]. This act is important for the USA where the creation or distribution of DRM circumvention tools is banned. The same law was applied in the European Union several years later by European Union Copyright Directive (EUCD) [European Parliament and Council 2001]. Some critics claim that the European act is even more restrictive [John Leyden 2002] than the DMCA.

Together with those directives, consumers lost some of their physical world privileges like fair use or first sale (see Section 2.5). Existing DRM systems do not support fair use; they offer only limited solutions. Usually, a purchased media file can be played only on one user's device. In the physical world, if we buy a magazine, we can read it, loan it or even sell it; however, we cannot legally copy it or change it without the permission of the copyright holder. Such rights, unfortunately, are not adequately supported by the digital world to date.

The biggest challenge for the software DRM systems is to attach a license to a content in a way that it cannot be removed, and the devices playing the content respect the license terms [LaMacchia 2002]. Therefore, significant research effort is focused on interoperability [Wang 2004; Chiariglione 2006; Koenen *et al.* 2004], specifically creating Rights Expression Languages (REL), and content protection, for instance digital watermarks. However, these efforts to date have led to an over-emphasis on the content protection aspects to the point that that many systems are overly restrictive [Samuelson 2003]. Thus in state-of-the-art approaches to DRM the fair use rights of users are not at all respected.

2.3.2 Digital Rights Management Software Architectures

Although there are many examples of independent DRM implementations, their architectures are similar. For instance, Liu [Liu *et al.* 2003] proposes a typical DRM architecture (see Figure 2.3) that consists of four main components:

- The content provider who represents the digital rights owner

- The distributor who is responsible for selling the provided content

- The consumer who retrieves the content

- The clearinghouse which is responsible for handling financial transactions and issuing licenses

Another model that was proposed by [Erickson 2003] also consists of four components: the content server which is similar to the distributor; the license server that acts in a role analogous to the clearinghouse; the rights escrow server that can be compared to the content provider; and the client side component which represents the consumer from Liu's model. The model proposes several improvements such as considering both clients' conventional and fair use requests.

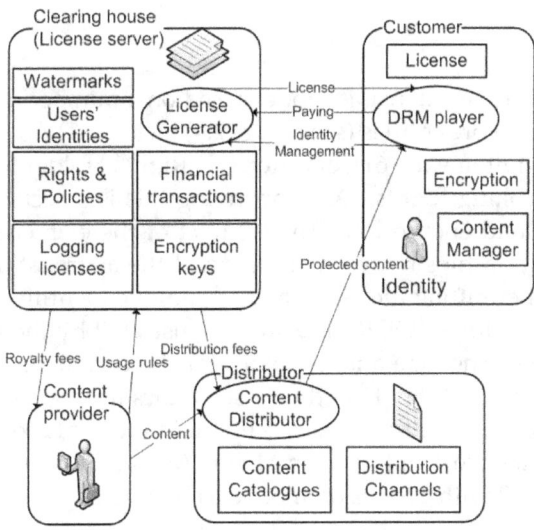

Figure 2.3: A typical-DRM architecture

The model applied in WMRM [Microsoft Corporation 2004] is also compatible with Liu's model. The main difference is the distributor component that was replaced with two modules: Web Server and Streaming Media Server.

[Michiels *et al.* 2005] presented a generalization of such a software DRM architecture and also identified relevant services that should be supported by DRM systems: License Service, Content Service, Access Service, Tracking Service, Import Service, Identification Service, Payment Service and Certification Authority. These services correspond to the aforementioned components.

2.3.3 Rights Expression Languages

Many current successful DRM developments and implementations contain some form of a well formulated and implemented Rights Expression Language (REL) to assist in the expression and understanding of authorized actions. The REL operates as a formal agreement between systems governing permitted activity which is generated by some defined authority and enforced by another. REL has been developed under competing standards, public and proprietary, with some adopted into commercial DRM solutions. Extensible Rights Markup Language (XrML) and Open Digital Rights Languages (ODRL) are the most notable [Rodriguez & Delgado 2006] solutions.

This section present the state of the art in this domain. In Chapter 7 we further define our own rights expression language taking advantage of Semantic Web technologies that we developed in our implementation.

ODRL

ODRL [Iannella 2002] is an extensible model based on a number of core entities and their relationships. The eleven core entities (see Figure 2.4) include: 1) Asset, 2) Party, 3) Permissions, 4) Constraints, 5) Requirements, 6) Conditions, 7) Rights Holders, 8) Contexts, 9) Offers, 10) Agreements, 11) Revoking Rights. Accompanying this is a security model for the security entities of signature and encryption. The Context of the elements provides for significant control over the relationships between entities and the aggregation of elements into Offers and Agreements by permitting the assignment of unique identifiers to the elements and sub-elements. The extensibility of ODRL is also demonstrated by the use of two XML schemas, one for the expression language and the other for the data dictionary. Flexibility of implementation comes with the ability to add new semantics through a data dictionary, extending the existing semantics. One of the most successful implementation of ODRL is the adoption of this standard into the work of the Open Mobile Alliance (OMA) producing the OMA REL[6] as part of their DRM v2 with a focus on mobile technologies.

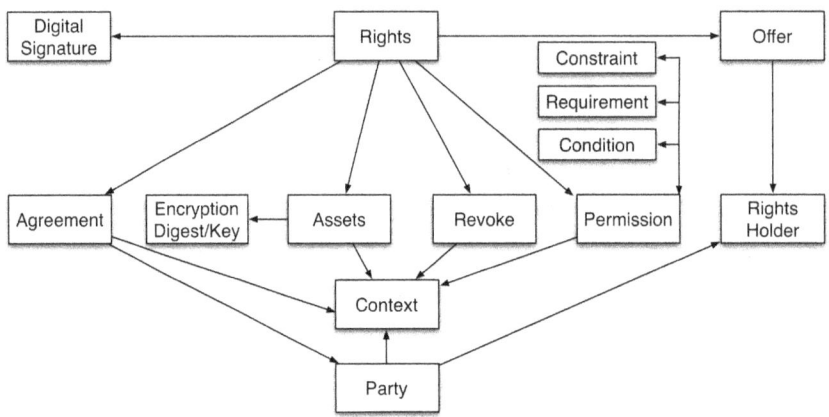

Figure 2.4: The entities of the ODRL model (based on [Iannella 2002])

NEMO

Networked Environment for Media Orchestration (NEMO) is also a developing standard in the same market, while some competing standards emerging from groups like Sun Labs with their DReaM-MMI[7] aiming to introduce an alternative to REL. Adobe (LifeCycle Policy Server) and Apple (FairPlay) also include REL, but maintain proprietary implementations at this time. Some authors [McKinley 2004; Barlas 2006] provide an introduction into the development of DRM with XML and REL, and the current marketplace for such technologies. The work discussed here focuses on the REL standards developments of XrML and ODRL, both of which are defined using XML Schema recommendations from W3C.

---

[6]OMA REL: `http://xml.coverpages.org/ni2004-05-31-a.html`
[7]DReaM: `https://dream.dev.java.net/`

XrML

XrML development is based on work by ContentGuard (formerly a Xerox technology) and has evolved on two paths: 1) v1.2 adopted by Microsoft and incorporated into the Windows Rights Management Services; and 2) v2.0 adopted by Moving Picture Experts Group (MPEG) and finalized into and ISO standard (ISO MPEG REL) as part of the MPEG-21 framework on standards for digital media. The ISO MPEG REL is a data model composed of four entities and their associated relationship using the basic assertion 'grant'. The entities are: 1) the principal to whom the grant is issued; 2) the right that the grant specifies; 3) the resource to which the grant applies; and 4) the condition that must be met before the right can be exercised.

2.3.4 Semantic DRMs

The large number of competing RELs have caused interoperability issues [Wang 2004; Chiariglione 2006; Koenen *et al.* 2004; Rosenblatt 2005] in the existing DRM implementations. Therefore, semantic solutions [García 2006] were introduced. Their main contribution was a copyright ontology and formal semantic that are helpful to overcome the interoperability problems.

One of the best known Semantic DRM projects is Rhizomik[8]. It is focused on interoperability between XML-based Right Expression Languages (RELs). It takes advantage of Semantic Web technologies to provide a shared ontology for copyright representation [García *et al.* 2007; García & Tummarello 2006]. The ontology is expressed using OWL-DL that provides a very expressive rights model. The model, for instance, includes economic, moral, and related rights. In this proposition, the end-users are unable to express their rights.

Work done by [Hilty *et al.* 2007] is also focused on interoperability problems and formal semantics definition, but focuses on digital usage control.

Other relevant related work was conducted in the area of audit logics. For instance, Cederquist et al. [Cederquist *et al.* 2007] proposed a framework that consists of a policy language, modeling ownership of data and administrative policies. Users can create documents, and authorize others to process the documents. However, this work is less aimed at fair use and semantic web.

To sum up, the proposed semantic approaches have the potential to overcome interoperability issues. These solutions, however, rely on complex models and introduce new rich vocabularies. The proposed ontologies are detailed and accurate. Thus, it is a challenging task for the consumers to learn and use them properly. This can be also the reason why semantic DRMs, such as rhizomik, have not been widely applied yet.

---

[8]Rhizomik: http://rhizomik.net/

2.3.5 Digital Watermarking

According to [Memon & Wong 1998], a digital watermark can be defined as *a signal added to digital data (audio, video, or still images) that can be detected or extracted later to make an assertion about the data*. In addition, there should be no difference between the original and the watermarked signals [Wolfgang *et al.* 1999].

The interest in this technology grew dramatically [Cox *et al.* 2002a] in early 1990s due to the need of copyright protection means. In 1998, the Digital Millennium Copyright Act (DMCA) [DMCA 1998] stated that any attempts to circumvent any technological measure are illegal, including digital watermarking. This law enforcement effectively protects intellectual properties of digital content owners and producers although digital watermarks do not prevent content from being viewed or played.

Digital watermarks and information embedding systems have been found useful in a number of applications [Podilchuk & Delp 2001; Cox *et al.* 2002b]:

- Ownership assertion: A digital watermark inserted to a file can be extracted only by the file creator.

- Fingerprinting: Distinct information can be inserted to each copy of disseminated content to trace sources of unauthorized duplications.

- Authentication and integrity verification: A watermark can be inserted to ensure that sensitive information is not changed.

- Usage control: Digital licenses or access rights can be represented by an embedded watermark.

- Content protection: Visible watermarks are often inserted to indicate that the obtained content is released with a purpose of preview or demo.

- Content labeling: An inserted watermark could give further information about the file, e.g., copyright notice.

A typical process of inserting a watermark has been depicted in Figure 2.5. It usually has two input parameters: a host signal and a watermark. A user-password parameter is optional. A typical process of detecting a watermark has been presented in Figure 2.6. It requires knowledge about the extraction algorithm and optionally the user's password.

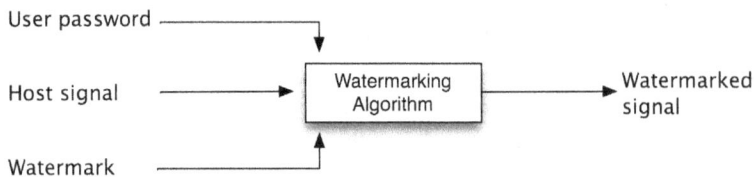

Figure 2.5: A watermark insertion algorithm

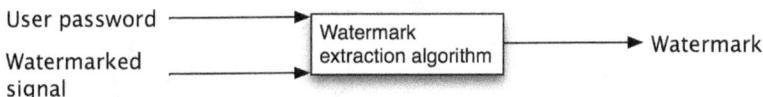

Figure 2.6: A watermark extraction algorithm

Digital watermarks are often classified from the perspective of resistance to media manipulation. We distinguish fragile and robust algorithms. The robust algorithms require that a watermark can be extracted even if the media file containing the watermark was modified, including signal degradation or transformation. When using fragile techniques, watermarks are prone to be lost or damaged as a result of any modifications in the media file. Digital watermarking algorithms are desired to provide imperceptibility, robustness, and capacity; those requirements, however, are mutually exclusive. To make watermarking techniques robust, the produced watermark should be inserted into the perceptually significant part of data [Cox *et al.* 1997]. However, this requirement is in contradiction with providing imperceptibility.

Watermarking algorithms are media type dependent. Therefore, algorithms designed for various media formats work using different principles. For example, watermarks for word documents are usually embedded in specific formatting or layout [Brassil *et al.* 1999]. When applying watermarks for web-pages, algorithms can be based on mixing upper and lower case characters in the HTML tags [Hua-jun *et al.* 2007]. Algorithms for other media types are also popular, specifically for images [Genov 2007], audio [Wang *et al.* 2008] and video [Jung *et al.* 2004].

2.4 Usage Control Models

In this section we present a typical structure of a usage control model. This structure is relevant for understanding the proposed improvements demonstrated in Chapters 5 and 7.

The most recent research efforts in the area of access control are directed towards Usage Control Models (UCON) [Park & Sandhu 2002; Park & Sandhu 2004]. Traditional access control systems focus on closed systems where all users and their hierarchy are known. In such systems, the authorization decision is made by servers that are equipped with reference monitors. UCON aims at the creation of a distributed usage model that spans many disciplines: authorization, trust management and DRM (see Figure 2.8). $UCON_{ABC}$ model [Zhang *et al.* 2008] has been depicted in Figure 2.7. The usage decision is made using six components:

- *Subjects and Subject Attributes* are entities that hold and exercise certain rights on objects. Subject Attributes are defined by [Zhang *et al.* 2008] as properties or capabilities that can be used during the usage decision process. For example, a user, a group, a role and a process are subjects, whereas credits/capabilities ($ 10 worth usage, print once), security clearance and usage log (the same file cannot be read twice) are examples of Subject Attributes.

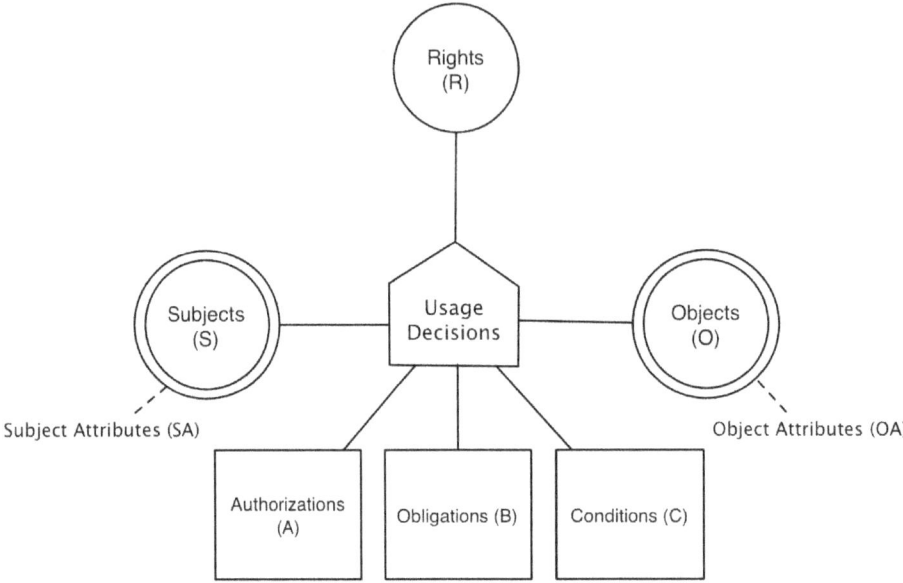

Figure 2.7: Usage Control Model [Zhang *et al.* 2008]

- *Objects and Object Attributes* can be used during the authorization process. Subjects hold rights on objects. Objects can be electronic documents (doc, pdf), media files (mp3, wav, jpg, dvd) or executables. Object attributes are, for example, security labels, ownerships and classes.

- *Rights* represent privileges that Subjects hold on Objects. They include rights for direct use of objects such as read, administration, access, delegation of rights, etc.

- *Authorizations* are rules that have to be met before allowing A Subject access an Object. There are two types of proposed authorizations: pre-authorizations and ongoing-authorizations. The former can, for example, include checking prepaid credit. The latter could be continuous usage time checking.

- *Obligations* represent mandatory actions for subjects to perform after obtaining rights on objects. Obligations have two types: pre-obligations and ongoing-obligations. The former can for example require a user to fill out some personal info, whereas the latter could demand the user to watch a given advertisement for the time the system is used.

- *Conditions* are sets of decisions that the system should verify during the authorization process along with authorization rules, before allowing usage of an object. They can evaluate the current state of the system to determine if relevant requirements are satisfied. For example, check the current local time, check the current location, evaluate the security status of the system, etc.

The main disadvantage of UCON is that Subjects are unable to disseminate Objects although they can delegate rights. Such a feature would be desirable from the perspective of fair use (see Section 2.5). UCON does not demonstrate how to attach rights to the object in a way that they could not be removed at the client side, which is crucial in DRM-based solutions. UCON also does not support tracing copyright infringement after the objects are disseminated. Although the model applies trust management solutions, it does not achieve its full

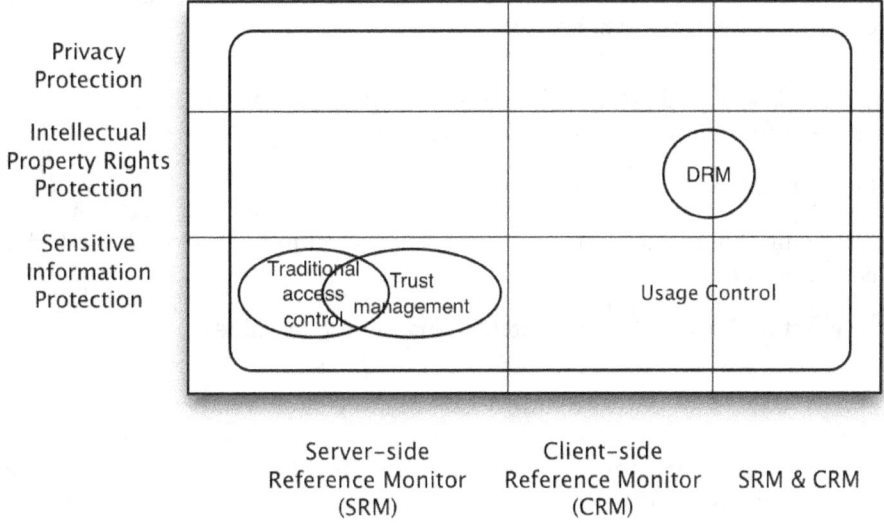

Figure 2.8: UCON coverage [Park & Sandhu 2004]

potential: users are unable to delegate permissions among themselves, even if they trust each other. Finally, according to [Park & Sandhu 2004] the reference implementation does not offer privacy protection (see Figure 2.8). [Park & Sandhu 2004] claim that privacy has been rarely studied in the context of controlling usage of digital information. They, however, expect it to get more attention. In Chapters 5 and 7 we further show how privacy of user identities can be implemented in usage control models.

2.5 Fair Use

Fair use [Felten 2003; Erickson 2003] policy allows legal owners to share products they bought with their acquaintances. It is based on the assumptions that the owners pass an original product and they cannot use it at the same time.

This section explain the fair use doctrine. It demonstrates how fair use is legislated in the U.S. and what are the implications for computer programs. It also demonstrates how existing DRM solutions implement it.

In Section 7.3 we describe how our approach addresses fair use. We also present application scenarios in Section 7.7.

2.5.1 Fair Use Definition

In various countries, fair use may be slightly different and have another name. For example, copyright exceptions, personal use and fair dealing have the same legal implications as fair use. In the U.S. fair use is incorporated as guidelines into the Copyright Act of 1976, 17 U.S.C. d' 107[9]. It states that to determine if a use is fair, a four factor test must be applied. The test consists of the following questions.

1. The purpose and character of the use, including whether such use is of a commercial nature or for nonprofit educational purposes;

2. the nature of the copyrighted work;

3. the amount and substantiality of the portion used in relation to the copyrighted work as a whole; and

4. the effect of the use upon the potential market for, or value of, the copyrighted work.

Courts are entitled to consider also other factors. None of these questions is a decision problem; for example, to evaluate question 4, we need to involve human expertise to measure the effect on the market. Furthermore, all of the questions belong to the class of non-algorithmic problems and thus we cannot answer the test questions by means of computers.

Only those policies that can be narrowed to yes/no decision can be automated successfully and without highly sophisticated intelligence we are not able to solve it [Felten 2003].

Although there are several approaches to this problem in the virtual world, existing DRM systems do not support fair use at all or provide very limited solutions. Since the users perceive the current restrictive solutions anachronistic and unrealistic [Jackson *et al.* 2005], many researchers demand a more consumer-friendly approach [Samuelson 2003] to the problem.

2.5.2 Fair Use in Existing Content Distribution Solutions

[Jackson *et al.* 2005] survey user experience with listening and sharing music in comparison with different copyright laws and DRM. In particular, they highlight 'how personal use rights [are] adversely affected by DRMs' and how the current design of DRMs 'restrict personal use activities'. An important facet to their survey was that the music sharing among friends were normally conducted within known networks, but that not all their activity would be permitted under copyright law - their choices in sharing were based on personal preference and simplicity.

During a recent working group conference held by the the Organization for Economic Co-operation and Development [Oecd 2006], members recognized this growing field of user-driven content creation, use and sharing that needs to be addressed: "The question is how to devise rules that allow for the coexistence of market and non-market creation and distribution and foster innovation without blocking downstream innovation." This rules development is clearly recognized by the Digital Media Project (DMP) started by MPEG founder

---

[9]17 U.S.C. d' 107: http://www.law.cornell.edu/uscode/17/107.html

Dr. Leonardo Chiariglione with the issuance of the 'Digital Media Manifesto' in October of 2003 [DMM 2003]. DMP also recognizes the requirement for social sharing as growing part of an effective DRM proofed by the listing of 'Mapping of rights traditionally enjoyed by users to the Digital Media space' as one of the four Policy Actions contained in the Major Actions of the Manifesto. DMP continues its work on DRM with the aim to create the DRM Standard and extends the architecture of ISO MPEG REL to help facilitate the growing usage scenarios.

Both ISO MPEG REL and ODRL use Rights Domains in their general form to assist in the distribution of media. These Domains can be of any form, such as home use, office, friends, library, etc. [Sheppard & Safavi-Naini 2006] demonstrated the benefit of such a system for ubiquitous computing with the extension of the authorized domain with the environmental role. Their review of using an environmental role to provide membership to the domain extends the context-aware functionality of the domain. This provides the opportunity for a user to be associated to a role that is granted the permissions, and not just to the user themselves. This approach highlights the flexibility of the current standards to facilitate usage in various environments. In particular, there is an apparent fit for extending such technologies to social networks for the creation or extension into social sharing domains; providing the user the control to actively share content based on accurate digital representation of copyright restrictions including a fair use opportunity [Grzonkowski *et al.* 2007; McCoy 2007; Rothman 2007].

[Arnab & Hutchison 2005] described a language extension for ODRL [Iannella 2002] to make it bi-directional. Such an extension enabled negotiations between a user and a content provider. It is based on license templates. In their proposition the user is also able to take advantage of some specific roles in order to negotiate a better contract.

Popescu et al. [Popescu *et al.* 2004] proposed "Authorized Domains" to define a network, in which legally acquired content can be played. The solution is suitable for home networks. However, it is not applicable to the web.

[Corcoran & Cucos 2005] proposed BAPTISM, a distributed system using biometric scanning technologies such as a customer's fingerprint to support fair use. In their scenario, each customer is given a personalized copy of digital content. The system provides facilities to share the copy with family members or friends by authorizing their public keys with the customer's private key. The solution requires additional hardware infrastructure to work, but it can be also deployed on the web.

FairPlay, a DRM created by Apple, is embedded in several Apple products. The most popular are iPod[10], iTunes, and QuickTime. Moreover, the iTunes music online store also sells music using FairPlay. The company has an agreement with American music industry. The most important condition of the agreement states that Apple has to use DRM to distribute content.

In order to store music, Apple uses "Protected AAC Files". The files are in MPEG-4 format encrypted using AAC format. Most of the algorithms applied in the encryption scheme are public: AES (Rijnadel) [Daemen & Rijmen 1999], the MPEG-4 file format. The exception to using public encryption algorithms was the user's key database component. The applied algorithm was broken by Jon Lech Johansen, who is also known for breaking DeCSS [Jonansen 1999] standard applied in DVD players.

---

[10]Apple. (2002). iPod, from `http://www.apple.com/ipod/`

Although an iPod allows the sharing of music among 5 authorized devices and also allows a user to copy it to an audio CD any number of times, several illegal systems that can omit the DRM protection exist: De-DRMS, PlayFair, QTFairUse, and Hymn. That was one of the reasons why Steve Jobs, Apple CEO, published his 'Thoughts on Music' [Jobs 2007], in which he demanded the 4 biggest American companies to cancel the DRM agreement. His calculation showed that the market of iPods is only 10% of the total music market. In addition only 3% of music files stored in iPods were purchased legally. Furthermore, he noted that the FairPlay encryption scheme relies on a secret that can be broken relatively quickly by the Internet community. His conclusion was that currently DRM in the music market does not work because it covers a very small part of it. The main problem of existing client-side DRM solutions is that they can be reverse-engineered and replaced with DRM-free code. Such code could be theoretically licensed and sold as a legal alternative [Rowel 2006]. It makes the existing solutions ineffective and also expensive.

Windows Media Rights Management (WMRM) [Microsoft Corporation 2004] offered by Microsoft is freely available, and therefore it is also the cheapest choice to start. It works, however, only under the Windows Operating systems and thus supports only Microsoft's media formats: WMA for audio, and WMV for video. The system works both with downloadable and stream-based files. User identities in this system rely on a unique identification numbers that are computed using the users' hardware; they are stored in DLL files. This idea affects the fair use doctrine since the identification number depends on a single device and thus files can be played only on one particular device. The core concept of Microsoft's approach is a software license that is responsible for specifying user rights and determining how many times a file can be played, possibilities of transferring a file to other devices, expiration date, permission to burn on a CD and others.

EMMS is a DRM solution by IBM. It offers an open architecture that enables content providers to adjust the system to future needs. The technology can be easily extended with watermarking, compression, or encryption. EMMS was successfully tested in 1998 in the first broadband music distribution trail. Three years later the technology was applied to NTT DoCoMo[11], the world's first mobile music service. The system was also successfully extended with SCORM and LOM metadata in order to apply the solution in the e-learning context [Mourad *et al.* 2005]. The system supports MP3, AAC, and ATRAC3. The main disadvantage is the lack of support for stream-based content.

We conclude that existing DRM solutions offer advanced cryptographic protocols which aims to make the content secure within the vendor's content players. They, however, do not provide fair use. Sharing content with friends is very limited or even impossible although some fair use support would satisfy the consumers' demands [Samuelson 2003].

2.6 Summary and Conclusion

In this chapter we described the state of the art of access control approaches and its main developments: Role-Based Access Control (RBAC), Trust Management, Digital Rights Management (DRM) and usage control models.

---

[11]NTT DoCoMo: http://www.nttdocomo.com/

We also introduced DRM-related technologies such as Rights Expression Languages (RELs) and Digital Watermarking because they are part of the conceptual model and its implementation.

We continue our introduction to trust management (see Section 2.2) in Chapter 4 in the context of Social Semantic Web technologies. We also further develop our definition of trust and related concepts such as a "stranger" and "friend".

Finally we also mentioned the fair use doctrine and demonstrated what are its implications for the existing content usage control solutions. We further take into account these implications to design our conceptual model in Chapter 5 and its implementation in Chapter 7.

We conclude that there are several approaches to fair use in existing DRMs, but the offered solutions are very limited. Another problem that we mentioned is interoperability. Semantic web could be used to solve this, but the solutions that have been proposed introduce complex models and vocabularies that are not widely applied.

Chapter 3

Web Authentication*

The classical way of authenticating users in web applications, is to request a login and the corresponding password. Then, the login and the password are sent directly to a server; and the server respond to the requests. If security is needed, the SSL/TLS protocol is applied, but the credentials are still sent through the Internet and servers are able to read them, even if the passwords are stored in a hashed form.

Very often a user visits a web site whose certificate cannot be verified by the user's browser. However, the browser usually enables the user to accept the certificate although its verification was unsuccessful [Xia & Brustoloni 2005]. To take full advantage of the potential of SSL/TLS, a user should buy a certificate issued by a well-known certificate authority and then the certificate should be installed on the user's browser. But because the users are still employing passwords, which are prone to technical (see Section 3.1) and social threats [Mitnick & Simon 2002; Adida 2007a], the use of SSL/TLS protocol has not really solved many of the problems that we demonstrate in this chapter.

In Section 3.1, we describe the main vulnerabilities of authentication protocols such as replay, interleaving, reflection, forced delay and chosen text attacks that were indicated by [Menezes *et al.* 1996] as the main threats for authentication protocols. Then, we also discuss the man-in-the-middle (MITM) attack which is often considered the main threat for generic web-authentication solutions [Berners-Lee *et al.* 1996; Franks *et al.* 1999]. Most effective defense techniques against this attack require additional infrastructure such as a Trusted Third Party (TTP), synchronized clocks or a centralized authentication service [Neuman & Ts'o 1994]. We conclude that such additional requirements represent significant disadvantages to the broad adoption of such techniques.

Section 3.2 introduces generic HTTP authentication solutions: Basic and Digest. Then, we present SSL/TLS that is widely used for e-commerce applications. Kerberos is also briefly described. It is often applied as a secure Single Sign-on solution. However, this idea was not widely deployed on the web. OpenID and OAuth, whose concepts resemble the original Kerberos, are becoming more and more popular as web authentication solutions. An authentication approach based on a browser plugin is also discussed. Finally, we briefly describe

---

*This chapter is partially based on [Grzonkowski *et al.* 2008b; Grzonkowski *et al.* 2010]

several Password-based Authentication Key Exchange (PAKE) solutions that aims at secure communication using short and memorable passwords. Their main security threats are the possibilities of dictionary attacks and lack of resistance to a server compromise.

We conclude the chapter with a short comparison of the existing solutions and discuss their advantages and disadvantages.

3.1 Vulnerabilities of Authentication Protocols

In this section we present the main vulnerabilities of authentication protocols. For designing an improved approach it is necessary to study and understand the deficiencies of known approaches to authentication and in how attack techniques can circumvent current approaches.

Firstly, we briefly describe replay, interleaving, reflection, forced delay and chosen text attacks that were indicated by [Menezes *et al.* 1996] as the main threats for authentication protocols. Then, we discuss the man-in-the-middle (MITM) attack (see Section 3.1.2) which is often considered as the main threat for web authentication solutions [Berners-Lee *et al.* 1996; Franks *et al.* 1999; Fielding *et al.* 1999]. Many successful protections against this attack, however, require additional elements of infrastructure such as a Third Trusted Party (TTP), synchronized clocks or a centralized authentication service [Neuman & Ts'o 1994]. We analyze and conclude those additional requirements as disadvantages. Finally, we present a number of Password-based Authenticated Key Exchange protocols (PAKE). Their main security threats are the possibilities of dictionary attacks and lack of resistance to a server compromise.

3.1.1 Design vulnerabilities

In [Menezes *et al.* 1996] analyzed and concluded several protocols vulnerabilities as the most important ones. Firstly, the replay attack which is an implication of the fact that data transferred on the Internet is routed through many peers. It poses a possibility of a replay attack, in which a malicious peer is able to read information and is further able to pretend as the message sender in the service that is the addressee of the message. The attack is possible, even if the data was encrypted. Additionally, [Denning & Sacco 1981] demonstrated that the attacker who intercepts the session, can attempt to compromise the session key and then use it for replay attacks and decrypting the new sessions, and as a result, timestamping extensions were introduced to many existing protocols. Other possible solutions to those kinds of attacks are cryptographic nonces, challenge-response techniques or embedding target identity in response.

Interleaving, which is another attack, can be performed by a selective combination of information from one or more previously or simultaneously ongoing protocol executions. A possible solution to this attack can be achieved by linking together all messages from a protocol run.

The Reflection Attack extends the interleaving attack in a way that it involves sending information from an ongoing protocol execution back to the originator of such information.

To defend it, [Menezes *et al.* 1996] suggested embedding an identifier of the target party into challenge responses, using unidirectional keys, and to avoid message symmetries.

In the attack known as *Forced Delay* an adversary intercepts a message and relays it at some later point in time. This attack is similar to the replay attack. However, the intercepted message was not used before. This attack can be countered by using time-outs and time-stamping services.

In the *Chosen-text* attack, the attacker chooses an arbitrary plaintext to be encrypted and obtains the corresponding cipher text. The attacker can also strategically choose the challenges and attempt to extract the victim's private key. This attack can be countered by using zero-knowledge proof techniques (see Section 6.1) and embedding random numbers in each challenge response.

Table 3.1 briefly summarizes the design vulnerabilities of authentication protocols.

Name	Description	Defense
Replay	A malicious peer replays previous messages. The attack is possible, even if the data was encrypted.	Timestamping, nonces, challenge-response techniques or embedding target identity in messages.
Session key	The possibility of using a compromised session key for replay attacks and decrypting the session data.	Timestamping, challenge-response.
Interleaving	It is a selective combination of information from one or more previously or simultaneously ongoing protocol executions.	Linking together all messages from a protocol run. For example in a form of chained nonces
Reflection	It extends interleaving by sending information from an ongoing protocol execution back to the originator of such information.	Embedding identifier of target party in challenge responses, using uni-directional keys or constructing protocols with each message of different form.
Forced Delay	An adversary intercepts a message and relays it at some later point in time	Time-outs, time-stamping services.
Chosen-text	An arbitrary plaintext is encrypted to obtain the corresponding cipher text. The attacker can also strategically choose the challenges and attempt to extract the victim's private key.	Zero-knowledge proof techniques, embedding random numbers in each challenge response.

Table 3.1: The main vulnerabilities of authentication protocols based on [Menezes *et al.* 1996]

3.1.2 Man-In-The-Middle Attack

The man-in-the-middle (MITM) attack is relevant for any authentication protocol using just one communication channel. The problem is caused by presence of intermediate hostile parties.

An adversary, who is able to observe and intercept messages exchanged between two potential victims, can read, modify and insert content at will. This situation is especially dangerous, if the messages are passed between two parties without either part knowing that the link between them has been compromised. Such attacks can even work if encryption is used. Several solutions to the MITM attack have been proposed. They, however, make establishing a communication link more complex requiring additional protocol steps. One such solution uses digital certificates. This approach requires a Third Trusted Party (TTP) to validate the digital certificates of the two parties. Some solutions such as Kerberos additionally require synchronized clocks of the network participants. Therefore, it increases the implementation cost and complexity. To lower the complexity, many protocols were designed in a way that an adversary is able to capture a single session; however, the user's credentials such as passwords are safe. An example of such a protocol is HTTP Digest [Franks *et al.* 1997] that is described in Section 3.2.2.

Other approaches to avoid MITM without increasing the complexity and cost are based on managing timeouts and delays during the authentication protocol execution [Beth & Desmedt 1991; Brands & Chaum 1993].

Other efficient ways of solving this problem include mutual authentication and two-factor authentication [Adida 2007a]. Such approaches can be often applied by redesigning existing solutions, but they increase the deployment cost as they usually require more infrastructure elements such as tokens or additional communication channels.

3.1.3 Dictionary Attacks

Recent research conducted by [Florencio & Herley 2007] has shown that end users tend to employ many passwords in their daily activities on computer networks. However, the majority of these passwords are of low quality and tend to be re-used and forgotten. It has been also demonstrated [Morris & Thompson 1979] that an attacker equipped with a dictionary of possible user passwords is able to perform a very efficient attack by checking all the password candidates. There are two main kinds of dictionary attacks:

- Offline attack in which the attacker records a session and then attempts to check the passwords candidates offline. The difficulty of this attack is that the attacker has to know the hash of the password and also the algorithm the password is computed.

- In online attack, the attacker tries to log in using the victim's username and a number of password candidates. In most cases, we are able to significantly slow down this attack by using *"Completely Automated Public Turing test to tell Computers and Humans Apart"* (CAPTCHA) [Pinkas & Sander 2002]. Such tests are easy to solve for humans, but very difficult for computers (e.g., image recognition). Thus, this challenge-response test are performed to ensure that the responses (e.g., usernames and passwords) are generated by humans.

If users tend to choose low entropy [Narayanan & Shmatikov 2005; Oechslin 2003] passwords, dictionary attacks are very effective. This has been the subject of many studies [Gong *et al.* 1993; MacKenzie *et al.* 2002; Ford & Kaliski 2000; Baudet 2005]. For potential defenses against offline dictionary attacks, which include public-key techniques, we refer an interested reader to [Halevi & Krawczyk 1999].

3.1.4 Server Compromise

To secure passwords in the case of a server compromise, they should not be stored in their plain-text form. Thus, servers store cryptographic hashes of passwords, computed using functions such as SHA1 or MD5. To introduce additional protection, authentication protocols designers introduced the technique of *"Salting"*. A *salt* is usually a short string that is added as a prefix to the string on which the hash is computed. This way two different users who choose the same passwords, have two different hash values stored in the server database. This small improvement protects from an attacker who possesses a dictionary of the all possible password candidates and pre-computed corresponding hashes. Because of the salt, the attacker has to pre-compute the hashes for each attempt to impersonate a user. Such a protection method is applied in unix-based systems [Menezes *et al.* 1996].

Another threat for plain-text stored password is that users tend to reuse the same login-password pairs for different web services. Thus, a malicious administrator would be able to steal their identities.

A general technique to take an arbitrary protocol and to make it provably resilient to server compromise, was provided for password-based solutions by [Gentry *et al.* 2006].

3.2 Web Authentication Solutions

In this section we first introduce generic HTTP authentication solutions: Basic and Digest. Then, we present SSL/TLS that is widely used for e-commerce purposes. We also briefly describe Kerberos that is often applied as a secure Single Sign-on solution (SSO). This SSO concept, however, was not widely deployed on the web. OpenID and OAuth, whose concepts resembles the original Kerberos idea, have become recognized web solutions. Although OpenID does not specify the authentication method, it implies some disadvantages we analyze in Section 3.2.5. Unlike OpenID, OAuth proposes a ticket-based authentication method that we present. Then, we discuss an authentication approach based on a browser plugin. It provides some advantages that are highlighted in Section 3.2.7. Finally, we give a brief description of the well known Password-based Authentication Key Exchange (PAKE) techniques that aims at secure communication using short and memorable passwords.

3.2.1 HTTP Basic Authentication

HTTP Basic authentication is the most widely used authentication method. It is supported by all web servers. It was originally specified in the HTTP RFC [Berners-Lee *et al.* 1996] and its limitations are further discussed in [Franks *et al.* 1999; Fielding *et al.* 1999].

To use this method, the server must know that some specific documents require authentication to work. Those documents must be put in a protected directory within the server. Such a directory must be labeled with a name. This name is called a *realm*. A single server can provide many realms. Then, users IDs should be assigned to corresponding realms that the users are entitled to access .

To access a document from the protected space, a user must provide correct credentials and the given user-id must be recognized within the realm.

Before the transmission the user's credentials are encoded as a sequence of base-64 characters. For instance, credentials for *Alice* who has a password *"enigma"* would be combined to "*Alice:enigma*" and encoded as "*QWxpY2U6ZW5pZ21h*". As a result of using base-64, the credentials are not sent in their plain-text form; however, anyone who sees the authentication request header from the transmission between Alice and the server can decode the credentials back to "*Alice:enigma*" by reversing the base-64 string.

This type of authentication was not designed to provide security, but to avoid breaking the HTTP protocol data because of unconventional characters, such as tabs and new lines, in the password [Franks *et al.* 1999]. There is also no effective way for a user to log out from a server because HTTP is not session-based.

3.2.2 HTTP Digest

The HTTP Digest authentication method was invented to replace insecure Basic authentication [Franks *et al.* 1997]. Instead of sending a reversible base-64 string, a cryptographic MD5 [Rivest 1992] hash of user credentials and other parameters is sent. Listing 3.1 describes the initial version of the protocol. Firstly, the username, realm and user password are concatenated and hashed using MD5 (A1). Then, the requested URL and the method for the request are also appended and hashed (A2). Finally, A1, A2 and a *nonce* are concatenated and hashed. The result is sent to the server. *Nonce* is a string generated by the server and sent back to the browser when a protected resources is accessed. For each user's request, this string is different. It is based on the user IP and request date. RFC2617 [Franks *et al.* 1999] proposed

```
A1 = MD5 (username : realm : password)

A2 = MD5 (method : url)

response = MD5 (A1 : nonce : A2)
```

Listing 3.1: HTTP Digest protocol

some improvements to the original protocol by introducing a client generated random *nonce*, a *nonce* counter incremented by client and also a Quality of Protection (qop) value. These enhancements are designed to protect against chosen-plaintext attack cryptanalysis, etc.

Listing 3.2 describes the improved protocol. According to the new protocol, if the qop directive's value in the response header is "auth-int". In comparison to CRAM-MD5 [Klensin *et al.* 1997], which is a similar solution proposed for LDAP, POP and IMAP [Franks *et al.* 1999], HTTP Digest is a step forward. However, it still cannot be consid-

```
A1 = MD5 (username : realm : password)

A2 = MD5 (method : url)

HA2 = MD5 (method : url : MD5 (entity - body))

response = MD5 (A1 : nonce : nonceCount : clientNonce : qop : A2)
```

Listing 3.2: HTTP Digest protocol

ered secure because the protocol resistance to replay attacks depends on the way the server implementation generates the nonce values [Franks *et al.* 1999]. In Digest authentication the replay attack, however, is usually limited to the requested document. If a protection from a replay attack is required, it can be provided by a slightly modified server-side implementation [Franks *et al.* 1997]. According to [Franks *et al.* 1997], both protocols are vulnerable to man-in-the-middle attacks. Thus, the main advantage of replacing Basic with Digest authentication is that the attacker can get access to the transaction data but not to the password. Therefore only one document at a time will be compromised, not the whole conversation.

[Garfinkel 2004] described a simple challenge-response solution very similar to HTTP Digest authentication. The server is supposed to store passwords in their plain-text form or to have corresponding hash values. However, even having only the hash, the server is still able to follow the protocol and to impersonate the user. Thus, this protocol offers a protection against MITM, but it is not resistant against dishonest servers.

3.2.3 SSL/TLS

The Secure Socket Layer (SSL) protocol was created by Netscape to stimulate the sales of the company's cryptographically enabled web servers by distributing a free client that implemented the same cryptographic protocols [Garfinkel & Spafford 2001]. Such a solution was necessary since solutions offered by HTTP [Berners-Lee *et al.* 1996; Franks *et al.* 1999] were prone to sniffing and man-in-the-middle attacks.

SSL provides authentication of both the client and server through the use of digital certificates and digitally signed challenges. SSL version 1.0 was never publicly released. Version 2.0 appeared in 1994 and was implemented in Netscape Navigator. Due to its security flaws, version 3.0 was released shortly after in 1995. Although SSL 3.0 is considered a valuable contribution, [Wagner & Schneier 1996] demonstrated that it still has some drawbacks such as change cipher spec-dropping, KeyExchangeAlgorithm-spoofing and version roll-back. In 1996 the IETF established a Transport Layer Security working group to create an open stream encryption standard based on SSL. This working group published RFC 2246 [Dierks & Allen 1999] in 1999 that defines "TLS Protocol Version 1.0" and then RFC 2818 [Rescorla 2000] to adjust TLS to HTTP/1.1. RFC 2712 [Medvinsky & Hur 1999] adds Kerberos authentication to TLS. SSL is located in between the raw TCP/IP and the application layer. TLS encrypts communication between a user and a server. Even if the user logs in to a server using TLS, the credentials are still sent. Thus, there is a possibility of obtaining them if the TLS session has been compromised, and also the server is able to read the credentials regardless of encryption.

3.2.4 Kerberos

Kerberos [Neuman & Ts'o 1994; Neuman *et al.* 2005] is an authentication protocol that requires a Third Trusted Party (TTP). The protocols was designed at MIT for project Athena. The protocol is currently in version 5 and requires parties to exchange 5 messages and an optional response. Kerberos provides an authentication service that acts as a trusted arbitrator. Kerberos shares secrets with every participant of the network and knowledge about this secret proves identity.

The protocol assumes that mutual authentication is performed. Therefore, some protection from man-in-the-middle attack is provided. However, in practice it is dependent on the client-side implementation. To exchange encrypted messages between parties, Kerberos uses DES, a symmetric cryptography protocol. The authentication part is provided using Needham-Schroeder's TTP protocol [Needham & Schroeder 1978] with some enhancements such as timestamps, a ticket-granting service, and a different approach to cross-realm authentication.

The basic idea of Kerberos is depicted in Figure 3.1. At the beginning of the communication, a client (C) requests a ticket for a Ticket-Granting Service (TGS) from the Authentication Service (AS). The ticket is sent to the client and encrypted with the client's secret key. To use a particular server (S), the client requests a ticket for that server from TGS. Then, the client is able to manage communication with the server using the obtained authenticator and ticket.

Kerberos has been deployed in Windows 2000 as the default protocol for network authentication[1]. However, it also attracted some criticism. The first problem is that the replay attack [Bellovin & Merritt 1990] was still feasible. The timestamps that were supposed to fix this problem, can be reused within the lifetime of the ticket. The lifetime of the tickets varies between 5 minutes and 8 hours which is enough for replay or forced delays attacks. Servers are responsible for storing and managing valid tickets. However, this requirement is no always satisfied.

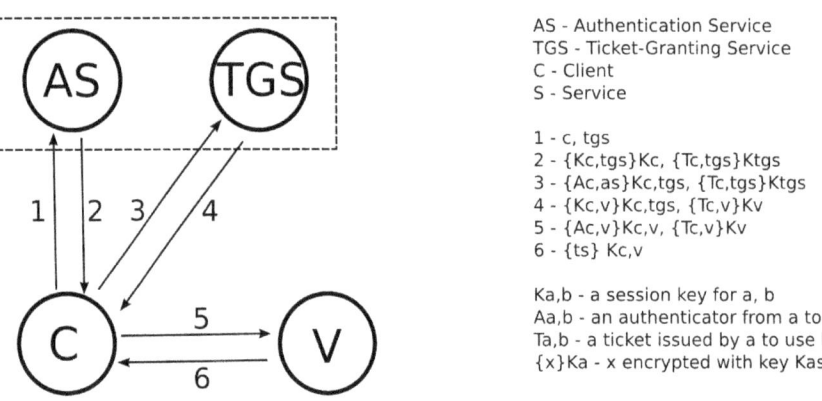

Figure 3.1: Kerberos authentication protocol

Another problem is that the protocol assumes that all the clocks in the network are approximately synchronized. The replay attack can be specifically successful if an attacker has the possibility of influencing the time on other hosts. Many network time protocols do not consider security as a major issue, and so this can be a serious weakness.

Kerberos is also prone to dictionary-based password-guessing attacks. Users passwords are often chosen from a small password space. Hence, an attacker who can record a complete authentication session can attempt to decrypt it with a high probability of success.

[Wen-Guey & Chi-Ming 1999] noted that the protocol is also prone to interleaving attacks. [Yu *et al.* 2004] have demonstrated how to perform an efficient chosen-plaintext attack.

---

[1]Windows 2000 Kerberos Authentication: `http://technet.microsoft.com/en-us/library/bb742431.aspx`

This attack was performed on version 4 of Kerberos, but the authors also demonstrated that it still can be performed on version 5. The protocol depends on the Authentication Service's (AS) availability. Thus, there is a single point of failure that can paralyze the whole network. Finally, all the user passwords are stored on a central server. If the central server gets compromised, all user secret keys will be compromised as well.

3.2.5 OpenID

The OpenID authentication protocol was designed in 2005 by Brad Fitzpatrick [Fitzpatrick 2005]. The main objective of OpenID was to provide a Single Sign-On feature for web pages. Therefore, it provides a decentralized user identification in a way that users can use the same logins at many websites. The protocol does not specify the method of authentication such as passwords, digital certificates, tokens, etc. The protocol introduced the use of URIs as user logins. For instance, *http://alice.deri.ie* would be a valid OpenId username, where *http://deri.ie* is the Identity Provider and *alice* is the End User name. The protocol also offers a mechanism to verify if a given URL belongs to its bearer.

Applying OpenID to a webpage is straightforward. It simply involves adding HTML tags to the page source (see Listing 3.3). There are three participants in the protocol (see Figure 3.2): End User (EU), Relying Party (RP), and the Identity Provider (IP). At the beginning of the protocol, an EU requests access to a web-site offered by an RP. To login, the EU is requested to type its username, which is a URI. Having this URI, the RP is able to determine the address of the corresponding IP for the given EU. Then, the EU is redirected to the determined IP which is able to verify the EU's identity. This result is sent back to the RP, which grants access for the requesting EU, if the authentication result was successful.

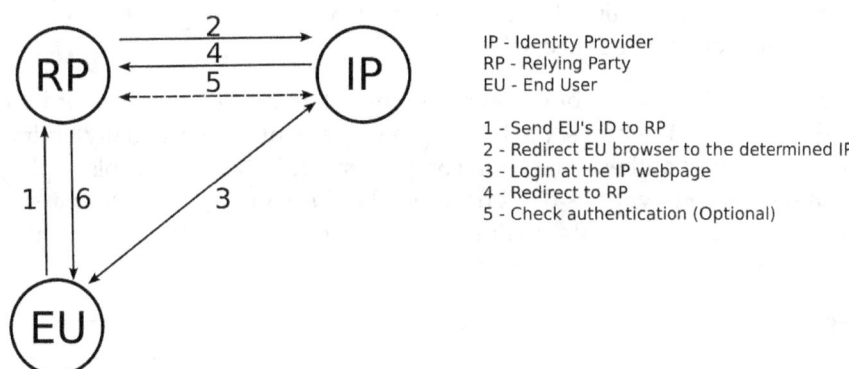

Figure 3.2: OpenID authentication protocol

```
<link rel="openid.server" href="http://www.deri.ie/openid/server.bml">

<link rel="openid.delegate" href="http://alice.deri.ie/">
```

Listing 3.3: An example use of OpenID in an HTML code

The protocol is currently in version 2.0 [Recordon & Reed 2006][2]. However, the future of this protocol and its applicability to e-commerce is somewhat unsure due to its phishing vulnerabilities [Adida 2007b].

3.2.6 OAuth

OAuth[3] is an protocol that aims at secure authorization on the web. Similarly to OpenID, OAuth provides a Single Sign-On functionality and hence it does not require users to retype their credentials at each visited website. Its aim was to delegate authorization from webpages to a central authority. Then the central authority generates tokens for the users. The tokens can be then used at each webpage.

This protocol uses nonce values, timestamps and signatures to increase security and to prevent a range of network attacks. The protocol resembles an implementation of Kerberos that operates using the HTTP environment. Hence, these two protocols have comparable advantages and drawbacks.

3.2.7 Browser Plugins

Halderman, Waters, and Felten [Halderman *et al.* 2005] proposed a client side solution to increase user security. They have developed a Firefox[4] plugin for generating many passwords from a single user password using a hash function. This solution proposes the use of a separate secret for each server the user wants to communicate with. Although this idea is browser dependent, it could be readily re-implemented for other browsers. Such solutions are also often version or even machine dependent since they may manage some local persistence to keep for example client-generated salts.

Because a web-browser is build on top of an authentication protocol, it inherits the underlaying protocol's drawbacks. Such a plugin implementation is usually built on the top of HTTP Basic or Digest authentication. In comparison with those protocols, a plugin provides additional resistance to various dictionary attacks since a plain-text user password is never stored on the server. Thus, it also maintains a greater level of security for the user, even if an end-server should become compromised.

3.2.8 Password-based Approaches

Password-Authenticated Key Exchange (PAKE) is a family of protocols that provides a reasonable level of security using short memorized passwords for protecting information over insecure channels. Such protocols are also a topic of the IEEE P1363[5] standard working group.

---

[2]OpenID 2.0 spec: `http://openid.net/specs/openid-authentication-2_0.html`

[3]OAuth protocol definition: `http://oauth.net/core/1.0/`

[4]Firefox: `http://www.mozilla.com/firefox/`

[5]IEEE P1363: `http://grouper.ieee.org/groups/1363/`

Encrypted Key Exchange

Encrypted Key Exchange (EKE) [Bellovin & Merritt 1992] combines both asymmetric and symmetric cryptography. The protocol has several versions.

In the most secure, the first communication stage uses the Diffie-Hellman protocol to establish a shared key, which aims at providing security against man-in-the-middle and other impersonation attempts. Then, the actual authentication stage is executed. It results in a symmetric key that is computed independently by both communicating parties.

Simplified Password-authenticated Exponential Key Exchange

The EKE protocol was followed by other propositions. The Simplified Password-authenticated Exponential Key Exchange (SPEKE) protocol was developed by [Jablon 1996] for commercial purposes.

The main difference in comparison to EKE is that the password is used to influence the selection of the generator parameter in the session-key generation function. Thus, the protocol introduced so-called *forward secrecy*. It means that an attacker to whom the password is revealed, is unable to access session keys of past sessions. Zhang [Zhang 2004] showed, however, that in SPEKE an adversary is able to test multiple password candidates using a single impersonation attempt. In the EKE protocol, an adversary can gain information about at most one possible password in each impersonation attempt.

Secure Remote Password

Secure Remote Password (SRP) [Wu 2000; Wu 1998] was developed in 1997. The security of this protocol depends on the strength of the applied one-way hash function. The protocol was revised several times, and is currently at revision six.

SRP is often applied to telnet and ftp. The protocol is more computationally intensive than EKE. It requires two modular exponentiations, whereas EKE requires only one. Moreover, the protocol is vulnerable to offline dictionary attacks, if an adversary intercepts session messages.

Other Improvements

A number of additional improvements to the initial EKE idea were proposed. For example, [Kwon 2000] proposed AMP (Authentication and Key Agreement via Memorable Password) to increase security against dictionary attacks by addressing the problem of low entropy passwords. Efficient Password-based protocol for Authenticated Key Exchange (EPA/EPA+) that additionally extends its resistance against server compromise was proposed by [Hwang *et al.* 2003]. The protocol uses amplified password file to offer more protection against dictionary attacks. Moreover, some confidential information such as salts is stored in an external storage device. Another group of authors [Gentry *et al.* 2005] proposed a technique that uses hidden smooth subgroups instead of Diffie-Hellman or RSA assumptions.

3.3 Summary and Conclusion

Table 3.2 summarizes our discussion, highlighting the advantages and disadvantages of each protocol.

According to [Menezes *et al.* 1996] protection from replay, interleaving, reflection, forced delay and chosen text attack is essential for secure authentication protocols. In the same way any secure authentication protocol must provide protection from the man-in-the-middle attacks.

The requirements of a TTP or synchronized clocks have been considered by us as disadvantages because they increase the solution deployment cost and complexity. A requirement of a centralized server is also considered as a disadvantage because it creates a single point of failure.

The table also informs, if a given protocol is version dependent. For instance, an attacker can force SSL version 2 instead of 3, and as a result, some of its security properties will be lost. The same situation happens in case of Kerberos, Plugins or PAKE-based solutions.

We note that in Table 3.2 we take into account the more secure version of the HTTP Digest authentication protocol.

The use of memorable passwords was considered as an advantage since many users do not understand digital certificates correctly [Xia & Brustoloni 2005]; and thus, they do not benefit from them. The support of memorable passwords, however, implies various possibilities of dictionary attacks such as offline attacks on session messages or public users' verifiers. There is also a threat of online dictionary attacks, but they are easier to eliminate.

Passwords should be kept secure in the case of a server compromise. This requirement is not satisfied by all the protocols.

The last column of the table summarizes PAKE protocols. Within this group their particular characteristics depend on the specific implementation of the PAKE protocol. As examples, EKE is resistant to offline attacks on the session messages, but the protocol is not secure against server compromise, unless additional security enhancements are applied. SRP had 6 revisions and each of them improved certain security aspects. Thus, we note that the overall reliability of password-based protocols is both protocol and version dependent.

All the presented protocols have various vulnerabilities. However, they are still widely used in a range of applications. In Section 7.6, we will develop an authentication protocol that aims to improve authentication on the web. Our approach will use the familiar mechanism of passwords, but removes practically all of the current vulnerabilities of password based authentication techniques.

Table 3.2 does not contain OpenID and OAuth since they do not introduce relevant security enhancements in comparison to Kerberos. We have introduced and described these protocols since they introduce TTP-based solutions for Web applications.

We also conclude that certain requirements are mutually exclusive. Support of passwords does not only increase convenience of a computer system, but also enables possibility of dictionary attacks.

Vulnerabilities and requirements	Protocol name					
	Basic	Digest	SSL/TLS	Kerberos	Plugin	PAKE
Replay	—	✓	✓	—	✓	✓
Interleaving	—	—	✓	—	—	✓
Reflection	—	—	✓	—	—	✓
Forced delay	—	—	✓	—	—	✓
Chosen text	—	✓	✓	—	✓	✓
MITM	—	—	✓	✓	—	✓
Require TTP	✓	✓	—	—	✓	✓
Req. sync. clocks	✓	✓	✓	—	✓	✓
Distributed topology	✓	✓	✓	—	✓	✓
Version dependent	✓	✓	—	—	—	—
Supports passwords	✓	✓	—	✓	✓	✓
Online dict. attacks	—	—	✓	—	✓	—
Offline dict. attacks	—	—	✓	—	✓	✓/—
Server compromise	—	✓	✓	—	✓	✓/—

Table 3.2: Various authentication protocols and their vulnerabilities. — stands for the lack of support of a given requirement or vulnerability. ✓ stands for resistance to a given problem or requirement support

At the moment there are two clear leaders among these authentication solutions: SSL/TLS and PAKE.

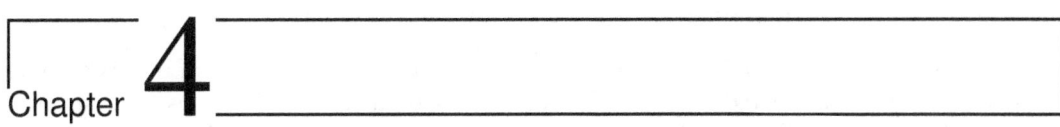

Chapter 4

Trust Issues in The Social Semantic Web*

This chapter presents infrastructure elements that are used to develop the prototype demonstrated in Part III.

In Section 4.1 we introduce Social Networks [Barnes 1954] that we use to represent relationships between people. Our presentation includes both practical examples and theoretical definitions. The advent of online social networks has enabled new types of applications that work on the top of them. Social networks combined with trust management have created the potential to authorize strangers. Thus, there is a new possibility of finding trusted users that are not directly connected with us.

In Section 4.2, we present the Friend-of-a-Friend (FOAF) vocabulary that enables the exchange of social data on the web. We specifically focus on its applicability for trust management and authentication.

4.1 Social Networks

The term "social network" was first mentioned in 1954 by J.A. Barnes [Barnes 1954]. The social network is a structure that consists of nodes that represent individual people or organizations. Such a structure depicts the ways in which people are connected through diverse social familiarities like acquaintance, friendship or close familial bonds.

The six degrees of separation theory [Newman 2000; Kleinberg 2001] has initiated the research in online social networks. The number six derives from an experiment performed in 1967 by social psychologist Stanley Milgram [Milgram 1967], who sent three hundreds letters to randomly selected people in America with the purpose of getting them delivered to target people. Each recipient was given some details about the target, such as their name and profession, and was asked to send the package to a personal acquaintance whom they believed was more likely to know the target personally. Unexpectedly, the experiment showed that the average length of chain of people was equal to six. [Barabasi 2003] argues that the hypothesis

---

*This chapter is partially based on [Grzonkowski *et al.* 2008a; Grzonkowski *et al.* 2008b]

of such a short social distance between two random people originates from a Hungarian book Chains (Láncszemek) written in 1929 by Frigyes Karinthy [Barabasi 2003].

Because Milgram's experiment had been rather small, it was questioned. As a result, [Watts *et al.* 2002] recruited over 60,000 participants from 166 different countries and performed tests within an Internet environment, which gave similar results.

The idea of creating online social networks and utilizing the concept of the six degrees of separation firstly appeared in 1998 at a website called *HotLinks*. The website was available for four years. Then, the members were moved to the Friendster [Boyd 2004] network, which was founded in 2002. Since winter 2002, the Friendster network has become more and more popular. As of September 2007, there are more than 21 million members.

Nowadays, there are many other online social networks that take advantage of the six degrees phenomenon. For instance, the idea was adopted to prevent spam. TrustMail [Golbeck *et al.* 2003] filters e-mails in a way that valid messages from unknown users still can be received, if there is a link between the sender and the receiver in the social network graph. Also a large growth of business oriented networks appeared, e.g., LinkedIn[1]. These websites manage professional contacts, enabling users to find employers or employees. There is a number of portals that helps to find new and manage existing social connections. For example, Facebook[2], MySpace[3] or Orkut[4]. Some of them such as Orkut or WIW [Csányi & Szendrői 2004] require invitations to join their network, this way the social network graphs are kept consistent and the portals guarantee that at least one relationship with the community exists for new members.

4.1.1   Trust Management using Social Networks

There is a growing number of wikis and community portals in the contemporary Web 2.0 [O'Reilly 2005; Musser & O'Reilly 2006]. Such portals use social networks that can be applied to define access rights in computer systems and also trust relationships between their participants. In Section 2.2 we introduced a number of trust definitions. To adjust them to the environment of social networks, we introduce our own trust definition in Definition 4.1.

Definition 4.1 (Trust in a Social Network).
Trust is as a personal ranking expressed by a social network member to other members. The ranking can take a number of values between complete distrust (0) and complete trust (1). We assume that if trust is not expressed, it is equal complete distrust (0).   ❖

This definition also implies that we consider some members of the social network as strangers. In Definition 4.2, we explain which social network members we classify as strangers for a given member.

Definition 4.2 (Stranger in a Social Network).
For a social network member $m_A \in M_{SN}$, a stranger is a member $m_B \in M_{SN}$ who is not directly connected with m_A in the social network graph that both of them coexist.   ❖

---

[1]LinkedIn: http://www.linkedin.com/
[2]Facebook: http://facebook.com/
[3]MySpace: www.myspace.com/
[4]Orkut http://www.orkut.com/

To effectively manage access rights using trust extracted from social networks, Golbeck [Golbeck 2005] highlights three desirable trust properties:

- Transitivity - although trust is not transitive in the mathematical sense, we often make this assumption for access control; for instance; the fact that Alice trusts Bob and Bob trusts Carol, do not implicate that Alice trust Carol. However, if there is no explicit statements saying Alice do not trust Carol, the advantage of transitivity is taken and the assumption that Alice trusts Carol is made.

- Composability - because trust can be gained from many sources, for instance different social network connections, one has to specify trust in each source. This way, trust can vary depending on the person for which a composability function is used.

- Personalization and asymmetry - trust is a personal opinion. Two different individuals may have completely different opinions about the same person. The same rule applies to trust in a relationship. Trust does not have to be symmetric.

We take into account these properties in our implementation. An authorization method that supports using these three properties, permits authorization of strangers, and thus, according to [Blaze *et al.* 1996], such a system becomes a trust management solution. However, the model proposed by these authors does not explicitly include social networks. It permits authorization for users having certain roles (e.g., admin, doctor, customer). To narrow this definition [Kruk *et al.* 2006b] introduced community driven access control (see Definition 4.3), which is a special case of trust management.

Definition 4.3 (Community Driven Access Control).
The service S that implements identity management based on social networks UPM_{SN} provides community driven access control over resources $\{r : r \in R_S\} \iff$ the changes introduced to the social network reflect the effective access rights $ACL(r)$ to the resource r. ❖

A simple digraph representation does not provide information about the quality and context of trust relations. To model social network more thoroughly each relationship can be annotated with metrics defining how long the friendship lasts, frequency of meetings, average time spent together. For example, Orkut supports a choice of four predefined types of friendship (*best friends*, *family*, *work*, *school*) and there is also a possibility of creating new groups.

There were also several approaches to twist scales. In theoretical works such as [Gambetta 1988] a probabilistic distribution between 0 (distrust) and 1 (trust) was proposed to express trust between two given persons. The FOAFRealm project [Kruk *et al.* 2006c] introduced a similar approach but in the context of social networks. The system proposes a friendship scale from 0% to 100% to describe connections between the social network members. The Trust Project[5] proposed using numbers from 1 and 10, where 1 means no trust and 10 means absolute trust. Instead of numerical scales, some other approaches [Davis & Vitiello 2005] proposed ontological trust representation for social networks members. It also provided more expressive vocabularies that support specifying for example, friends, enemies, siblings, coworkers, etc.

---

[5]Trust Project: `http://trust.mindswap.org/trustOnt.shtml`

In this thesis we use the friendship level metric introduced by [Kruk *et al.* 2006b] (see Definition 4.4). The friendship values can be expressed in various *contexts*. For example, home or work.

Definition 4.4 (Friendship Level Metric).
Each friendship relation $r \in R_{SN}$ between social network member $m_A \in M_{SN}$ and member $m_B \in M_{SN}$ can be annotated with a quality measure $FLM_{context}(m_A, m_B) \in < 0, 1 >$ representing a friendship level metric within given *context*.   ❖

Many web applications provide access rights control to particular resources defined with access control lists (see Definition 4.5). Community driven access control systems take into account not only the resource's owner, but the whole social network. Such an approach means that a distant node in the social network digraph could be given more trust than a directly neighboring node due to the social connections. This possibility was expressed in for instance FOAFRealm/D-FOAF (see Definition 4.1).

Definition 4.5 (Social Networked Access Control List).
Access control list $ACL_{SN}(m, d, l : m \in M_{SN}, d_{max} \in D_{SN}, flm_{min} \in FLM_{SN})$ defined within user profile management system based on social networks defines access rights delegation within a maximal distance $d_{max} \in D_{SN}$ and a minimal friendship level metric $flm\_context_{min} \in FLM_{SN}$. Both values are computed across the social network SN from the one member $m \in M_{SN}$ to the member requesting access to the resource.   ❖

This definition means that a person is granted access to a resource when the friendship level and the distance between the resource owner and the service requester meet the required constraints. The distance is computed as the shortest path from the owner to the requester. The friendship level is computed by multiplying all metric values (which are all $\in < 0, 1 >$) on the path from the resource owner to the requester. Since there is a possibility of several such paths in the social network digraph, only the highest found product is taken. Access rights can be delegated further only if other requesters conform to the given distance and friendship level constraints.

4.2   Friend-of-a-Friend Vocabulary

The Friend-of-a-Friend (FOAF) [Dan Brickley and Libby Miller 2005] vocabulary was created to support the publication of machine readable user profile descriptions as well as describing online social networks. For example, a profile describing that Alice knows Bob is given in Listing 4.1.

Because of using RDF, statements can occur many times, for instance, by repeating the *foaf:knows* statement with another attribute, Alice can easily express "knows" relationships with more people. This way she is able to specify outgoing connections from her social network node.

The FOAF vocabulary specifies about 60 elements that belong to several categories: FOAF Basics, Personal Info, OnlineAccounts / IM, Project and Groups, Documents and Images (see Table 4.1).

```
<foaf:Person>
    <foaf:name>Alice</foaf:name>
    <foaf:mbox_sha1sum>9485f8a93ec9284a541c0581b48d7a193a74ef89
    </foaf:mbox_sha1sum>
    <foaf:homepage rdf:resource="http://example.org/Alice/" />
    <foaf:depiction rdf:resource="http://example.org/Alice/photo.jpeg" />
    <foaf:knows rdf:resource="mailto:bob@bobsemail.org" />
</foaf:Person>
```

Listing 4.1: An example FOAF profile

	FOAF Basics	Personal Info	Online Accounts / IM	Projects and Groups	Documents and Images
Category					
Classes	Agent Persons		OnlineAccount OnlineChatAccount OnlineEcommerceAcc. OnlineGamingAccount	Project Organization Group	Document Image PersonalProfileDoc.
Properties	name nick title homepage mbox mbox_sha1sum img depiction surname family_name givenname firstName	weblog knows interest currentProject pastProject plan based_near workplaceHomep. workInfoHomep. schoolHomepage topic_interest publications geekcode myersBriggs dnaChecksum	HoldsAccount accountServiceHomep. accountName icqChatID msnChatID aimChatID jabberID yahooChatID	member membershipClass fundedBy theme	topic primaryTopic tipjar sha1 made thumbnail logo

Table 4.1: Classes and properties of FOAF grouped into categories (based on [Dan Brickley and Libby Miller 2005])

4.2.1 Trust Management using FOAF

The *foaf:knows* property enables FOAF to describe relations in social networks. The usability of this information is rather negligible because it does not specify the context or quality of the relationship between two connected individuals. However, the reference FOAF model can be extended with new vocabularies such as XHTML Friends Network (XFN)[6] to make it suitable for an application's needs.

The *foaf:knows* property, which specifies that a given individual knows another one, can be also adapted to other needs such as an access control solution to resources. Since we naturally tend to like some people more than the others, the main consideration is the trust level between two nodes in the social network digraph. However, the FOAF vocabulary does not support trust levels. Such extensions were proposed by other re-

---

[6]XHTML Friends Network: http://www.gmpg.org/xfn/

searchers [Golbeck *et al.* 2003; Davis & Vitiello 2005; Kruk 2004].

As explained in Section 4.1.1, [Kruk *et al.* 2006b] proposed using a real scale between 0 and 1 to represent a trust between two members of a social network. An alternative method is provided by Trust Ontology[7] which rates trust on an integer scale from 1 to 10. Alternative approaches include research work that proposes using an ontological representation [Davis & Vitiello 2005]. This approach enables more a greater level of detail and expressivity but requires additional AI components, known as "reasoners", in the network to enable it.

The FOAF concept of "describing graphs" for members, where they specify their connections, causes privacy issues. In a distributed environment such as the Web, one can publish additional *foaf:knows* information that could be acquired by web-crawlers and in some cases enable them to violate security constraints set up by resources owners. To prevent such situations, additional security enhancements are needed.

Such enhancements were considered in the FOAFRealm project [Grzonkowski *et al.* 2005; Kruk *et al.* 2006a; Choi *et al.* 2008; Choi *et al.* 2006; Grzonkowski *et al.* 2009] that proposes some FOAF vocabulary extensions such as digital signatures, password SHA1 sum, and attaching numerical representations to *foaf:knows* predicate.

Using FOAF for trust management also requires revealing users' email addresses. Even if email addresses are stored in encrypted form using SHA1, they can still be compared with possible match candidates by performing simple hash computations. Thus, their privacy could be compromised.

4.2.2 Authentication using FOAF

Due to the lack of authentication information in the initial FOAF specification, the standard FOAF vocabulary can not be used to provide authentication services. For this reason, in 2007, FOAF was extended by its authors with a *<foaf:openid>* property containing information about users' OpenID logins. Although this property can be used for providing authentication, its usability is marginal: OpenID has been perceived as a convenient, but insecure authentication method [Adida 2007a].

FOAFRealm, which provided a FOAF-based authentication service, considers the *<foaf:mbox>* property as user login. To slightly increase privacy, the system stores only *<foaf:mbox_sha1sum>*. Therefore, the value of *<foaf:mbox>* is never revealed to strangers. Since the FOAF vocabulary does not contain any property for storing password-verifier information, FOAFRealm introduces *<xfoaf:passowrd_sha1sum>* to the vocabulary. During the authentication process, passwords provided by the users are compared with the password SHA1 sum stored in the user's profile at the server side.

This way of authentication does not provide strong security. The users have to send their passwords to the server over a network link. Thus, someone who possesses the user's hash, may attempt a dictionary attack and so this method is prone to phishing [Jagatic *et al.* 2007].

To achieve more secure authentication, [Story *et al.* 2009] proposed combining FOAF with

---

[7]Trust Ontology: `http://trust.mindswap.org/trustOnt.shtml`

SSL. The proposed protocol requires users to own domains and then to issue self-signed certificates using the URL of their domain. These certificates are used during the authentication procedure, in which a user proves that they own the domains embedded in the certificates thus confirming their identities. Although the protocol uses SSL, the applied trust model differs from a standard public key infrastructure (PKI) in the way that the users are responsible for signing and revoking their own certificates. In comparison with traditional PKI infrastructures, the complexity of such a system is much lower. However, this protocol inherits drawbacks typical for certificate-based authentication: certificates can be stolen by other parties, they are much more difficult to install and issue for inexperienced users and most tools support only a command-line interface.

4.2.3 Necessary FOAF extensions

In this chapter we concluded that the existing FOAF techniques are not sufficient to provide authentication and authorization services for end users. To address those issues we list the main requirements that have to be addressed:

- the context or quality of *foaf:knows* has to be specified;

- there is a need for trusted sources of FOAF data;

- the users' privacy has to be addressed to prevent SPAM and unauthorized alterations of their profile information;

- to authenticate a user, there is a need for a property for storing a hash of user's password or a certificate;

- to avoid dictionary attacks, such a property should be kept private within the originating server (or server-side infrastructure).

Part III

Core

*"The effort of using machines to mimic the human mind
has always struck me as rather silly.
I would rather use them to mimic
something better."*

— Edsger Dijkstra

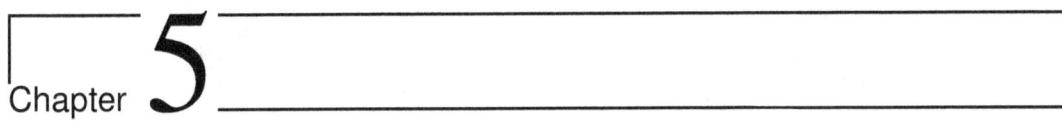

Chapter 5

Conceptual Model*

In this chapter we present the foundations and the conceptual model of Fair Rights Management (FRM). This is our contribution towards fair use in the digital world. To achieve this goal, we propose taking advantage of social networks and semantic techniques of terms negotiation.

Our approach is demonstrated through a use case scenario (see Section 5.1). Then we show how to apply and implement the proposed improvements within a standard DRM model (see Section 2.3.2). FRM introduces a model in which subjects are capable of specifying their own policies (see Section 5.2). Recursive rights delegation to trusted subjects is possible. We demonstrate our improvements to user authentication and its associated semantic infrastructure (see Section 5.3). The model works in distributed environments ensuring that a user's credentials and objects are secure. Finally, in Section 5.4 we define the necessary conceptual foundations to deliver and enable FRM.

5.1 Existing Usage Control Solutions

In Section 2.3.1 we showed that the biggest challenges [LaMacchia 2002] for current DRM systems is to attach a license to a content in a way that it cannot be removed, and to ensure that the devices playing the content respect the license terms. This is a reason why a lot of research effort is focused on interoperability, specifically creating Rights Expression Languages (REL), and content protection mechanisms such as digital watermarks. This situation has the result that many DRM systems are over restrictive [Samuelson 2003]; and efforts to support fair use remain aspirational.

Figure 5.1 depicts a simple scenario, in which users form a social network of trusted friends. They buy electronic items such as books or online courses and create personal sharing policies that are consistent with the purchased licenses. They share those items with their trusted friends. At the same time, if the license agreement is violated for example by making such items available for mass distribution via a website or a peer-to-peer (p2p) network, the

---

*This chapter is partially based on [Grzonkowski *et al.* 2008b]

relevant content provider(s) are able to trace the source of copyright infringement and act accordingly. Furthermore the social network can punish such breeches of trust by penalizing the trust rating of an offender or barring them entirely from the social network.

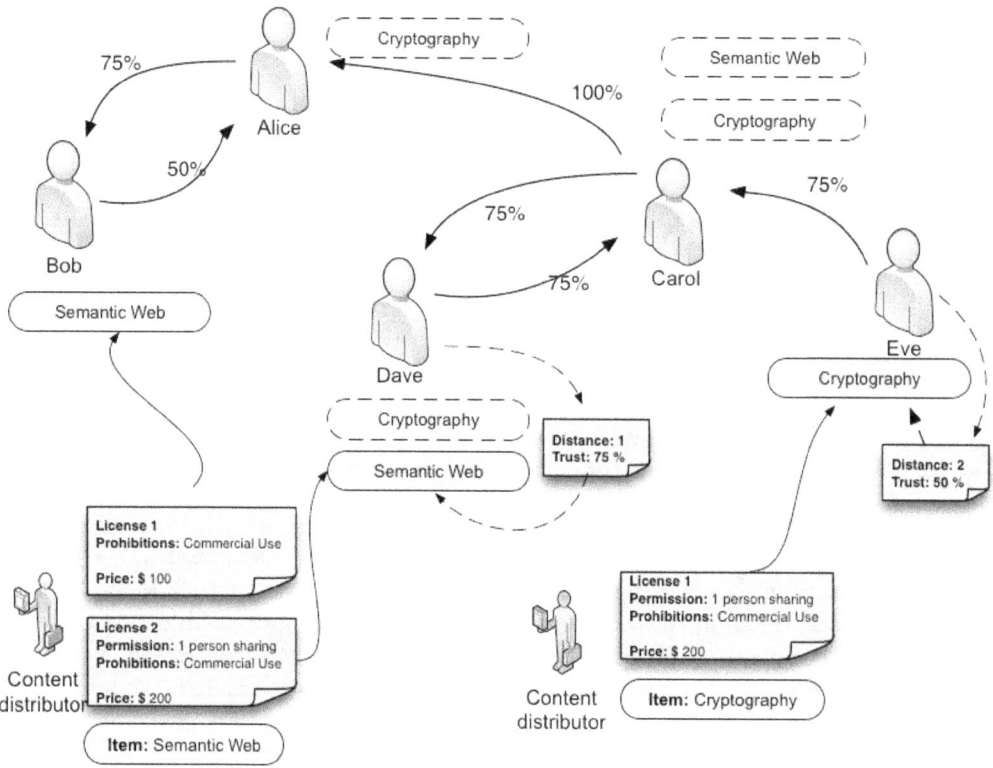

Figure 5.1: Conceptual scenario

This simple scenario is not satisfied by existing DRM or UCON solutions. To address it we created the Fair Rights Management (FRM) platform whose conceptual model and implementation are described in this chapter and in Chapter 7. The main challenges for such a solution are related to security and usability. This scenario operates within a distributed environment, in which data is stored and transmitted via the Internet. The electronic data items must have non-removable licensing components and the users should be able to prove their identities in a safe manner which protects individual privacy. A detailed discussion of these system requirements was presented in the earlier sections of this thesis (see Sections 2.5.2, 3.3 and 4.2.3)

5.2   FRM Usage Control Model

The usage control model that is applied in FRM extends $UCON_{ABC}$ [Park & Sandhu 2002; Park & Sandhu 2004] (see Section 2.4). Figure 5.2 depicts the model using the notation introduced by [Park & Sandhu 2002]. Thus, the meaning of most entities in the model is similar; however, new components were necessary to achieve the new goals. The model offers trust management that allows the usage decision component the calculation of a trust level between two given Subjects. This can be calculated directly where two users have a direct relationship, or by deriving it indirectly from other members of the social network when the users are strangers (see Definition 4.2). The FRM Usage Control Model has the following

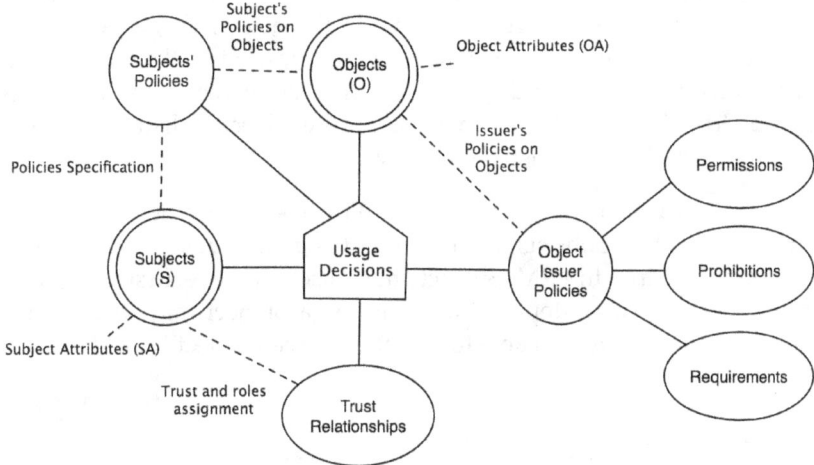

Figure 5.2: FRM Usage Control Model

elements:

- **Subjects**: there are two crucial differences in comparison with $UCON_{ABC}$. Firstly, a Subject may own and delegate obtained rights on Objects. Secondly, a given Subject is able to specify trust relationships with other Subjects. Those relationships are taken into consideration when making the usage decision. A Subject becomes an owner of Objects as a result of a transaction within the system, for example by paying fees. Thus, Subjects are consumers of digital content. Depending on the license agreement, a given Object may be owned by a Subject under different terms of ownership. The terms and policies applying to ownership are ultimately determined by the object issuer. Some terms and policies can entitle the Subject to share the acquired digital Object with other Subjects this providing a means of limited sharing of the digital Object.

- **Objects**: in FRM, Objects are digital media components that Subjects can poses. Usually in DRM-like solutions, Subjects have to pay for using them. In the prototype implementation of the FRM usage model, Objects are enriched with invisible watermarks to provide means for tracing sources of copyright infringement. Any two Subjects acquiring the same object from a content provider have two different copies. The Objects carry the information given by the Object Issuer's Policies because its nature is static. The Subjects' policies are dynamic because they can be changed at any time. Hence, there is always a need to evaluate them, if the Object is to be used by a stranger.

- **Trust Relationships**: the trust relationships are set by Subjects. Trust specified in such a way creates a directed graph that is in fact a social network. The Subjects are able to change the trust relationships at any time. Therefore, the nature of this component is dynamic. This creates an engineering problem, in distributed environments, when passing Objects that require derived authorization to strangers.

- **Object Issuer Policies**: the Object Issuers' Policies specify the terms on which the Object can be used by a Subject. The policies consists of permissions, prohibitions and requirements. *Permissions* describe rights granted by the license. For instance, they may give some extra rights for the subject, e.g., rights delegation. *Prohibitions* disallow the subject from performing certain actions on the object, e.g., a public display is one of these. *Requirements* are additional restrictions imposed by the license. After the transaction between the Subject and the content provider is made, the Object Issuers' Policies are embedded into the object. Therefore, if the Object is distributed by the Subject the policies are attached and distributed as well.

- **Subjects' Policies**: if the Object Issuers' Policies grant a Subject the right to delegate their rights to other Subjects, then a Subject is able to delegate the object through their Trust Relationships. In FRM, Subjects may also enable recursive rights delegation and determine its maximal depth. For example, a Subject may decide that only directly connected Subjects are also able to delegate a given Object.

5.3   Structure of Authorization Decision

In this section we describe how the authorization process works in FRM. We describe the main components involved in the process and compare our solution with other models proposed in the literature. A survey of Authorization in Trust Management solutions was presented in [Chapin *et al.* 2008]. These authors proposed a generalized structure for an authorization decision (see Figure 5.3(a)). Compared to UCON, this is an alternative model.

An *Authorization Decision* has been defined as the determination of whether a given requester possesses the necessary attributes to access a particular resource as mediated by local policy, based on well-defined semantic of policies and credentials. The output of the model is a boolean "yes" or "no" decision. The components are defined as follows [Chapin *et al.* 2008]:

- L - Authorization mechanism: the automated means by which an authorization decision is reached. Depending on the context, this refers to an algorithm or a module of software executed by the authorizer.

- P - Policy: local policy that can be defined in some specification language

- T_P - Policy Compilation: Compile statements in a hight-level policy language into lower level terms for the core semantics

- C - Certificates: define credentials for a particular requester

- V - Certificate Validation: determines if a certificate is valid. For example, most of the certificates define lifetime information.

- T_C - Credential Encoding: transforms certificate credentials into credentials defined in terms understood by the core semantics

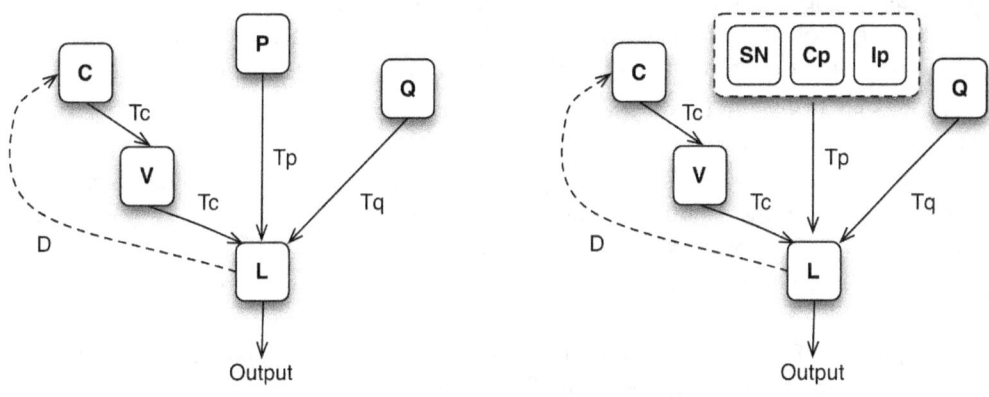

(a) Generalized structure [Chapin *et al.* 2008]   (b) The way FRM extends the generalized structure

Figure 5.3: Structure of Authorization Decision

- *D* - Distributed Certificate Discovery: represents the possibility of attempting to discover and collect credentials that are missing

- *Q* - Authorization Query: a question or goal that is specialized for a particular access request

- T_Q - Query Compilation: translates the goal into terms understood by the core semantics

To map FRM on this model, the policy model needs a social network extension. Therefore, new parameters have to be taken into consideration in the *Policy* module when making an authorization decision. Figure 5.3(b) shows how FRM fits and extends the proposed model with the following components:

- C_P - Customer Policies: specific policies of access to a resource expressed by the user

- SN - Social Network: trust connections between the user and other users. Trust can be computed using transitive values of the social network digraph.

- I_P - Issuer Policies: policies expressed by the license. They define limitations for C_P.

The implementation details of the applied Usage Control Model are presented in Section 7.4.

5.4 Model Definitions

To formalize trust relationships between Subjects, we use the *Friendship Level Metric* (FLM) introduced in Section 4.1.1. We additionally provide a more accurate definition of a *social network member* (see Definition 5.1). A *social network member* is a special case of a Subject that participates in a system using social networks. This way we highlight the difference between FRM and other Usage Control Models. We also use the terminology introduced in Section 5.3, specifically Customer Policies (C_P), Social Network (SN), and Issuer Policies (I_P). Then, we introduce the notion of a service (S). The service is responsible for storing Social Networks, usernames (u) with their corresponding verifiers (v), and roles (UPM_{ROLES}).

Definition 5.1 (Social network member).
A social network member $m \in M_{SN}$ is distinguished from other members $m_n \in M_{SN}$ by a different username $u : u \in Ur$ that is registered at the service S. Each u has a corresponding verifier v which is the result of a one-way function f that $v = f(m, p)$. The password p is known only to m and is not revealed to the service S in any point of time of the *authentication procedure* (see Section 7.6.1). ❖

In FRM, we use FOAFRealm-like definitions of a friend that implements FLM. Thus, it goes beyond FOAF and extends it with a quality parameter.

Definition 5.2 (Friend).
Member $m_a \in M_{SN}$ is considered as a friend of member's $m_b \in M_{SN}$ if there is a direct connection from m_b to m_a within the social network M_{SN}. Each friendship relation has a corresponding value defined within the given *friendship level metric*. ❖

Hence, the modeled social network [Barnes 1954] is a digraph, in which edges have assigned labels that represent friendship quality. Additionally the model contains Objects $o : o \in O_S$ that can be added to the service S by social network members who are assigned to role *uploader* $u_{ROLE} \in UPM_{ROLES}$.

In FRM, the social network members are not allowed to access objects o in their original form. A personalized copy o' is created each time a social network member requests o.

Definition 5.3 (FRM Object).
A personalized FRM Object o' is prepared for each Subject's request by using a watermarking function fw. As an input, the watermarking function takes the original Object $o \in O_S$, the username u of a social network member m who is the owner of the Object o and the issuer's policies I_P on which the transaction between the service S and member m was made. o' is computed as $o' = fw(o, u, I_P)$. ❖

In this definition fw is a private function known only to S. Possession of o' is not sufficient to calculate o. I_P can be read from o', but u can be read only when having a secret key that is set up by S.

I_P are composed of various terms. The terms include permissions, prohibitions, and requirements, which are specific for each transaction. Thus we introduce the notion of $P_{terms_{agreed}}$, $Pr_{terms_{agreed}}$, and $R_{terms_{agreed}}$ which respectively represents permissions, prohibitions, and requirements agreed in a given transaction. We also introduce the concept of a $FRMPlayer$ (see Section A.7). Its objective is the capability of using or playing $FRMObjects$ in a meaningful way.

Definition 5.4 (Permission).
A permission $perm \in P_{terms}$ for an Object $o \in O_S$ can be issued to a social network member $m \in M_{SN}$ as a result of Buy Item (see Section A.5) or Borrow Item (see Section A.4) procedures. The set of permissions $P_{terms_{agreed}} \subseteq P_{terms}$ assigned to m is evaluated by the $FRMPlayer$ when playing the FRM Object o'. ❖

Definition 5.5 (Prohibition).
A prohibition $proh \in Pr_{terms}$ for an Object $o \in O_S$ can be issued to a social network member $m \in M_{SN}$ as a result of Buy Item (see Section A.5) or Borrow Item (see Section A.4) procedures. The set of prohibitions $Pr_{terms_{agreed}} \subseteq Pr_{terms}$ assigned to m is evaluated by the $FRMPlayer$ when playing the FRM Object o'. ❖

Definition 5.6 (Requirement).
A requirement $req \in R_{terms}$ for an Object $o \in O_S$ can be issued to a social network member $m \in M_{SN}$ as a result of Buy Item (see Section A.5) or Borrow Item (see Section A.4) procedures. The set of requirements $R_{terms_{agreed}} \subseteq R_{terms}$ assigned to m is evaluated by the $FRMPlayer$ when playing the FRM Object o'. ❖

An issuer of an Object may define many usage terms for the same Object. During the purchase phase, the Subject and the issuer make an agreement about the terms and the price. Hence, the license is expressed as a set of terms:

$$I_P = P_{terms_{agreed}} \cup Pr_{terms_{agreed}} \cup R_{terms_{agreed}}$$

The member $m \in M_{SN}$ can also specify the customer policies (C_P) that are a subset of issuer policies ($C_P \supseteq I_P$). If an Object o' can be shared with the social network members, the member m who bought or borrowed the Object, can specify the maximum distance in the social network and minimal required trust level that is necessary to enable further sharing. Each member that is given access to the Object through the social network M_{SN}, can also set his/her own sharing policies C_P on the borrowed Object. Each time the Object is accessed, recursive calculations are made to determine if social sharing is granted. Hence, the rights on the Object R_{OBJ} for a member m are calculated as a function of several parameters:

$$R_{OBJ} = (I_P, C_P, Id, u, SN)$$

where u is given and confirmed during the authentication procedure. Id represents the identification number of the member bought the object. I_P, Id are read from o' when a member m with the username u attempts to play the object o. C_P is calculated recursively on the path from Id to m in the given social network SN.

In FRM, *memberA* can borrow an Object $Object2 \in objects_{memberB}$ from *memberB*, if there is a direct or derived trust relationship between them. In addition *memberB* must enable and set the minimal trust level that permits sharing. If *memberA* satisfies the distance and the trust level requirements, the sharing operation is permitted and the object can be download (see Section A.2). As a result of this operation, *memberA* is given a personalized $FRMObject$ based on the requested *Object2*.

In order to buy an Object, a member must successfully complete a financial transaction. The member acquires with a personalized version of the purchased Object on the terms that were agreed during the transaction and are expressed in the object license. The object license and the member *id* are permanently attached to each downloaded object. In turn such an object can be shared by this member. Depending on the value of R_{OBJ}, the object can be also shared by this member's friends. To download the Object, a member must authenticate in a secure way.

5.5 Summary

In this chapter we have identified several problems with existing Usage Control and DRM solutions. Specifically, the need for a more flexible usage control model that keeps the usage process and associated workflow secure.

We also note that there is a need for a trust management and explored how this can be implemented using social networks. The need for a secure and convenient means of user authentication in a distributed environment was motivated.

In the context of digital content it was emphasized that licenses should be attached to the content in a way that makes it difficult to remove them. It was also observed that existing solutions cause interoperability and legal conflicts. In particular DRM solutions fail to provide any meaningful support for a consumer's fair use rights for digital content.

We proposed Fair Rights Management (FRM) to deal with those issues. It is demonstrated how FRM differs from existing UCON solutions. Then, we described how an authentication decision is made. Finally, the conceptual foundations for a working FRM implementation are explored.

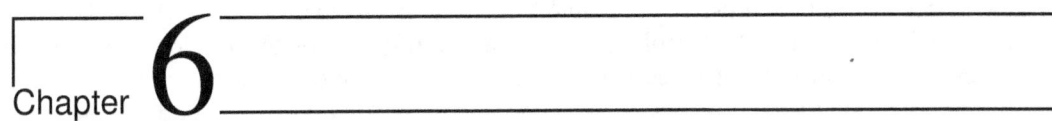

Chapter 6

Zero Knowledge Proof Authentication*

This chapter introduces the reader to Zero Knowledge Proof (ZKP) authentication protocols, which are secure methods of claiming identity. In ZKP, the verifier is unable to learn anything from the authentication procedure and the prover is unable to repeat the procedure with another verifier. In Section 6.1, we describe the foundations of the ZKP idea. We also present a generic ZKP protocol. In Section 6.2, we present the main mathematical problems that could be used to create such a protocol. In particular our considerations include classical problems, elliptic curves, and graph isomorphism. We present those three approaches since they differ fundamentally in the way they operate on data structures: numbers, points and matrices. We then focus on graph isomorphism describing various approaches to attack it. Section 6.3 describes some practical implementations of the ZKP protocols. In Section 6.4, we discuss usability issues for a web deployment of ZKP.

6.1 Zero Knowledge Proof Authentication

The zero-knowledge proof term has been formalized by Goldwasser, Micali, and Rack-off [Goldwasser *et al.* 1985]. It describes a group of challenge-response authentication protocols, in which parties are required to prove the correctness of their secrets, without revealing these secrets. Such protocols exist for any NP problem, provided that one-way functions exist [Goldwasser *et al.* 1985].

The use of zero-knowledge proofs as a mean of proving identity was first proposed by [Feige *et al.* 1988]. The protocol depends on prime numbers and uses modular arithmetic. The protocol was further developed by [Guillou & Quisquater 1988] to lower the bandwidth and memory requirements. [Schnorr 1989] proposed an alternative for the protocol using the intractability of the discrete logarithm problem. The work of these three groups of researchers supports the use of ZKP in a network environment, but they all require digital certificates to work. Therefore, users are unable to use their login and passwords pairs and also the presence of a trusted third party is required to confirm the validity of digital certificates. Thus,

---

*This chapter is partially based on [Grzonkowski *et al.* 2008b; Grzonkowski & Corcoran 2009]

existing usage of ZKP techniques would appear to suffer from the same complexity of use as many of the authentications techniques examined in Chapter 3.

The ZKP protocol can be described in several general steps. Firstly, a requirement of the protocol is that a prover who can be a user, say *Alice*, has to register her name and public key. Those credentials must be accessible to the server which acts as a verifier. The user's key-pair depends on an NP problem that is used in the protocol. All her login attempts can be described in several steps (see Figure 6.1), in which *Alice* requests server authentication. During the authentication procedure, a client-side application must respond to a number of challenges issued by the server:

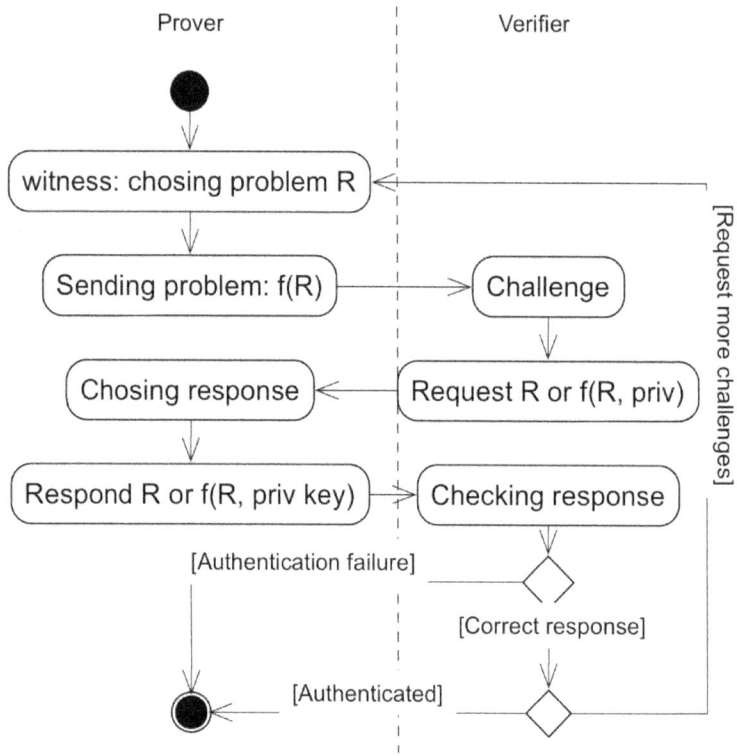

Figure 6.1: A generic zero-knowledge proof protocol

- Step 1 - *Alice* generates a random problem R and she computes f(R) using a one way hash function. The problem and the function are specific to the NP problem the protocol uses.

- Step 2 - She sends f(R) to the server where she wishes to be authenticated. She keeps R secret.

- Step 3 - The server stores the received f(R) function and sends a request to *Alice*. The request contains a challenge. The challenge is a random decision that requires *Alice* to be capable of answering one of two questions: one of which demonstrates her knowledge of the private key (f(R, private key)); and the other, an easy question, to prevent her from guessing (R). Thus, the server randomly chooses the question.

- Step 4 - *Alice* sends back the answer that depends on the challenge: f(R, private key) or R. She always reveals only one parameter.

- Step 5 - The server verifies her answer. If the answer is correct, the server can authenticate her or she can be queried for another challenge to decrease the probability of guessing; if so, the algorithm starts over with Step 1.

In this protocol, Step 1 is also called *witness*, Steps 2 and 3 are *the challenge*, whereas step 4 is *the response*. If the protocol is repeated t times, all t rounds must be answered successfully to prove *Alice's* identity. The server is always convinced with probability $1\text{-}2^{-t}$. In zero-knowledge proof protocols, the verifier cannot learn anything from the authentication process. Moreover, the verifier is unable to cheat the prover because he only has a single value from two possible challenge responses. This is not sufficient to calculate the prover's secret. Furthermore, a dishonest prover cannot cheat the verifier because the protocol is repeated as long as the verifier is not convinced. Due to random challenge selection, a dishonest verifier cannot pretend to be the prover to another verifier.

To satisfy the aforementioned properties, any zero-knowledge protocol must satisfy three conditions:

1. Soundness - if a statement is true, an honest prover will be able to convince a verifier of this fact

2. Correctness - if a statement is false, a dishonest verifier will not be able to cheat the verifier with any significant probability of success

3. Zero-knowledge - if a statement is true, a dishonest verifier is unable to learn anything about the prover's secret

We note that in this thesis we focus on interactive zero knowledge protocols. However, there is also a variant of non-interactive zero-knowledge (NIZK) protocols. Some authors [Blum *et al.* 1988] have shown that it is enough for two parties to share a common random string to achieve zero-knowledge without interaction. NIZK protocols are also robust in a concurrent setting (see Section 6.3.2). They preserve zero-knowledge even if the same string is shared globally [Feige *et al.* 1990]. However, NIZK require stronger cryptographic assumptions (trapdoor one-way permutations as opposed to arbitrary one-way functions) and in general they are much less efficient than interactive ZKP [Damgard 1999].

Later in this chapter we discuss three variations of interactive zero-knowledge protocols. Each of them uses different data structures, thus having unique properties that we briefly describe.

6.2 Approaches to ZKP

We present three approaches since these differ in the way they operate on data structures: numbers, points, matrices. We then focus on graph isomorphism since it does not cause round-off errors; it does not rely on prime numbers; and the necessary calculations are performed on integers. We also describe how graph isomorphism can be used to construct a ZKP protocol. Thus, we present various approaches to solve the problem of finding isomorphism of two given graphs.

6.2.1 Classical Problems

There are two main classical problems that enable zero-knowledge proofs [Menezes *et al.* 1996]: the discrete logarithm problem [ElGamal 1985] and the square-root problem [Rabin 1979]. Recent findings in quantum cryptography [Ambainis 2004], however, show that their complexity, and thus their usefulness, can be significantly decreased by using Peter Shor's algorithm. For a detailed description of the algorithm, we refer the interested reader to [Shor 1997]. These problems strongly depend on generating prime numbers. Moreover, the security of a key that is 1024-bits-long is comparable with the security of a 160-bit key in elliptic curve cryptography [Barker *et al.* 2007]. Therefore, the classical approach is considered to have been replaced with other solutions. Nevertheless we will briefly explain the basis of each technique for completeness.

Discrete logarithm problem

The discrete logarithm problem is defined as finding an x such that

$$g^x = b \bmod n$$

where g, b, and n are known for both the prover and verifier. Additionally, x must be coprime to n [ElGamal 1985]. Solving this problem is known to be computationally infeasible [ElGamal 1985; Menezes *et al.* 1996].

Square-root problem

The square-root problem is defined as

$$x^2 = b \bmod n$$

for known b, and n. In addition, x must be coprime to n [Rabin 1979].

6.2.2 Elliptic Curves

Applicability of Elliptic Curve in Cryptography (ECC) was proposed independently in 1985 by Victor Miller [Miller 1986] and Neal Koblitz [Koblitz 1987]. It is an efficient and attractive alternative to the classical public key cryptosystems. A public-private key-pair on an elliptic curve is defined as

$$y^2 = x^3 + ax + b$$

where $4a^3 + 27b^2 \neq 0$.

The security of ECC depends on the difficulty of solving the Elliptic Curve Discrete Logarithm Problem. The security of keys used in ECC is much higher than the security of the same size keys for classical problems [Barker *et al.* 2007]. Additionally, the keys can be compressed: if we have one of the coordinates of a key, we can compute the other one using the elliptic curve equation.

The main operation involved in ECC is point multiplication. For example, n is a scalar and P and Q are two points on an elliptic curve such that $nP = Q$. It is computationally infeasible to calculate n for sufficiently large numbers. In practice, Q acts as a user's public key, whereas P becomes the private key. In order to make the computations fast, they are performed using finite fields. This involves finding a multiplicative inverse of a number, which is the main barrier to provide an efficient implementation. To avoid many multiplicative inverse operations, points can be represented in projective coordinates [Blake *et al.* 1999]. Although this eliminates the need to compute many multiplicative inverses, it requires more scalar multiplication than with affine coordinates.

6.2.3 Graph Isomorphism

Graphs $G_1 = (V_1, E_1)$ and $G_2 = (V_2, E_2)$ that have the same sets of vertices $V_1 = V_2 = \{1,2,...,n\}$ are isomorphic, if there exists a permutation π on vertices $\{1, 2, \ldots, n\}$ so that $(u, v) \in E_1 \leftrightarrow (\pi(u), \pi(v)) \in E_2$. Therefore, to produce an isomorphic graph G_2 of graph G_1, we have to rename its vertices. An example is depicted in Figure 6.2. The problem is not likely to be

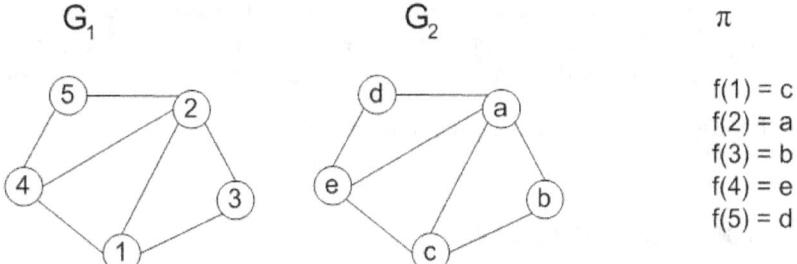

Figure 6.2: An example graph isomorphism for $G_2 = \pi(G_1)$.

NP-complete [Schöning 1987], but it is NP. There are no known polynomial-time algorithms that can solve it (see Section 6.2.4).

The first zero knowledge proof protocol for graph isomorphism was given by [Goldreich *et al.* 1988]. In this protocol, a public key is composed of two isomorphic graphs G_1 and G_2, whereby the permutation π_p

$$G_2 = \pi_p(G_1)$$

is a private key. A prover generates a random permutation π_R, and sends a graph $G_R = \pi_R(G_1)$ to the verifier. Then, depending on the verifier's challenge, the prover sends back π_R or π_{R2} such that

$$\pi_{R2} = \pi_R \circ \pi_p^{-1}.$$

Thus, π_{R2} is a product of the permutation π_R and the inverse of the permutation π_p^{-1}. The verifier is able to check one of the conditions:

$$G_R = \pi_R(G_1) \text{ or } G_R = \pi_{R2}(G_2)$$

Knowledge about only one parameter π_{R1} or π_{R2} does not let the verifier compute the prover's private key.

Such a protocol operates on graphs; there is no need to use additional field arithmetic and the computations do not have round-off errors.

6.2.4 Algorithms for Determining Graph Isomorphism

Efficient algorithms for graphs of restricted types were proposed; For example, probabilistic algorithms were discussed by [Babai *et al.* 1980; Babai & Kucera 1979]; [Gil & Zibin 2005] proposed efficient algorithms, but only for isomorphism of simple types; [Spielman 1996] proposed a solution only for strongly regular graphs. There is also a polynomial-time algorithm for determining the isomorphism of graphs of fixed genus [Filotti & Mayer 1980] and for trees [Aho *et al.* 1974]; another group of approaches are brute-force algorithms for sub-graph isomorphism [Ullmann 1976]. Furthermore, [Corneil & Gotlieb 1970] described algorithms for determining if two graphs are isomorphic; however, very often the problem is to find the permutation, not to determine if two given graphs are isomorphic. There are also informal publications claiming that there are polynomial algorithms for graph isomorphism [Czerwinski 2007; Duda 2008], but they were already questioned by counterexamples.

We further discuss graph isomorphism in Sections 8.5.3 and 8.6.

6.3 Protocol Compositions

To provide practical solutions, there were many attempts to optimize the generic protocol (see Section 6.1), especially by introducing parallelization and permitting concurrent executions. However, many researchers have demonstrated that such improvements might cause specific protocols to lose their zero-knowledge properties [Goldreich & Krawczyk 1990; Bellare *et al.* 1990; Canetti *et al.* 2000]. Thus, there is an important question regarding zero-knowledge interactive proofs: whether they preserve their zero-knowledge properties in a specific protocol composition. This determines if a given security protocol is applicable for practical realizations. We distinguish three main compositions of zero-knowledge proofs protocols: sequential, parallel, and concurrent. In all compositions we assume that both parties: the prover and verifier follow the prescribed protocol. We also assume that the actions of the honest parties in each executions of the protocol are independent from their actions in other executions of the protocol. An adversary may, however, run various executions of the same protocol and try to take some advantage from each execution. Therefore, it is crucial to create protocols that can preserve their zero-knowledge property in various networked environments. In a perfect situation, the users should keep track of the protocol executions. However, this is unrealistic in practice. There might be also a need for a coordinator, but trying to coordinate the protocol executions is problematic and requires additional infrastructure. Thus, in a practical solution the number of possible interactions between a prover and a verifier must be large enough to ensure each protocol cycle is different from previous cycles.

It was noted by [Canetti *et al.* 2000] that all known zero knowledge protocols are breakable, if an adversary can reset the prover to its initial state and force to use the same random coin or tape. This problem is particularly interesting in case of implementing smart cards. Thus, [Canetti *et al.* 2000] proposed the notion of resettable zero-knowledge (rZK). The rZK protocols remain zero knowledge even if an adversary can interact with the prover many times, each time reseting the prover to its initial state. According to [Canetti *et al.* 2000], to design protocols resistant to this attack, protocol implementations have to deliver their own random numbers generators. In addition, these generators should take challenges from verifiers as input values for their algorithms.

6.3.1 Sequential and Parallel Compositions

In a sequential compositions the protocol is invoked many times and each invocation follows the termination of the previous one. The original formulation of zero-knowledge is not closed under sequential composition [Goldreich & Krawczyk 1990]. The applicability of such protocols is, however, very limited since they cannot be used safely more than once.

In a parallel composition, many instances of the same protocol are invoked simultaneously. It means that *ith* messages of many instances of the protocol are sent at the same time.

In general, the zero-knowledge condition is not satisfied under parallel composition. [Goldreich & Krawczyk 1990] gave examples of protocols that are zero-knowledge with respect to the strongest known definitions, but their parallel compositions are not zero-knowledge. A naive approach to parallelization is not sufficient to preserve zero-knowledge. To make it possible, the verifier must commit the challenge questions before receiving the commitment from the prover [Bellare *et al.* 1990].

6.3.2 Concurrent Composition

A concurrent zero knowledge [Dwork *et al.* 2004] is a generalization between sequential and parallel ZKP composition. It is based on the use of multiple instances of the protocol but invoked at arbitrary times and each proceeds at an arbitrary pace.

Concurrent zero-knowledge takes into account situations in which a malicious verifier can interact several times with the same prover in an interleaved way (see Section 3.1). To preserve zero knowledge, [Dwork *et al.* 1998] proposed using so-called timing assumptions. Under these assumptions, there are a-priori known bounds on the delays of messages with respect to some global clock. Each party has also a local clock whose rate is within a constant factor of rate of the global clock. Thus in some cases parties delay response messages or alternatively consider messages outdated (time-out). [Dwork *et al.* 1998] argue that using these timing assumptions of concurrent protocols preserve zero knowledge. Such a solution limits the possibility of nesting sessions by dishonest parties. Further, [Dwork & Sahai 1998] showed that the timing assumptions can be even pushed to the preprocessing phase. [Richardson & Kilian 1999] demonstrated how to construct a zero knowledge protocol under the concurrent assumption. However, their protocols are not constant round.

[Goldreich 2002] notes that proving that a protocol is parallel zero-knowledge suffices for concurrent composition: it is reasonable to assume that the parties' local clock have approximately the same rate, and that drifting is corrected by occasional clock synchronization; the global time can be divided into phases and each of them can consist of a constant number of rounds; thus each party wishing to execute the protocol just delays its invocation to the beginning of the next phase; subsequently, concurrent execution of constant-round protocol in this setting amounts to a sequence of time-disjoint almost-parallel executions of the protocol [Goldreich 2002].

For practical implementations of zero-knowledge protocols, it is desirable that they preserve their security properties under the concurrent composition.

6.4 Usability Considerations of using ZKP Protocols

ZKP authentication protocols cause additional computational and communication overhead. Therefore, in computational and bandwidth limited environments such as web-browsers, and mobile phones, there is a need for efficient protocols in terms of messages sent and steps performed.

For usability purposes, the integration of ZKP solutions with existing web applications should be transparent from the user's perspective. Thus, installation of additional plugins or protocols would not satisfy this requirement.

We note that Web users are accustomed to use logins and password pairs. It would be desirable to have a similar interface to ZKP protocols to simplify their presentation to end-users. However we note that ZKP was originally created to provide a reliable PKI infrastructure and did not envisage the use of plaintext usernames and passwords.

Introducing passwords also introduces additional risks which were not considered by the originators of ZKP techniques. Such risks are mainly dictionary attacks on low-entropy passwords (see Section 3.1). If we are to adapt ZKP techniques for standard Web usage it is desirable to minimize these risks or the significant benefits of ZKP security will be lost.

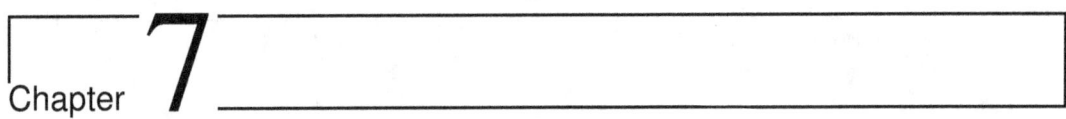

Chapter 7

Implementation*

In this chapter we present our implementation of Fair Rights Management (FRM). This provides the basis for a comprehensive semantic content distribution and usage control platform. This platform uses and extends existing semantic web standards to satisfy contemporary usage control requirements for digital content. Furthermore, FRM has been designed with a view to supporting the more significant fair use scenarios. It also provides a reliable identity management system, supports machine-readable digital licenses and incorporates methods for protecting the content that is distributed.

In Section 7.1 we describe in detail the implementation of the FRM conceptual model developed in Chapter 5. Then, in Section 7.2 the applied trust management module is presented. In Section 7.3 the Rights Expression Language employed by FRM is described. Section 7.4 describes the key classes and properties of the core ontology model for FRM. Section 7.5 provides details on the digital watermarking implementation employed in our FRM prototype. The most significant design and development efforts were spent on developing the authentication service for FRM, employing the Zero-Knowledge Proof protocol and described in Section 7.6. Finally, in Section 7.7 we present application scenarios for FRM.

7.1 Conceptual Model Implementation

This section presents the building blocks of FRM. They are compatible with the four components-based architecture explained in Section 2.3. We also demonstrate how the improvements introduced in Sections 5.2 and 5.3 are implemented.

The layered structure of the FRM is depicted in Figure 7.1. The bottom layer of the model is composed of four data sources:

- Users' Identities: this data is required by the authorization and authentication services. The authorization service stores not only user profile information, but also informa-

---

*This chapter is partially based on [Grzonkowski & Zaremba 2008; Grzonkowski *et al.* 2008b; Grzonkowski *et al.* 2009]

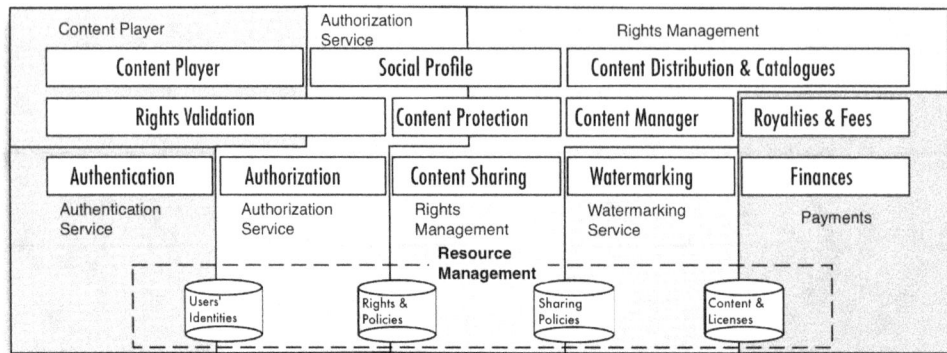

Figure 7.1: The conceptual model of the FRM platform

tion on how these profiles are connected to one another. It computes social network distances and trust levels. The authentication module stores bindings between user identities and their corresponding public keys

- Rights and Policies: persistent storage of contracts that are agreed between the customers and the content owners. This data is accessed when authorization or content sharing services are requested

- Sharing Policies: this storage is responsible for storing user sharing policies C_P (see Section 5.4) that are crucial when content is shared across a social networks

- Content and Licenses: this repository stores catalogues of digital content. The catalogues consist of both resources r and their corresponding issuer policies I_P (see Section 5.4). This data is required to facilitate financial transactions between customers and content owners

The first layer of the model is composed of essential services that are building blocks for the upper-layers

- Authentication: the authentication module executes a zero-knowledge proof protocol to confirm user identities

- Authorization: the key component of the authorization service is the social network component. To complete the authorization process, this component also analyzes sharing policies C_P

- Content Sharing: this module analyzes both the issuer policies I_P and the corresponding customers policies C_P

- Watermarking: this module embeds additional meta-data into the files that are distributed through FRM. This embedded metadata consists of the buyer's identity and the agreed license. There are also metadata components that can be read solely by the content provider. Watermarking is crucial to provide security of distributed items

- Finances: this service is required for performing online payments and ensuring that the transactions are made correctly

The next layer integrates the output of the bottom layer components. It does not have direct access to the primary data sources.

- Rights Validation: this module analyzes information relating to a requester's identity, the content owner and the social network (see Section 5.4). The *Rights Validation* module acts on behalf of the upper layers to provide a determination if a given content satisfies all the criteria to allow it to be legally displayed, played, rendered or otherwise "activated"

- Content Protection: the protection of the given content is provided in a passive way, which means that the distributed content has one or more digital watermarks incorporated. Thus, a content player performs an authentication procedure to determine if a given user is permitted to play the content

- Content Manager: this module is necessary to provide content providers with the possibility of uploading new content to the system. In FRM, the content providers have the same possibilities as regular members. However, they additionally perform an *uploader* role. This role acts as an indicator for the system of their extra capabilities and permissions

- Royalties and Fees: this module is responsible for performing online transactions between the content uploaders and the customers. In FRM we only simulate this functionality and provide required API that could be used by other systems

The top layer of the model consists of three main components that are the end-point services and user interfaces:

- Content Player: this is the user interface created on top of the *Rights Validation* module. It enables users to prove their identities in a zero-knowledge proof way; and then to use this established identity in the authorization module to determine if the content can be played for the established identity

- Social Profile: is the user interface for managing the user's social network

- Content Distribution and Catalogues: this is a service delivered by the content provider for an efficient and convenient content search and browsing

The FRM platform implementation has been split into six functional modules (see Figure 7.1):

- Rights Management: the implementation of this module covers Content Sharing, Content Manager, Content Distribution and Catalogues, partially Social Profile, and also Content Protection. This component is described in Section 7.4

- Authorization Service described in Section 7.2 includes trust management and also partially Social Profile, Content Protection and Rights Validation

- Content Player and Watermarking modules are described in Section 7.5

- Authentication Service: this is based on Zero-Knowledge Proof (ZKP) protocols and is described in Section 7.6

- Financial module that is simulated. However, this topic is explored in more detail in [Grzonkowski & Corcoran 2009]

7.2   Trust Management and Access Control

The FOAF vocabulary alone is not sufficient to provide trust management using social networks. The main problem is that the contexts or qualities of the relationships are not expressed (see Section 4.2.1). Various approaches to this problem were proposed [Golbeck 2005; Kruk *et al.* 2006b; Davis & Vitiello 2005] (see Section 4.2.1). In FRM, to provide trust management and access control, we have applied Distributed FOAFRealm (D-FOAF) [Grzonkowski *et al.* 2005; Kruk *et al.* 2006b; Grzonkowski *et al.* 2009]. The system is a result of collaboration between DERI Galway and Gdansk University of Technology (GUT). Its first centralized version (FOAFRealm) was developed in 2004 [Kruk 2004]. The system was later extended to a distributed service by other researchers participating in the collaboration. The main component that made the system distributed across multiple FOAFRealm instances was a hypercube-based peer-to-peer (P2P) network [Grzonkowski & Kruk 2006]. Using this P2P network, D-FOAF purses the idea of single registration, in which users have accounts in one of the member services called the registration server [Hardt 2004; Shen & Dewan 1992]. Then, the user can easily login to the other member services of the distributed identity management system. Users have to remember only one set of credentials representing their identities while the system performs a distributed authorization [Woo & Lam 1993] using the underlying p2p topology.

Thanks to D-FOAF, the members of web communities who are spread across a number of different web applications are able to have single credentials and single lists of friends [Kruk *et al.* 2006b; Grzonkowski *et al.* 2009] contained in FOAF-style profiles.

Such a social network and distributed profile management system must be protected from many threats. These threats can be divided into several categories [Grzonkowski *et al.* 2005]:

- Fundamental problems: this group includes the aforementioned authentication problems described by [Menezes *et al.* 1996], MITM, encryption cracking, etc

- Technical problems: most of problems in this category are related to the TCP/IP architecture, for instance, DoS, DNS Spoofing, sniffing

- Browser problems: they are mainly related to cookies and various possibilities cookies theft

- Human related problems: such as choosing weak passwords and usernames, not understanding systems security, phishing

- Other problems: they are caused by software bugs, trojans or malware

Because the definition of access rights in community driven access management (see Definition 4.3) is based on the structure of the social network, this information must be robustly protected by an identity management system [Kaye 2004]. Improved security within such a distributed social network can be achieved by signing user profiles with a private keys issued by the registration server for each user [Thompson *et al.* 2003]. To allow a user to access protected resources, the service has to check the presented credentials and confirm that the user satisfies the requested access control list restrictions. Thus, the service has to check if the given distance and friendship level meet the required constraints. Distance and friendship level metrics computations are executed each time the user requests access to the protected resources. In D-FOAF, the process of calculating user rights in a distributed network is based on the modified Dijkstra algorithm [Dijkstra 1959; Kruk *et al.* 2006b].

D-FOAF provided an infrastructure for a distributed trust management. However, it was still necessary to build new components on top of it to provide a DRM solution that is less restrictive than existing approaches. There was also a need to create additional components to keep this less restrictive model secure.

7.3 Applied Rights Expression Model

In Section 2.3.3 we have introduced the most prominent Rights Expression Languages (REL), namely ODRL and MPEG REL. In this work to describe the usage rights on resources, we decided to use the Creative Commons [Lessig 2004] (CC)[1] licensing scheme. In this Section we justify our choice of the CC rights model for the Fair Rights Management prototype.

Creative Commons licenses (CC) were proposed and released by Creative Commons, a non-profit organization founded by Lawrence Lessig [Lessig 2004]. The licenses allow the content creators to indicate if they would like to waive any of their normal legal rights - primarily copyright - for the benefit of others.

Instead of labeling copyrighted content with an "All Rights Reserved" notice, with CC, authors may label the copyrighted content with a "Some Rights Reserved" notice. This enables other individuals to mix or reuse their works. Terms and conditions expressed by CC licenses can be easily modeled using ontologies and Semantic Web techniques. Thus, a corresponding RDF vocabulary (CcRdf) was proposed[2]. It is slightly enriched with other vocabularies, mainly Dublin Core[3] [Weibel *et al.* 1998].

The main classes of this vocabulary are *Work* and *License*. *Work* can have several predicates such as *title*, *description* and a link to the corresponding *license*. *Licenses* can express permission, prohibitions and requirements given by the content creators. These terms specify, for example, the nature of distribution of the digital work, if the character of the use is commercial, or if a new digital work containing CC licensed material can still be distributed. The Creative Commons [Lessig 2004] RDF License format enables the expression of permissions,

---

[1]Creative Commons, `http://creativecommons.org/`
[2]CC RDF License Validator: `http://validator.creativecommons.org/`
[3]Dublin Core Metadata Initiative: `http://dublincore.org/`

Type	Identifier	Description
Permissions	Reproduction	Multiple copies of the object can be made
	Distribution	Permits distribution, public display, and publicly performance
	Derivative Works	Distribution of derivative works is permitted
	High Income Nation Use	Rights might be exercised in nations defined as high-income economies by the world bank
	Sharing	Permits commercial derivatives, but only non-commercial distribution
Requirements	Notice	An indication to the license governing the work must be provided
	Attribution	Requires giving credit to the copyright holder and/or author
	Share Alike	Derivative works must be licensed under the same terms or compatible terms as the original work
	Source Code	Redistribution of this work requires the source code to be included
	Copyleft	Requires that derivative and combined works must be licensed under specified terms, similar to those on the original work
	Lesser Copyleft	Requires that derivative works must be licensed under specified terms with at least the same conditions as the original work; combinations with the work may be licensed under different terms
Prohibitions	Commercial Use	Prohibits using the work for commercial purposes

Table 7.1: Summary of the principle Creative Commons licenses

prohibitions, and requirements (see Table 7.1):

- The permissions can, for example, express the possibility of Distribution, Reproduction or Derivative Works.

- The CC license can, in addition, define that commercial use or public preview is prohibited. Possible values of prohibitions do not affect permissions granted by copyright law, such as fair use [Abelson *et al.* 2008].

- The vocabulary allows requiring certain behavior of the customers, for instance, including source code, attribution, share alike or notice.

Licenses which enable more elaborate terms and conditions than currently supported by the standard CC syntax can be expressed as RDF extensions to the original CcRdf code. Listing 7.1 depicts an example of a CC license. This sample license permits distribution and derivative works, but it requires a notice and it prohibits commercial use.

It was indicated by [Parrott 2001] that there are four main components of RELs: 1) subjects that are actors who perform actions on objects; 2) objects that represent content on which subject's actions are performed; 3) operations that represent what a given subject can do on a given object; 4) constraints that are conditions under which the subject can perform the operations.

Creative Commons licenses were not designed to act as a REL. However, their expressiveness covers very well these requirements: *Objects* can be represented by the class *Work*; *operations* permitted for the *Subject* can be represented using the class *License* that contains requirements, permissions and prohibitions; the set of *Constraints* can be represented by instances of *permissions*, *prohibitions* and *requirements*. The CC license does not provide a proper class for representing subjects, but as we demonstrate in Section 7.4, this can be done by combining CC licenses with FOAF vocabulary. Figure 7.2 depicts the mapping.

```
<rdf:RDF xmlns="http://creativecommons.org/ns#"
    xmlns:dc="http://purl.org/dc/elements/1.1/"
    xmlns:rdf="http://www.w3.org/1999/02/22-rdf-syntax-ns#">
<Work rdf:about="http://www.drmlab.org/confidential/">
    <dc:title>The DRM lab blog</dc:title>
    <dc:description>This is a blog of the DRM lab</dc:description>
    <license rdf:resource="http://creativecommons.org/licenses/by-nc/3.0/" />
</Work>
<License rdf:about="http://creativecommons.org/licenses/by-nc/3.0/">
    <requires rdf:resource="http://web.resource.org/cc/Notice" />
    <permits rdf:resource="http://web.resource.org/cc/Distribution" />
    <permits rdf:resource="http://web.resource.org/cc/DerivativeWorks" />
    <prohibits rdf:resource="http://web.resource.org/cc/CommercialUse" />
</License>
</rdf:RDF>
```

Listing 7.1: Creative Commons RDF license example

This contribution was described in [Grzonkowski & McDaniel 2008]. We also note that other authors proposed using FOAF together with CC [Samwald & Adlassnig 2008] in the domain of life sciences. However, their paper does not explain how they combined these ontologies.

According to [Rodriguez & Delgado 2006; Delgado *et al.* 2005], mappings between CC and other Rights Expression Languages (RELs), such as MPEG-21 REL [DeMartini *et al.* 2003] or ODRL [Iannella 2002], are feasible and known. To provide a full mapping from CC to MPEG-21 REL, the vocabulary of the latter has to be extended with the following expressivity: 1) to enable control of copyrights and license notices; 2) to credit the copyright holder and the author of original work; 3) to license derivate works under the same terms and conditions as the original work; and 4) to provide source code of derivate works.

The core CC semantics can be also expressed by ODRL [Iannella 2005]. CC Permissions and Requirements map directly to ODRL Permissions and Requirements. The semantics of CC Attribution is also already covered. There are two solutions to express Prohibitions [Iannella 2005]: using negative constraints, such as non-Commercial use; providing references to human-readable CC licenses. However, the ODRL 1.1 model [Iannella 2002] does not support the concept of CC Prohibitions. The model assumes that only explicitly given Permissions or Rights are allowed. As a result, if something is not mentioned in the item's description, it is prohibited.

Initially CC licenses were designed to provide licenses for creative works such as music, film, images, etc. The idea was to make such works cheaper and easier accessible. Because the proper metadata was designed, there are already in existence search applications to find works satisfying the given criteria.

[Chiariglione 2006] indicates two main advantages of CC licenses over the RELs: 1) CC licenses have legal value when expressed in the form required for specific jurisdiction, licenses expressed in REL do not achieve the same goal; and 2) CC licenses grants users their *fair*

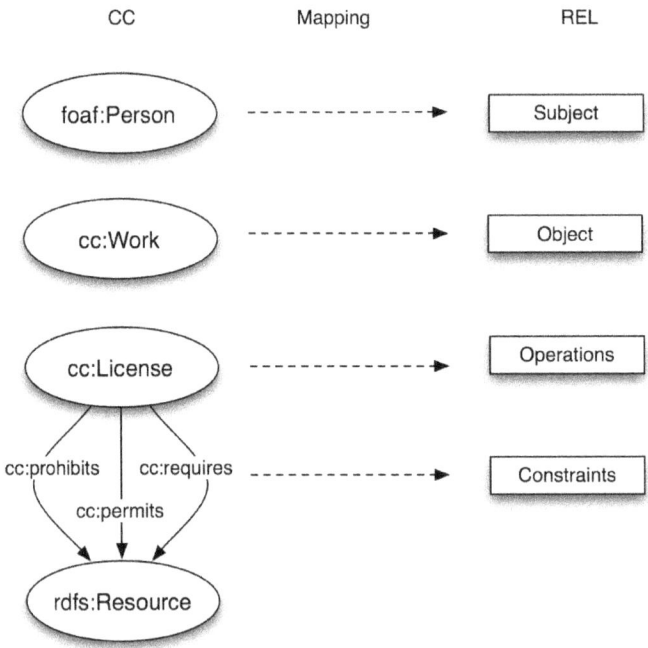

Figure 7.2: The proposed mapping of Creative Commons licenses to Rights Expression Languages (REL)

use. This way not only technical protection is provided for the users, but also protection enforced by law. In addition, every CC license applies worldwide, lasts for the duration of the copyright and it is not revocable.

7.4 Rights Management Vocabularies

To store, manage and discover digital media components, we have adopted and combined a set of semantic web standards. The key classes and properties are shown in Figure 7.3. The main data components that are stored in the repository are *Licenses*, *Works*, *Subjects* and *purchases*.

Licenses are necessary to support the possibility of contracts between the content providers and the consumers. A typical CC license consists of *permissions*, *prohibitions* and *requirements*. In addition, FRM adds specific predicates to the ontology such as *frm:price*.

Work implements the idea of Objects. Thus, this class represents the digital media components that are uploaded by the content provider. To describe them, we use the Dublin Core [Weibel *et al.* 1998] vocabulary. This ontology provides predicates for describing uploaded works: title (*dc:title*), keywords (*dc:subject*), abstract (*dc:description*), and so on. *Dublin Core* is also used to connect Objects (*dc:references*) and licenses (*dc:license*) terms that have been purchased by Subjects. To express access control policies on resources, we applied the *s3b* vocabulary that originates from FOAFRealm [Kruk *et al.* 2006b]. For example, if the value of the

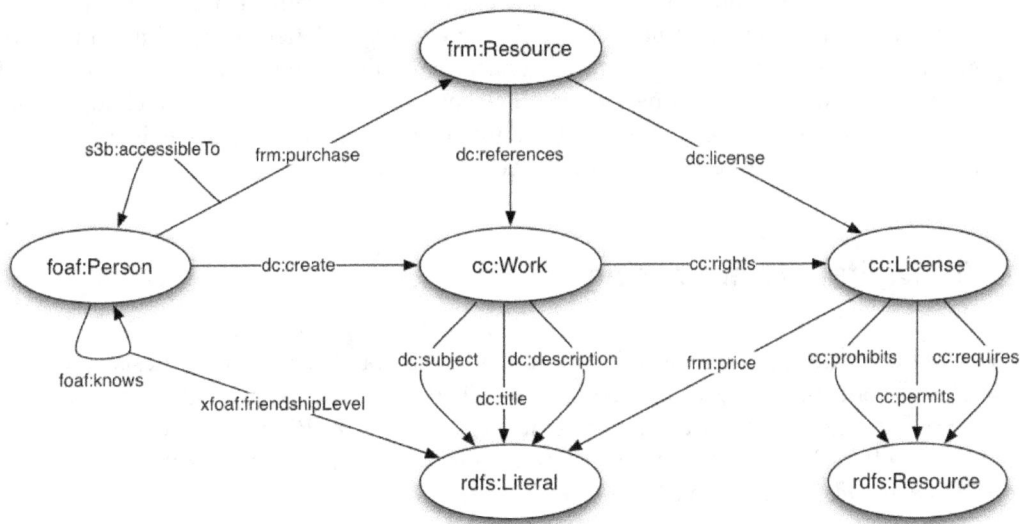

Figure 7.3: Key classes and properties of integrated ontology for rights management

predicate in the Alice's profile is set to F[mailto:alice@frm.drmlab.org]2.7, according to FOAF-Realm, friends of Alice's who are two degrees of separation from her and who are trusted at 70% or more can access the Objects. FRM adds the predicates of a purchase (*frm:purchase*), price (*frm:price*), and a digital signature of a license (*frm:signature*).

To describe *Subjects* we use FOAF[4] [Dan Brickley and Libby Miller 2005], which is suitable for describing their profiles and social network information (*foaf:knows*, *foaf:name*, *foaf:mbox*). To introduce the concept of trust, social networks are expressed in a more detailed way using the XFOAF[5] vocabulary [Grzonkowski & Kruk 2007] that was introduced by FOAFRealm. Its predicate *friendshipLevel* represents the acquaintance value between two given members of a social network. Note that this term is often used interchangeably with trust between the Subjects. It lies in a range between 0 and 100 %.

The rights management component is able to process this information stored in the description of the digital media components. This functionality enables the consumers to transfer their copyrights to somebody else. The transfer details are dependent on the license agreements. The licenses offers a possibility for the content distributors to specify various details about sharing content the acquaintances of a member. This information includes the maximal social distance between them and the required trust levels. In our proposed approach, the information about acquaintance, trust levels and relationship types is provided by Subjects to the license server. Once the subject's data is delivered, it must be signed and stored securely.

All copyright transfers must be done by means of the license server which is responsible for updating the profile information. The licenses allow content distributors to specify various details about sharing constraints as well as typical constraints that are delivered by the ODRL specification [Iannella 2002] (see Section 2.3.3).

---

[4]FOAF: http://www.foaf-project.org
[5]http://www.foafrealm.org/documentation/xfoaf/

It is worth mentioning that all current DRM solutions cause privacy problems because they require consumer identities to be publicly exposed [Cohen 2003]. Emerging technologies may be able to resolve such privacy concerns to a certain extent [Kruk *et al.* 2006b], but to realize the full potential of new hybrid markets for digital content legal changes and new business models are needed. This problem, however, requires changes in existing legal frameworks otherwise it will remain unsolved [Cohen 2003].

7.5 Digital Watermarking

The digital watermarking module was outside the core work of this thesis. The module was also contributed by other researchers. Thus it found applicability in other projects such as Amulet, which is an implementation of a Digital Rights Management system for eLearning [Ureche *et al.* 2008]. For a more detailed description, we refer the interested reader to [Ureche *et al.* 2008; Ureche 2009].

For this thesis, the main function of this module is to produce an *FRM Object* (see Definition 5.3). The FRM platform uses digital watermarking [Podilchuk & Delp 2001; Cox *et al.* 2002b] for a number of applications, specifically *ownership assertion*, *usage control*, and *content labeling* (see Section 2.3.5). The FRM platform stores Objects in their plain form. However, the consumers are always given personalized files that enable the tracking of copyright infringement and also perform authorization. The portion of FRM related to authorization and authentication is readable for trusted platforms [Erickson 2003] and it is cryptographically signed by the FRM platform. The part that enables tracing of copyright infringement is hidden from the players and requires knowledge about the password used during the watermarking process. To protect a file, our prototype implementation uses invisible watermarking techniques. These are used to insert the license terms into the distributed content. This is necessary for the trusted platforms to check the usage rules before playing the content. If a file does not have usage rules attached, the trusted platform will not play the content. Then, the invisible watermarking techniques are also used to insert extra control information to the content. This information is inserted using the given password. Only with the knowledge of the original password, the control data be extracted. The digital watermark insertion procedure depends on the type of media file and requires three parameters to produce a protected file:

- text - that is the information that we aim to insert in the content. In our use case scenarios, this information is usually a Creative Common [Lessig 2004] license that describe customer's usage rules

- media object - the file that will have the content embedded

- password - a secret information that is necessary to read control values inserted to the content

The process of generating a protected file can be described in three steps (see Figure 7.4):

1. Add - in which the given license is embedded to the given content

2. Sign - the given usage rules (license) are signed by the content provider using the customer's id.

3. Control - additional information is attached using the password. Protecting this information from attackers is crucial to prevent the content compromise.

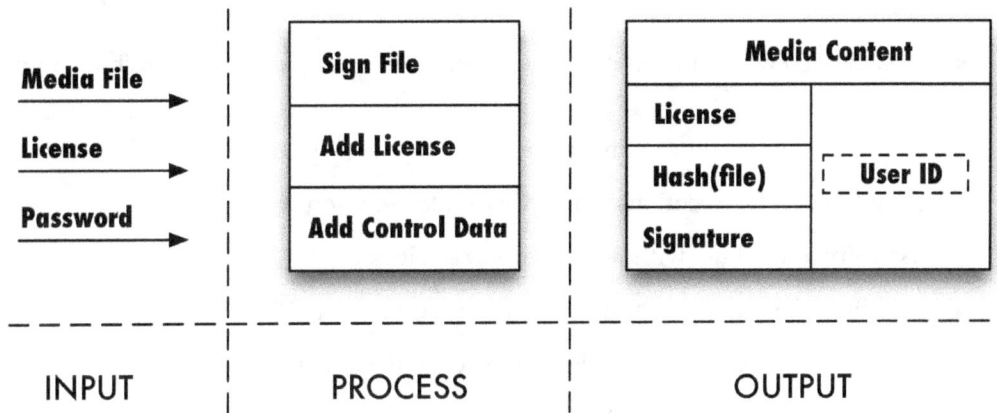

Figure 7.4: Applied file watermarking method

In FRM, the end user receives a collection of protected files. The FRM player is a user interface (UI) level application. It is able to play uploaded content only if it has a valid machine-readable license. The consumers must be first authenticated in order to play the content. Authentication is based on FOAFRealm/D-FOAF [Kruk *et al.* 2006b; Grzonkowski *et al.* 2005], a semantic identity management platform based on FOAF. In FRM, there is a one-to-one mapping between the subjects in FRM and FOAF-based profiles obtained from D-FOAF. This distinguishes FRM from a conventional DRM system because of the members' personal trust ranking, a relational trust ranking and social distance as additional metrics over the conventional DRM and usage control models.

The authorization process depends on the users' social network. Since its structure is dynamic, it can generate different results at different points in time. Immediately after the *Rights Validation* process, a decision is made if the given item is permitted to be played or not.

The consumer component functionality is provided with an ability to transfer copyrights to other consumers. The subjects are able to specify sharing policies, if they obtain such a permission. The policies must be corresponding to the earlier agreed license terms. Each content has a unique watermark embedded. Thus attempts at copyright infringement can be easily detected and traced to the originating infringer. The simple fact that such infringement is readily detectable should serve to discourage a majority of active infringers and a range of measures can be taken to discourage persistent offenders. Such measures might range from a gradual degradation of their trust metric, to barring them from the social network and, in extreme cases, real-world legal actions may be mandated.

7.6 Authentication Service

In this section we describe a web authentication service that uses zero-knowledge proof technology to confirm the identity of the requester. The service is called SEcure DIgital CredentIals (SeDiCi) [Grzonkowski 2010]. We use this service to offer enhanced security and privacy. We describe the authentication procedure including the private key algorithm. Then, we present the applied authentication protocol. In the previous sections we determined a number of desired security requirements (see Section 3.3) that have to be satisfied to provide both secure and relatively fast, to the users' perception, authentication on the web:

- Resistance to known attacks on authentication protocols or at least possibility of protection

- Possibility of protection against man-in-the-middle (MITM) attack

- Possibility of safe executions within distributed environments

- Possibility of working without synchronized clocks

- Possibility of working without a Third Trusted Party (TTP)

- Support of the use of memorable passwords in the authentication process

- Protection from dictionary attacks

- Users' passwords security even when the server is compromised (this is necessary to avoid impersonation attempts)

We also concluded that there are usability requirements that have to be satisfied to deliver a practical solution (see Section 6.4):

- The protocol should be fast enough [Miller 1968; Nielsen 1999] for practical realizations

- Integration with existing web applications should be easy and straightforward

- Communication between a user and a server should be performed using widely accessible and supported technologies

We suggest that an efficient ZKP-based protocol can satisfy those requirements. Firstly, ZKP offers best protection against common attack on security protocols [Menezes *et al.* 1996] such as replay attack, session key attack, interleaving, reflection attack, forced delay and chosen-text attack (see Section 3.1).

MITM is possible against some ZKP protocols since the man in the middle could simply relay communication between the prover and the verifier. However, it was argued by [Beth & Desmedt 1991] and [Brands & Chaum 1993] that this problem can be addressed by introducing time limits on the authentication time.

In case of ZKP authentication, there is also no need for synchronized clocks, but as we mentioned earlier both parties could count the response times to detect possible MITM attempts.

The presence of a TTP increases the security of the authentication process at it protects against MITM without the need for timing assumptions [Beth & Desmedt 1991; Brands & Chaum 1993]; it, however, requires both the prover and the verifier to keep and manage digital certificates. ZKP protocols typically use public key cryptography and thus they do not support passwords. Therefore, the problems of dictionary attacks and compromised servers are not really related to conventional ZKP solutions.

In Section 7.6.2 we propose a private-key algorithm that enables using ZKP together with user logins and passwords. Such a protocol is lightweight enough to be implemented in web browsers and deployed within computationally limited handheld devices. Therefore, we claim that our approach addresses the stated requirements without additional compromises. We note that in our approach, the public and the private key pairs are created by the user's browser during each authentication attempt. Therefore there is a question if such a protocol is still secure and also if it is fast enough for practical realizations. We further investigate and provide an answer to this question in Chapter 8.

7.6.1 Authentication procedure

To start the authentication procedure, a user, say *Alice*, must first register. Then, in order to login after her initial registration, *Alice* types her username and password. Note that her password never leaves her browser. The browser uses the password to calculate her private key (see Section 7.6.2) and then to generate a set of challenge graphs (see Section 7.6.3). These graphs and her username are then sent to the server and are used to complete the challenge-response authentication protocol described in Section 7.6.3.

A sequence diagram is presented in Figure 7.5 and shows our top-level approach in detail. When compared with other ZKP implementations, the browser is now responsible for a number of new tasks: firstly, calculating private keys from passwords; secondly, generating challenge graphs, and challenge responses. Furthermore, the server has the additional responsibility of generating random challenges for any registered authentication clients (browsers). Finally, there is an additional interaction step between a browser and a server when compared to classical approaches (see Section 3.2): the request-response interaction is replaced with request-challenge-response interaction. We note that a user's browser must perform more additional operations and communication tasks than in conventional authentication procedures. The main question is whether this new approach is feasible and, in particular, will not cause long waiting periods for end-users. This requires a very efficient implementation of the underlying algorithms and the use of distributed computing at the client-side (browser). A detailed evaluation and testing of our algorithms and the answers to these questions is given in Chapter 8. Here we focus on a detailed description of the various elements of our optimized authentication protocol and the prototype authentication service built on top of it.

7.6.2 Private-key algorithm

A user's private key is a permutation. Since we want to keep users using login and password pairs, we transform passwords to corresponding permutations using a one-way function.

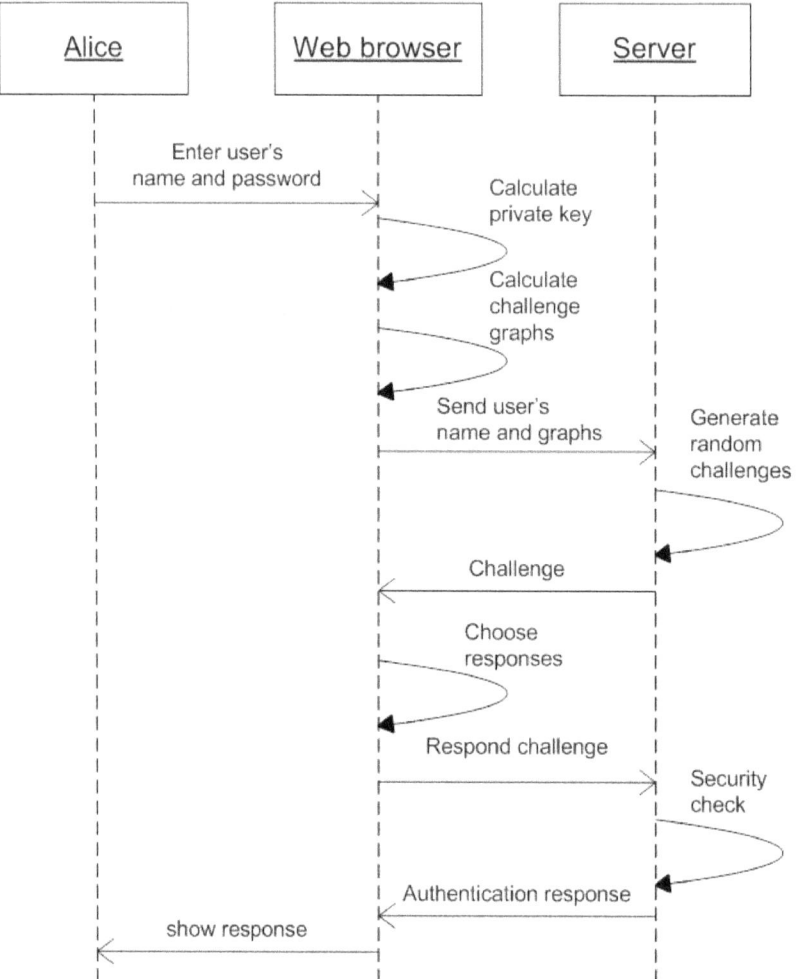

Figure 7.5: ZKP implementation on the Web

Such a transformation must always generate same-size permutations to ensure they can be used together with users' public keys. The transformation we use has been depicted in Figure 7.6 and is explained in the following section.

Transformation

In our protocol (see Section 7.6.3) we have used Secure Hash Algorithm - Version 1.0 (SHA1) [Eastlake & Jones 2001]. The family of SHA algorithms was designed by the National Security Agency (NSA)[6]. The National Institute of Standards and Technology (NIST)[7] published these hash functions as a U.S. Federal Information Processing Standard [Dang 2009]. The SHA1 algorithm computes a 160-bits-long hash for any string that is no longer than 2^{64}-

---

[6]NSA: http://www.nsa.gov/
[7]NIST: www.nist.gov/

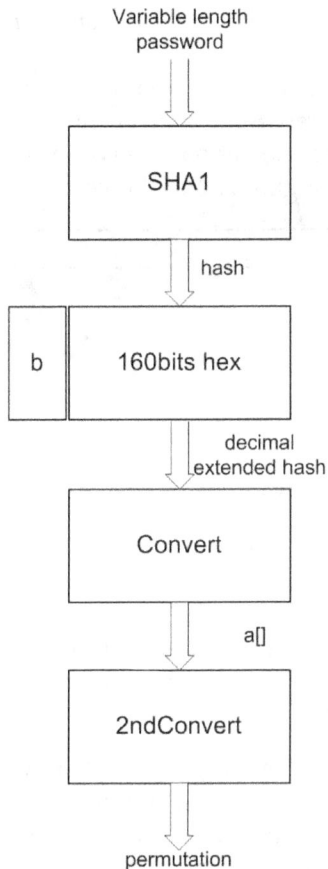

Figure 7.6: The process of conversion a password to permutation

bits. Such a hash is composed of numbers 0-9, a-f; and therefore, we can interpret the hash as a hexadecimal number. We use this number as a seed for our algorithm. The proposed algorithm groups together permutations that have the same size; n-long permutations are always in positions from *n!+1* to *(n+1)!* (see Section 7.6.2).

If the hash alone was used as an index into a table of permutations, different hashes would be mapped to permutations of varying lengths. Thus, we extend all the hashes with a hexadecimal character *b* at the beginning of each obtained string. This modification causes that all the hexadecimal numbers that we obtain from hashes correspond to values between *41!+1* and *42!*; therefore, all the generated permutations have the same length, which is *41*. The key size, of course, can be changed, if another hash generation algorithm is used. That would result in a different bracket of values and also permutation size.

Calculating a permutation at a certain position

The web-application calculates permutations in two steps. The first being based on the observation that all the natural numbers can be represented as:

$$a_0 0! + a_1 1! + a_2 2! + \ldots + a_k k! \text{ for any natural number k}$$

Such a representation is unambiguous and it is also known as factorial number system [Knuth 1997]. Thus, to represent a given number in it, there is a need to find the $a_1, a_2, \ldots a_k$ factors. In our implementation, this is done by using Algorithm 1, which converts a given decimal number (see Figure 7.6) to the vector a[]. The algorithm uses the Greatest-

---

Algorithm 1 Convert($number$)

---
  var $i := 0$
  var $factor := 0$
  var $a[] := newArray()$
  while number > 0 **do**
    $factor := GreatestFactorial(number)$
    $a[i] := number/factor$
    $number := number - a[i] * factor$
    $i = i + 1$
  end while
  return a

Factorial() function that returns the smallest factorial that is greater than the given number. For efficiency reasons, we suggest an implementation that uses a predefined table of factorials and a binary search algorithm.

The second step of the conversion is performed by Algorithm 2. It takes the table a[] as an input and returns as the output a table permutation[] that contains the created permutation. This task is performed by Algorithm 2. The algorithm requires a temporary structure s, on which the following functions can be performed:

- insert (x) - adds a number x to the structure

- remove (x) - removes a number x from structure

- elementAt (j) - returns a number i that satisfies the condition: there are exactly j-1 smaller numbers than i in the structure

- full(n) - return a structure with integers $0,1,\ldots.(n-1)$

For example, with s=0,1,2,3 by removing an element at second position we get s=0,1,3, and if we repeat the operation we have s=0,1.

The structure s could be a simple table, however, the complexity of operating the table would be $O(n)$. A B-Tree, and in particular, an AVL tree, which is a special case of a B-Tree, is used for the structure s. In such structures, the computational complexity of removing elements is $O(log\ n)$.

7.6.3 Authentication Protocol

To execute an authentication protocol, two parties must have the prover's public key, which is calculated during the registration procedure. This procedure is usually executed once, un-

---

Algorithm 2 2ndConvert($a[]$)

---

var $n := lengtha$
var $s := full(n)$ {returns a structure with integers 0,1,....(n-1)}
var $a[] := newArray()$
for $i = 0$ to $n - 1$ **do**
   $s.insert(i)$ {Initializing our temporary structure}
end for
for $i = 0$ to $k - 1$ **do**
   $permutation[i] := s.elementAt(a[i])$ {getting an element at a certain position}
   $s.remove(a[i])$ {removing the taken element}
end for
return permutation

---

less there is a need for a change of the prover's password. For instance, the prover might forget it or the verifier might require the prover to change the password on a monthly basis. Once both parties have on the public key, the authentication protocol can be executed. The authentication steps depend on the applied protocol (see Chapter 3).

In this section we describe both the registration and authentication protocols that we applied in our solution. We assume that *Alice* is the prover, whereas *Bob* is the verifier. *Alice* knows the permutation π_{priv} between two graphs G_1 and G_2. *Bob* also knows the graphs. *Alice* wants to convince *Bob* that she knows the permutation, but she is going to keep it secret.

Registration

The registration procedure requires *Alice* to generate and send her public key to *Bob*. She does not reveal to anybody nor store her private key. Her private key is generated by her browser every time after she types the correct password. If she enters an incorrect password, a corresponding incorrect private key will be generated. Her keys have to be created each time she requests authentication because web browsers do not have permissions to access the underlaying file systems. Without additional plugins, web browsers can store information only in cookies, which do not provide sufficient security for storing confidential data such as private keys [Grzonkowski *et al.* 2005].

1. *Alice's* browser transforms her password to a permutation π_{priv} that is her private key (see Section 7.6.2).

2. *Alice's* browser generates a random graph G_1

3. *Alice's* browser computes graph $G_2 = \pi_{priv}(G_1)$

4. *Alice's* browser sends graphs G_1, G_2, and her username to *Bob*. She keeps π_{priv} secret

Alice is able to convince anybody that she is the publisher of such credentials, while she keeps the password secret (see Section 6.2.3).

Authentication

To authenticate, *Alice* obtains the number of challenges from *Bob*. This number influences the security of the protocol. It has to be sufficiently high to ensure secure authentication, but also, the number of challenges cannot be too high to make sure the protocol does not take too long to complete each authentication request.

In our description we assumed that both parties validate each other's messages; and if the validation fails, the validating party interrupts the protocol.

We also introduce the timing constraints of the following types:

- *Timeouts* (α). The prover requires the verifier to deliver certain messages before time specified by the *timeout* value. If that does not happen, the verifier interrupts the protocol.

- *Delays* (β). The prover delays its responses to the verifier according to the time specified by the *delay* value. This way the prover is protected from dishonest verifiers who could nest many sessions.

- *Current time* (δ_i). Each party must be able to measure how long the protocol is being executed to be able to calculate *timeouts* and *delays*. The parties measure this time independently and there is no need for synchronization of their local clocks.

These timing constraints are necessary to preserve zero-knowledge in the concurrent composition (see Section 6.3.2). Values for α and β must be agreed before the protocol execution in a way that $\beta \geq \alpha$ and they do not cause long waiting times for the user. The protocol is composed of five constant rounds, in which the participating parties exchange messages:

1. *Alice's* browser is acquiring the number of challenges t from *Bob*

    - *Alice's* browser randomly selects γ_0 and γ_1; and then calculates $A_0 = \gamma_0(G_1)$ and $A_1 = \gamma_1(G_1)$
    - *Alice's* browser sends A_0 and A_1 to *Bob*
    - *Alice's* browser checks current time δ_1
    - *Alice's* browser sets β and α ($\beta \geq \alpha$)

2. *Bob* receives A_0 and A_1

    - *Bob* selects t random permutations $\mu_1, \mu_2, ..., \mu_t$
    - *Bob* randomly generates $v_1, v_2, ..., v_t$ such that for all $i \in \{1, 2, ..., t\}$,$v_i \in \{0, 1\}$
    - *Bob* calculates $Q_i = \mu_i(A_{v_i})$. He sends Q_i to *Alice*

3. *Alice's* browser receives and stores the *Bob's* message

    - *Alice's* browser generates t random permutations $\pi_{R1}, \pi_{R2}, ..., \pi_{Rt}$
    - *Alice's* browser calculates t graphs $G_{R1}, G_{R2}, ..., G_{Rt}$ such that $G_{Rn} = \pi_{Rn}(G_1)$ where $n \in \{1, 2, ..., t\}$

- *Alice's* browser sends the generated graphs to the *Bob*

4. *Bob* stores the graphs

  - *Bob* sends $v_1, v_2, ..., v_t$ and $\mu_1, \mu_2, ..., \mu_t$ to *Alice*

  - *Alice's* browser checks current time δ_2 and checks if $(\delta_2 - \delta_1 \leq \alpha)$. If this condition is not satisfied, *Alice's* browser considers the session as timeout and interrupts the authentication procedure

  - *Alice's* browser checks if $Q_i = \mu_i(A_{v_i})$ are correct. If all the equations are satisfied, *Alice's* browser constructs a response vector $R_1, R_2, ..., R_t$. If $v_1 = 0$, then $R_i = \pi_{Ri}$, otherwise $R_i = \pi_{Ri} \circ \pi_{priv}^{-1}$

  - *Alice's* browser stores current time δ_3 and waits until $(\delta_3 - \delta_1 \geq \beta)$

  - *Alice's* browser sends the response vector to *Bob*

5. *Bob* checks her response

  - *Bob* expects that if $v_i = 0$, then $Ri(G_1) = G_{Ri}$. If $v_i = 1$, then $Ri(G_2) = G_{Ri}$

  - *Bob* sends her a response. She is authenticated, only if all the challenge questions are responded correctly

The concept of this protocol is derived in part from [Goldreich *et al.* 1988] and is introduced in Section 6.2.3. To adjust this protocol to the web environment and to handle higher latencies which are experienced on the web, there is a need to execute multiple challenges in parallel. However, [Goldreich & Krawczyk 1990; Goldreich & Krawczyk 1996] argue that a simple parallelization results in a protocol that may not be zero knowledge. Thus we have decided to apply extensions introduced by [Bellare *et al.* 1990]. These extensions ensure that the verifier commits on random challenges before obtaining the prover's message; and this way the prover's graphs do not influence the selection of the challenge questions.

Our final ZKP protocol requires the parties to perform five constant rounds. Each round contains a number of challenges requested by the verifier at the beginning of the protocol. We combine it with the private-key algorithm described in Section 7.6.2, and in this way we obtain an interactive ZKP password-based protocol using isomorphic graphs. We further evaluate the applicability of this protocol to web environments in Chapter 8.

7.7 Application Scenarios

We present some fair use scenarios that have been identified as important use cases for DRM implementations [Grzonkowski *et al.* 2007; Arnab & Hutchison 2005]. However, we remark that their support is poor or non-existant (see Section 2.5.2).

In the given scenarios Alice is a customer, Dave is a trusted friend of her and Bob is a content provider.

7.7.1   Fair Use Scenarios

Sharing Content: Alice is familiar with physical world rules. She usually buys magazines, she reads them and then often shares them with Dave who is her boyfriend. She expects the same rights when she buys electronic content. Since she participates in an online Spanish class, she would like to share the access with Dave who also considers buying a full membership. However, Dave would like to try the service before buying it. Such guest memberships are often possible in the physical world, for example, when learning a foreign language or going to the gym.

The partial sharing of training materials is a practical problem that was experienced by the emerging multimedia training industry [Grzonkowski *et al.* 2007; Ureche *et al.* 2008]. This new industry sector wants to give their customers flexibility in their use of customized content within their organizations, but they equally need to avoid the illegal use of such specialized content by third parties.

Content Redistribution: It happened several times that Alice sold a book at an online auction because she read it or became disinterested in the topic. Hence, she expects that the content or the membership she buys, can be sold, if it is no longer needed. Alice may even be willing to pay more for such a permission from the content distributor.

Price Negotiation: The content provider may offer less restrictive license terms for some groups of people. For example, if Alice is a math teacher, the content provider could offer her a math course for a lower price. Alice could be also interested to pay more for a less restrictive license that would allow her to share her purchase with Bob.

Fair Use Requirements: Those scenarios identify essential fair use requirements:

1. *Content sharing:* Alice would like to share the content with Dave. However, she does not want to use it at the same time.

2. *Content Redistribution:* Alice would like to sell an item when it is no more needed.

3. *Negotiations:* Alice is willing to pay more if she is given more rights. She also expects to pay less if she gives some rights up.

7.7.2   Scenario Implementation

To provide interoperability and the possibility of deploying FRM in a web environment, we base FRM on semantic web technologies. The user's profile has been based on modified FOAF that provides possibility of expressing social network as a directed graph (see Section 7.2). Figure 7.7 presents an example of Alice's profile in which she defines Dave as a friend with a 75% level of personal trust. Both users are instances of the FOAF class Person. Her profile is composed of FOAF and FOAFRealm vocabularies (see Section 7.4).

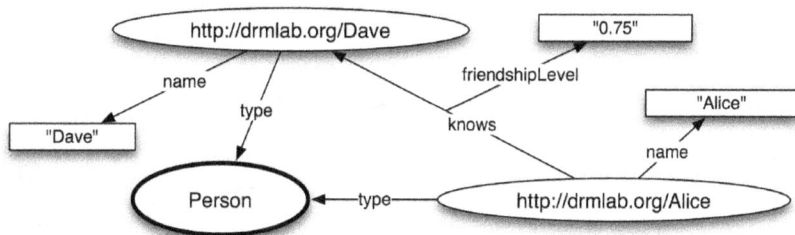

Figure 7.7: An example of an initial Alice's profile

Content Sharing and Redistribution

In FRM, the possibility of sharing the purchased content is expressed in the attached licenses. For example, license 1 (see Figure 7.8) offers the permission to distribute and reproduce the content. Therefore, it costs more than license 2 which does not have such permissions. The distribution rule, defined in the Creative Commons vocabulary (see Section 7.3), means also that it can be publicly displayed and publicly performed, whereas the reproduction permission enables making multiple copies.

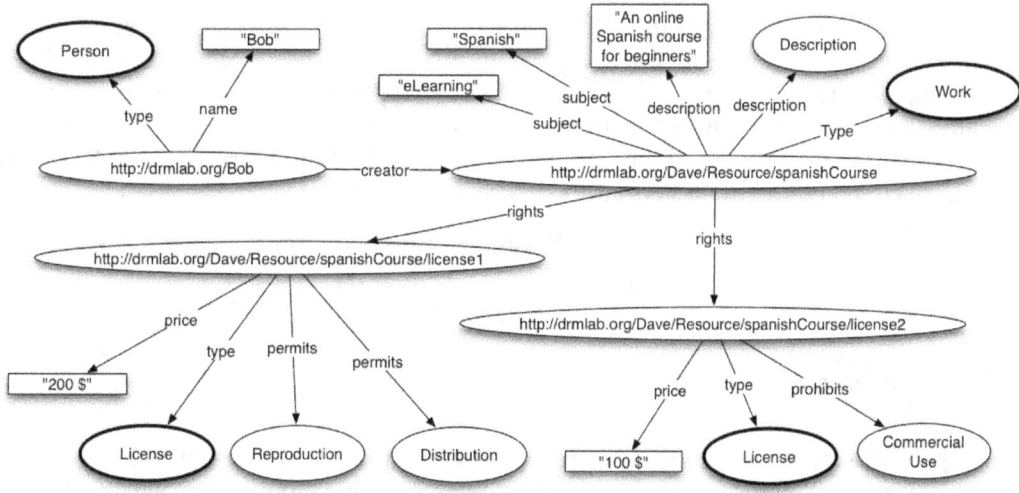

Figure 7.8: An example of a Bob's offer containing the sale offer accessible on two different terms and conditions

Figure 7.9 shows that Alice has enabled sharing with friends that are two degrees of separation from her and trusted at 70%. If Alice purchases the Spanish course on the terms expressed by *license 1*, she will be able to distribute the item to Dave because she defined Dave as a friend of hers and she specified the friendship level to be 75% (see Figure 7.9). Alice expressed the sharing constraints in a way that also trusted friends of her friends' can access this resource if they are two degrees of separation from her. Consequently, a direct friend of Dave trusted at 94 % or more would be able to access the course.

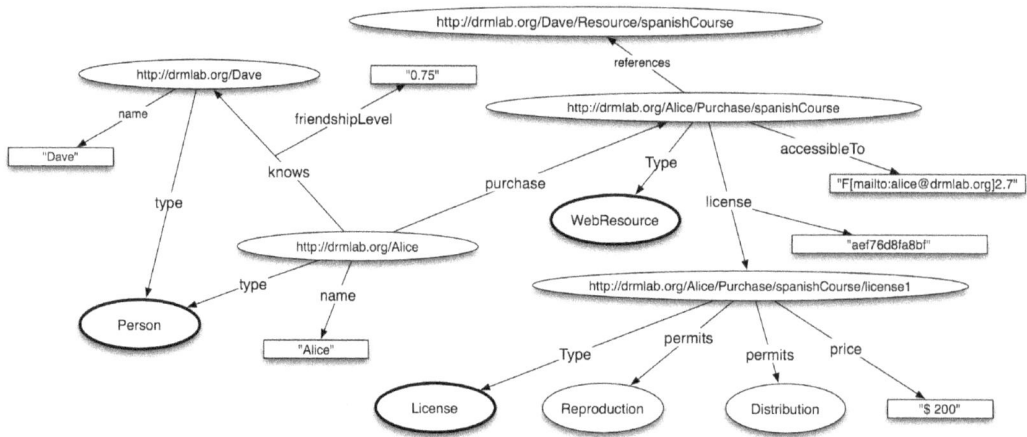

Figure 7.9: The Alice's profile after the transaction with Bob

Price Negotiation

Using FRM, Bob is able to attach many different licenses to a single content. Each license can differ in price and terms. For instance an inexpensive license can be restricted to personal use only, whereas the possibility of sharing the content with friends may cost more. Such a situation is depicted in Figure 7.8: Bob presents his offer and he agrees on more flexible rules for a higher price. Therefore, Alice has a choice if she agrees on the restrictive terms for a relatively low price or if she is willing to pay more for less restrictive terms. Figure 7.9 shows that she has finally decided to pay more to obtain the ability of sharing legally her purchase with Dave who is a friend of hers although *license 2* was cheaper.

In Appendix B, we provide the RDF listings corresponding to the examples depicted in Figures 7.7 - 7.9.

7.7.3   Threats

While FRM is very convenient in use, there is a high risk that without additional security measures the model is vulnerable to malicious users. For example, the users could create a "super user" that would be connected with everyone and having 100% trust or they could set trust to 100% among each other in a large group. This way the users would be able to share content for only a fraction of the original price.

The maximal social distance that can be specified in FOAFRealm [Kruk 2004] does not solve the problem either since it is set up by the users. The solution could be delivered by client-side solutions such as DRM, but they do not have long life time and sooner or later DRM solutions are cracked [Jobs 2007]. Thus in our solution we rely on digital watermarks that enable tracing of copyright infringement. Further, the encryption algorithm for these watermarks is kept secret by the provider of the content (see Section 7.5).

The problem of unfair collaborative online communities has been also considered by other researchers. [Yang *et al.* 2009] proposes analyzing various histograms of users' connectivities, whereas [Hogg 2009] suggests taking into account friends of friends when calculating users' reputations.

Although providers of content should not blindly accept end-user specified trust levels, according to [Gambetta 1988] *"asking too little of trust is just as ill advised as asking too much"*.

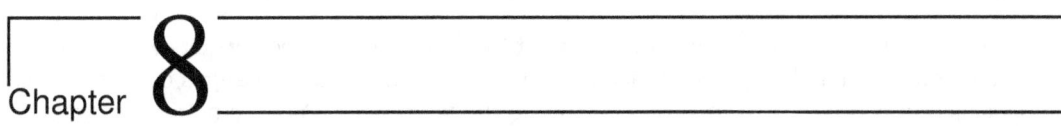

Chapter 8

Evaluation*

In this chapter we evaluate our Zero-Knowledge Proof approach to determine if its implementation is fast and secure enough for practical realizations. In Section 8.1, we introduce our goals, we describe the evaluation environment and the test methodology. We test performance for four different web browsers. We analyze stability and predictability of the the algorithm. We also verify if the protocol satisfies the existing response-time standards. We also measure data overhead that is caused by our implementation.

We analyze three protocol compositions: sequential in Section 8.2; parallel in Section 8.3; and finally concurrent in Section 8.4. We use the obtained results to verify if existing browsers are fast enough to perform a secure authentication that is still transparent for the users. Then, in Section 8.5, we verify our approach against a number of authentication protocol threats. We model an attack in which an attacker is able to break the authentication procedure with a given confidence. We perform our analyses by performing a dictionary attack and also a naive brute-force attack. Finally, we attempt to estimate the number of required ZKP rounds that guarantee both a secure and usable solution.

8.1 Usability of a Web-based ZKP implementation

As a proof of the concept of our ZKP protocol we implemented a prototype. Its server side is a Java servlet that was deployed within a Jakarta Tomcat server. The code is not platform specific and can be easily ported to other languages. The client side was implemented in JavaScript; thus it is portable across all contemporary web browsers. We note that the code is also working efficiently on various mobile devices [Grzonkowski & Corcoran 2009].

8.1.1 Evaluation Goals

We implemented a working proof of concept to demonstrate the practicality of our ZKP protocol for use in real-world applications. Our key consideration was to verify if it could be

---

*This chapter is partially based on [Grzonkowski *et al.* 2008b; Grzonkowski & Corcoran 2009]

successfully implemented across a range of web browsers; and thus, if such a system can be transparent to users in web applications. Performance and response times are in line with what users have come to expect from typical Web applications without compromising the strong security provided by ZKP. We also aimed to provide cross-browser functionality and evaluate performance across multiple browsers.

Typical usability studies are comprised of four components: performance tests, accuracy, recall, and emotional response. Since our authentication protocol changes only the invisible aspects of the way how users authenticate on the web, we focus only on performance measurements to verify if the proposed method satisfies existing response-time requirements.

To conduct the performance tests, an important challenge for our application was to satisfy the accepted response-time guidelines. One such set of guidelines was proposed in 1968 by [Miller 1968] and appears to have stood the test of time. Three decades after his findings, those rules are still applicable for web applications [Nielsen 1999; Bouch *et al.* 2000]. Therefore, we base our performance evaluation on those guidelines.

Miller defines three main time constraints:

- 0.1 second for keeping the user attention attracted - the user has the impression that the responses from the system are coming immediately

- One second for keeping a user flow though uninterrupted - the users notice latencies when using the system, but they do not lose the feeling of freely using it

- 10 seconds for keeping the user's attention on the dialog - if the response takes longer than 10 seconds, users will want to perform other tasks

8.1.2 Evaluation Environment

We performed our tests on four different web-browsers:

- Firefox 3.5.3

- Safari 4.0.2

- Internet Explorer 8

- Opera 9.64

The browsers were run on the same machine - a Macbook Pro, with an Intel CPU and an installation of Mac OS X 10.5.8. In case of Internet Explorer, we tested it under Windows XP service pack 2 on the same Macbook. The tests were automated and run using a script. The obtained results are presented in Appendix C.

To verify usability of our approach in a typical web authentication scenario, we evaluated our implementation in two ways: (i) we measured the authentication time for a given amount of challenges, and (ii) we counted the amount of data that was exchanged in order to achieve certain security levels. We note that Java/JavaScript performance results are specific for each browser, but in the case of data tests, exactly the same amount of information was exchanged by each browser. Thus we did not repeat the data tests for each browser.

8.1.3 Tests Methodology

To perform our tests, we developed an extension for our client-side script. The extension was responsible for executing the script for a given number of times for using a given amount of challenges. Time and other parameters were also measured by the script. Respective values were displayed by the script after each run. This way we were able to collect many data samples and analyze our implementation efficiency, stability and also the number of bytes exchanged.

We performed tests for various protocol compositions introduced in Section 6.3, in particular: sequential, parallel and concurrent.

Detailed data samples of the performed tests for various browsers are attached in Appendix C.

8.2 Sequential Composition

The protocol proposed in Section 7.6 can be implemented in a sequential ZKP workflow. In such a case, each browser's request contains only one challenge graph and also timing assumptions (α, β) are not taken into consideration. However, such a method of authentication causes longer authentication times. Our tests showed that the time necessary for performing one challenge was between 115 (Opera) and 408 (Firefox) ms. Assuming that the authentication process should not be longer than 10 seconds, the Firefox browser is able to execute a maximum of 24 challenges. Opera that is faster and in such a setting is able to execute 24 challenges in 2.76 seconds.

In the following subsections we further investigate if such results are secure enough for practical realizations.

8.2.1 Interrupted Session Attack

There is a possibility that an attacker could prepare a set of graphs knowing permutations to only one of the public key graphs G_1 or G_2; and then, attempt to authenticate, expecting a certain sequence of responses from the verifier. The attacker would stop and restart the authentication procedure right after receiving a question challenge that is unable to respond to.

If we define the time that is necessary for one round as s, then the time that is necessary for an attacker to verify all the possibilities can be calculated as the number of possible zeros and ones in a string of a given size. Thus, we use the following formula to find the exact number:

$$s \sum_{k=0}^{n-1} 2^k$$

where n is the number of challenges. For example, in case of 24 challenges, there are 10^{24} possible authentication scenarios. According to the introduced formula, the attacker would interrupt 10^{23} sessions after the first verifier question, 10^{22} after the second question, etc. Taking into account the Opera one-challenge-time, the attacker would need approximately 22.3 days to issue 10^{24} authentication requests.

Because the challenges are generated in a random manner, it is not guaranteed that the attacker would be successful. However, we can consider that such an attack could be feasible in the near future. This level of security could be acceptable for existing web applications used for non-commercial purposes (i.e., no associated financial transactions).

8.2.2 Conclusion

Sequential composition requires more time than 10 seconds to perform secure authentication on some browsers. Thus we note that such an implementation can barely satisfy existing response-time standards. However, we note that in many security solutions the users expect some latencies because they know that something is going on. Thus, in security applications 0.1 seconds authentication time may not be desirable for most users. [Bouch & Sasse 1999] argue that users may even judge a relatively fast service to be unacceptable unless it is also predictable, visually appealing and reliable. Thus, in our studies we aim to determine not only the authentication time, but also the level of security delivered within given time constraints.

In Section 8.3 we introduce necessary modifications to realize a parallel realization of the ZKP authentication workflow. We also investigate which protocol, serial or parallel, provides users with more security.

8.3 Parallel Composition

This protocol composition extends the sequential one in the way described in Section 7.6.3. However, we do not take into consideration timings (α,β,δ) as they are necessary only in the concurrent protocol composition. The main difference between the sequential and parallel version is that in parallel many challenges and responses are synchronously sent in one message. Such an enhancement leads to significant performance improvements. This enables faster authentication cycles, or more authentications to be squeezed into the same time window thus enhancing ZKP security. In turn, these improvements make the parallel composition useful for a broader spectrum of applications for ZKP authentication.

8.3.1 Performance tests

We performed a number of tests with different settings for various web browsers. We present our data samples using box plot-style charts. On Figures 8.1 - 8.4 each box plot represents 10 data samples obtained for a given number of challenges. Thus, each chart presents a group of 110 samples. In the case of Firefox (see Figure 8.1(a)), the median value of a one second long

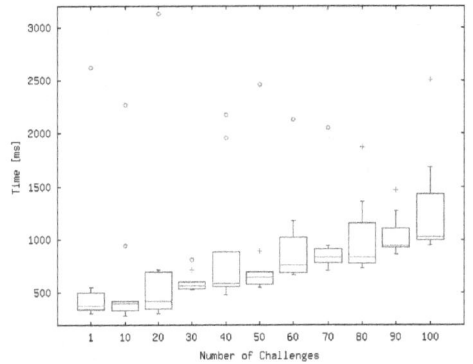

(a) Data distribution for the Firefox browser up to 100 challenges

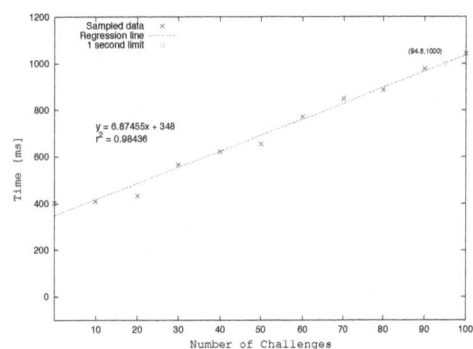

(b) Median data samples and illustration of linear regression for Firefox

Figure 8.1: Tests for Firefox

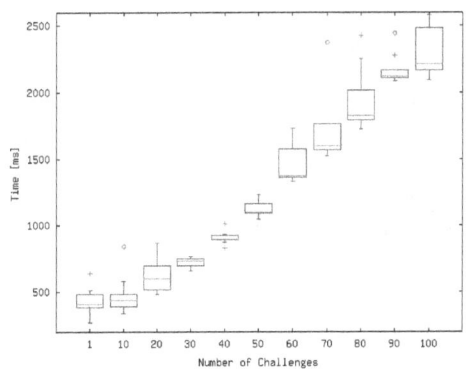

(a) Data distribution for the Safari browser up to 100 challenges

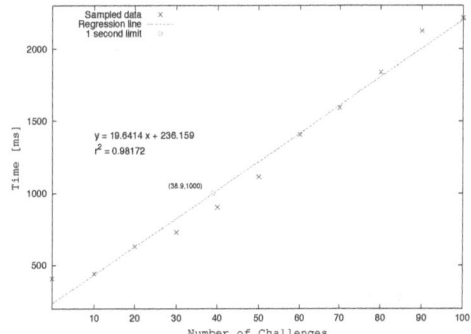

(b) Median data samples and illustration of linear regression for Safari

Figure 8.2: Tests for Safari

authentication time was missed for 100 challenges. Among 110 data samples, the one second limit was missed 24 times. This was caused mainly due to some random system events: only five data samples of 24 were inside the representative box plots range (outliers); the remaining 19 were classified as extreme outliers (outside the representative range).

Thus, assuming predictable and more stable system behavior, and also excluding extreme outliers from the data sample, we had 95 % authentication attempts below one second. If we, however, consider all the samples, only one sample was above 3 seconds (3.126) and two other samples were above 2.5 seconds. Figure 8.1(b) demonstrates that the data we sampled can be represented by a linear regression with 98.4 % confidence. Performing tests on the Safari browser, we obtained more stable data samples, but their median values were higher (see Figure 8.2(a)). Two samples were slightly above 2.5 seconds. The one second limit of the median value was missed with a setting of 50 challenges. Up to 40 challenges, 39 of 40 data samples were below one second. The linear regression of the obtained data (see Figure 8.2(b)) was calculated with 98.2 % confidence.

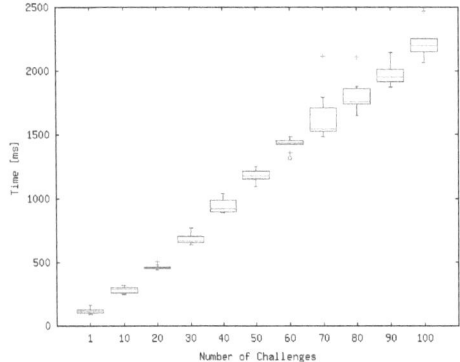

(a) Data distribution for the Opera browser up to 100 challenges

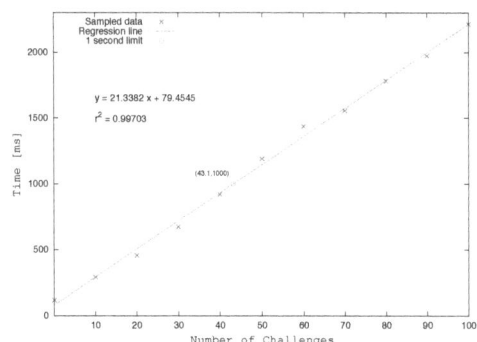

(b) Median data samples and illustration of linear regression for Opera

Figure 8.3: Tests for Opera

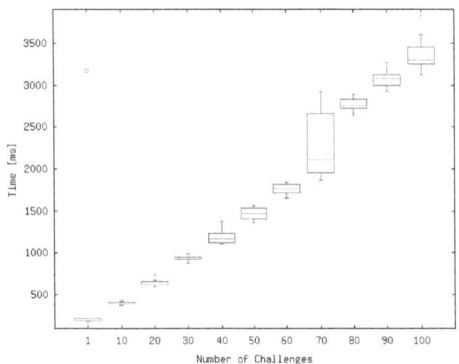

(a) Data distribution for the Internet Explorer browser up to 100 challenges

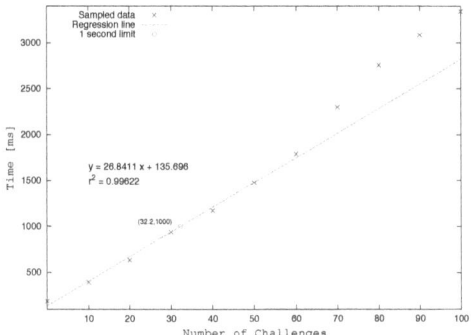

(b) Median data samples and illustration of linear regression for Internet Explorer

Figure 8.4: Tests for Internet Explorer

In the case of Opera, we observed even more stable results than in the previous test. The data distribution of the obtained samples showed little variance (see Figure 8.3(a)). Similarly to Safari, the one second limit was exceeded when changing the number of challenges to 50. All the obtained samples were below 2.5 seconds. The fact that the results were very stable resulted in a linear regression calculated with 99.7 % confidence level (see Figure 8.3(b)).

Finally, we tested Internet Explorer. Its results were the most stable and we also observed the smallest number of outliers (see Figure 8.4(a)). The one second response-time limit was reached when the number of challenges was set to 40, which was slightly worse than in the case of other browsers. Further analyses of the obtained data samples shows that there are only three outliers and one extreme outlier. Therefore, 109 of 110 data samples of the experiment were within the representative range. The obtained linear regression parameters were calculated with confidence of 99.6 %.

8.3.2 Authentication Cost

Our additional calculations on the obtained data and regression models showed that one challenge in Firefox costs approximately 6.5 ms (start-up time 408 ms), 21 ms for Opera (start-up time 115), 19 ms for Safari (228.5 ms start-up time) and finally 26 ms for Internet Explorer (start-up time 188). Low additional challenge cost in Firefox was obtained with longer start-up time comparing to other browsers.

This means that depending on the number of challenges necessary to authenticate the user, a given browser might be unresponsive for one or two seconds after clicking the "login" button. According to [Miller 1968], the user flow though is not interrupted within this time constraint. We also note that in most applications authentication is performed once and then there is no need to repeat it.

8.3.3 Performance Test Conclusions

We note that all the obtained authentication-time samples were longer than 0.1 seconds. Therefore, we focused on the second time constraint defined by [Miller 1968]: one second *for keeping a user flow though uninterrupted.*

We also observed another problem: when the computation lasted longer than 2.5 seconds, the user's thoughts flow was always interrupted by the browser warning message (see Figure 8.5). If the computation were not cancelled and if we kept clicking 'no' every 2.5 seconds, the browser returned the correct results. We observed that the authentication process was transparent from the user's perspective up to 60 challenges, for which the median value of the response-time was 1.766 seconds. In case of 70 challenges (the median value of 2.11 seconds) some authentication requests were causing the user to additionally click 'no' in the appearing alert box. Taking into account the browser's stability, we consider the median value of 1.7 seconds as a threshold for keeping the authentication process transparent from the user's perspective. In our experiment, 1.7 second median time guaranteed that all the samples were below 2.5 seconds and this was crucial to keep the process transparent. We note that this threshold can be modified through a manual change in the system registry (for Windows).

Calculating linear regression for Internet Explorer (see Figure 8.4(b)), we excluded samples obtained for 70 challenges and more since they were influenced by the user's clicking speed (see Figure 8.4(a)). We conclude that all the tested browsers can perform a transparent authentication process from the user's perspective up to 60 challenges. Taking into account the regression models presented in Figures 8.1b - 8.4b, we also note that time required to process these tasks, is a linear function of the amount of challenges. From our tests we conclude that our algorithm executed with significantly greater speed on the Firefox browser and that the lowest one-challenge time that was observed for Opera. However, Firefox has significantly longer start-up times which make this browser unsuitable for a sequential protocol implementation.

In Sections 8.3.5 and 8.5, we use this information in the further examination of the protocol's resistance to various attacks.

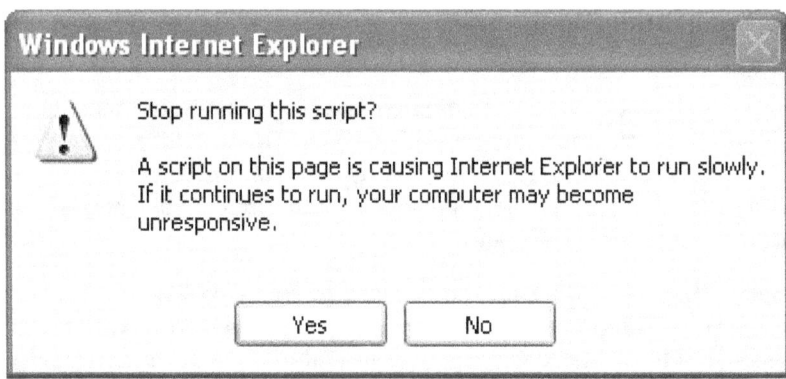

Figure 8.5: An alert box informing that a script works too long under Windows

8.3.4 Data measurements

To exchange graphs between a browser and the server, we encoded graphs into Java's String representation. The operations on both sides were performed on matrices. Our objective was to count the data that was exchanged between the browser and the server. In the classical authentication approaches (see Section 3.2), we cannot set the authentication confidence level; and consequently, the browsers always sent logins and passwords. In zero-knowledge proof approaches, the browser sends more data, if higher security is required. To measure the amount of data exchanged, we have removed the HTTP header from our considerations since this parameter has always a fixed length. Figure 8.6 shows that the total amount of data sent from the browser to the server was mainly determined by the first stage of the protocol (see Section 7.6.3) performed by the user's browser. The ratio between data sent in the authentication request and the challenge response is 71% to 29%. This parameter is neither browser nor hardware dependent. A single data challenge costs approximately 400 bytes. Moreover, the data transmitted by our server in round 4 (see Section 7.6.3) was equal to the amount of challenges, whereas in round 5 (see Section 7.6.3) the server always sent four or five bytes depending on the authentication result, respectively *true* or *false*.

8.3.5 Interrupted Session attack

Interrupted sessions are the main threat for interactive Zero-Knowledge Proof protocols in which all challenge questions are sent in parallel. In this attack scenario, an attacker prepares a set of graphs and corresponding permutations to G1 or G2; consequently, the attacker is able to respond to only one a priori chosen challenge for each graph. Then, the attacker sends the graphs to the verifier and waits for the response to determine if it matches the prepared set. As long as the expected response does not come, the attacker interrupts the authentication procedure and restarts it with the same graphs, expecting again to obtain the assumed response. In this scenario, the attacker's chances drop exponentially, with the linear growth of the number of challenges requested by the verifier.

This attack is slightly less efficient in the case of a sequential ZKP composition (see Section 8.2) because the attacker is more likely to perform some challenges before the session

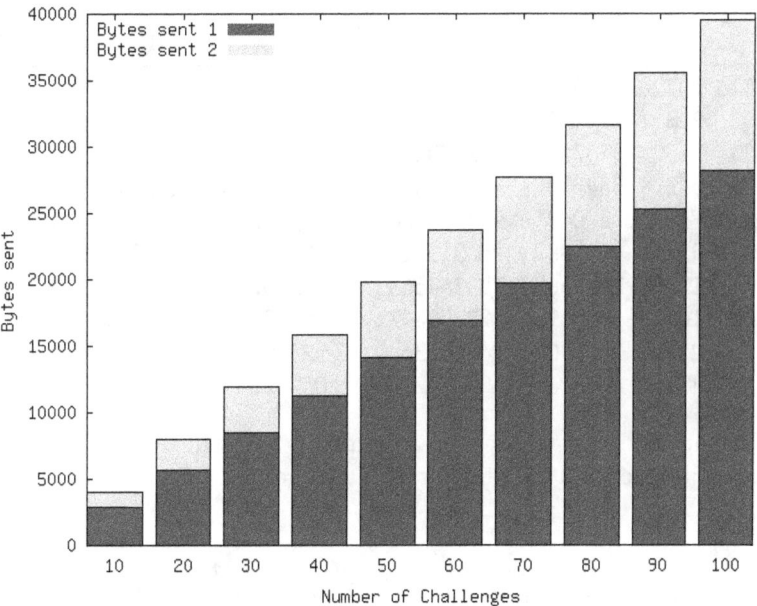

Figure 8.6: Bytes sent from a browser to a server during an authentication request (Bytes sent 1) and responding to the challenge (Bytes sent 2)

interruption. However, due to the long start-up times, which are between 115 and 408 ms, a sequential ZKP protocol composition would support only several challenges in the assumed one second time limit. If we consider our goal as 10 seconds: *for keeping user's attention on the dialog*, the browser would be able to perform at least 24 challenges - 408 ms for performing one challenge-response round (see Section 8.2). This way, according to the existing rankings [Miller 1968; Bouch & Sasse 1999; Nielsen 1999; Bouch *et al.* 2000], the usability of the protocol is kept. However, it would be no longer transparent from the user's perspective. Further in this section, we take into account the interrupted session scenario and determine the lowest possible amount of challenges that guarantees secure authentication for parallel ZKP protocols.

In protocols based on probability, the attacker has always a possibility of guessing the challenge question with a given confidence. We can easily calculate this confidence using the Bernoulli scheme: the probability of at least one success in N trials of nested session impersonation attacks can be expressed as

$$P(N,p) = \sum_{k=1}^{N} \binom{N}{k}(p)^k(1-p)^{N-k}$$

where p is equal to $1/2^t$, where t is the number of challenges. Taking advantage of the fact that this probability is supplemented by the probability of zero successes in N trials (k = 0), we are able to simplify the formula to

$$P(N,p) = 1 - (1-p)^N$$

To depict this formula, Table 8.1 contains sample values for the given number of challenges

		Challenges					
		10	20	30	40	50	60
	10 %	107	109568	112197632	1.1489E+11	1.17648E+14	1.20471E+17
	20 %	228	233472	239075328	2.44813E+11	2.50689E+14	2.56705E+17
	30 %	365	373760	382730240	3.91916E+11	4.01322E+14	4.10953E+17
Confidence [%]	40 %	522	534528	547356672	5.60493E+11	5.73945E+14	5.8772E+17
	50 %	710	727040	744488960	7.62357E+11	7.80653E+14	7.99389E+17
	60 %	937	959488	982515712	1.0061E+12	1.03024E+15	1.05497E+18
	70 %	1232	1261568	1291845632	1.32285E+12	1.3546E+15	1.38711E+18
	80 %	1647	1686528	1727004672	1.76845E+12	1.8109E+15	1.85436E+18
	90 %	2350	2406400	2464153600	2.52329E+12	2.58385E+15	2.64586E+18
	99 %	4710	4823040	4938792960	5.05732E+12	5.1787E+15	5.30299E+18

Table 8.1: The approximate number of attempts to perform the interrupted sessions attack with a given confidence and the number of challenges

and confidence level. For example, in case of 10 challenges requested by the server, an attacker has to perform 710 attempts to achieve confidence 50 % of an impersonation attempt ($0.5 \simeq 1 - (1 - \frac{1}{2^{10}})^{710}$).

To authenticate securely, the number of necessary attempts should be high enough to make such an attack impractical and infeasible. To perform the attack, we chose Firefox since, despite a slow start-up time, it behaved best in the multiple challenge performance tests. Thus, it would be also a wise choice for an attacker who needs to generate multiple responses as fast as possible.

Here, we show more detailed analyses of the authentication times for this browser. We separated the time of sending the challenge graphs and obtaining the server challenge vector from the total time. Table 8.2 and Figure 8.7 present the obtained results. We note that this partial authentication time also increases linearly, but much slower than the total authentication time; their arctangent values are equal respectively 35.96 and 81.72 degrees. Therefore, time necessary for the attacker to verify the server's response increases slower than the total time (see Table 8.2). In Table 8.3, we combine these results with Table 8.1 to predict the time that is necessary to perform a successful impersonation attempt with a given confidence level. We note that in case of 30 challenges and a computer used for this evaluation, the attacker would need at least half-a-year to perform an interruption attack of only 10 % success probability. In the case of 40 challenges, a successful attack is infeasible even assuming a very small success probability.

8.3.6 Parallel Composition Summary

Figure 8.8 summarizes our performance tests, which helps us to determine the maximal number of challenges for the authentication process that keeps it usable for practical realizations. To measure how the browsers' times increase, we calculated the arctangent of each regression. For Firefox, Safari, Opera and Internet Explorer, its value is respectively 81.72, 87.09, 87.32 and 87.87 degrees. It confirms that together with the increase of the number of chal-

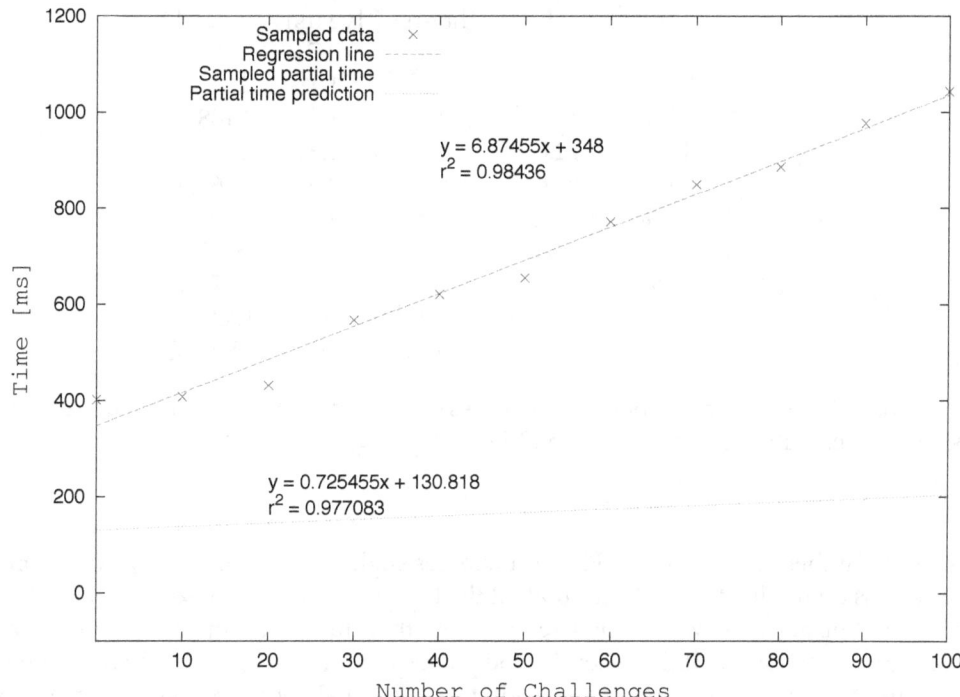

Figure 8.7: Time necessary in Firefox to send graphs and receive challenge question (partial time prediction) and authentication time based on sampled data

Challenges	Time to obtain challenge vector [ms]	Total time [ms]	Times ratio [%]
10	138	408	33.8
20	145	431.5	33.6
30	148	566.5	26.1
40	160	621	25.8
50	165	655	25.2
60	182	771.5	23.6
70	187	849.5	22.0
80	189	886.5	21.3
90	192	977	19.7
100	201	1043	19.3

Table 8.2: Obtained time results for requesting the challenge vector from the verifier using the firefox browser

| | Challenges | | | |
	10	20	30	40
	[seconds]	[hours]	[years]	[years]
10 %	14.8	4.4	0.5	582.9
20 %	31.5	9.4	1.1	1242.1
30 %	50.4	15.1	1.8	1988.4
40 %	72.0	21.5	2.6	2843.7
50 %	98.0	29.3	3.5	3867.9
60 %	129.3	38.6	4.6	5104.5
70 %	170.0	50.8	6.1	6711.6
80 %	227.3	67.9	8.1	8972.4
90 %	324.3	96.9	11.6	12802.1
99 %	650.0	194.3	23.2	25658.7

(left axis label: Confidence [%])

Table 8.3: Estimated time to perform a successful impersonation attempt using the nested sessions attack with a given success confidence

lenges, the authentication time in Firefox increases slightly slower than in the other browsers. The regression model demonstrates that all the browsers are able to execute 37 challenges in one second or even below it. However, we note that due to the Internet Explorer warning message (see Section 8.3.3), 1.7 second is the practical limit to keep the authentication process transparent. This time constraint enabled at least 63 challenges in each tested browser. In Section 8.3.5 we further investigate if this is enough to provide secure authentication.

The time constraints of 10 seconds: *for keeping user's attention on the dialog*, enables the browsers to execute even more than 350 challenges. We cannot, however, assume that 10 second is transparent for all users given the problem with the Internet Explorer timeout dialog. Finally, we note that in all interactive ZKP protocols together with the linear growth of the number of challenges (t), the cheating probability drops exponentially (2^{-t}). To satisfy Miller's one second requirement [Miller 1968], 37 challenges represent a practical and acceptable limit for today's computers.

Note that in Section 8.3.5, we determined the minimal number of challenges that are necessary to provide secure authentication and also satisfy the aforementioned response-time guidelines.

8.4 Concurrent Composition

Concurrent composition is particularly interesting for distributed environments such as the Internet. In comparison with the parallel composition, it ensures the validity of the protocol under stronger security assumptions.

According to [Goldreich 2002], proving that a given protocol can preserve zero-knowledge in a parallel composition is sufficient for creating its valid concurrent composition (see Section 6.3.2). There is, however, the necessity to introduce the notion of delays (β) and time-outs (α)

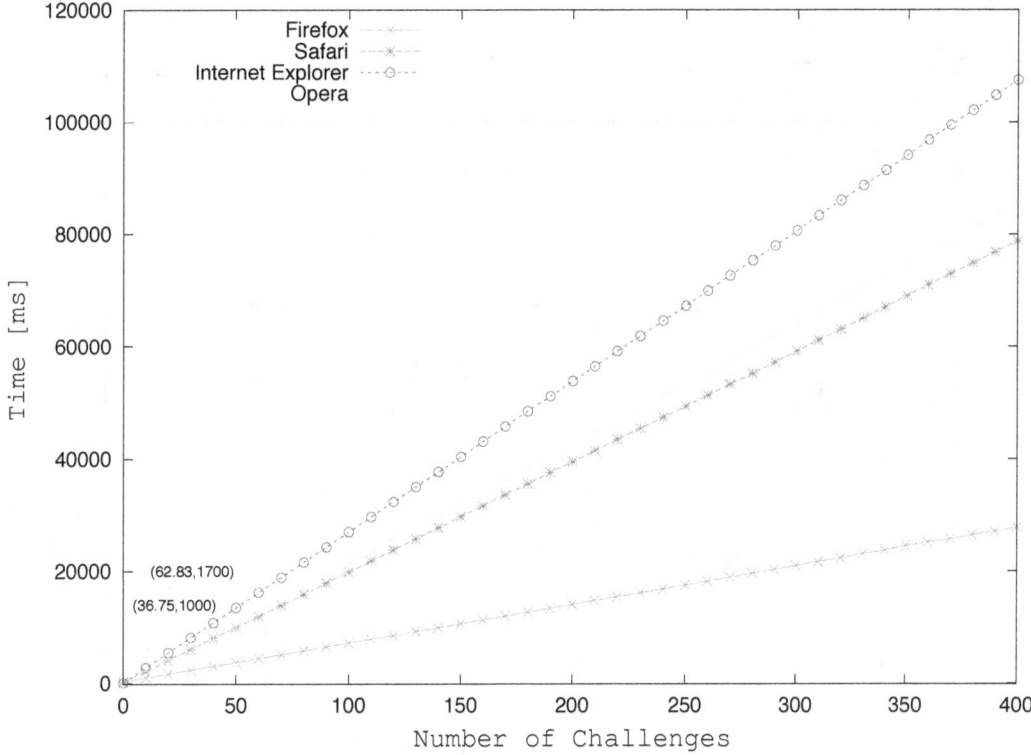

Figure 8.8: Regression models of the expected number of challenges for various browsers during authentication

to the protocol. Both α and β must be agreed by the prover and the verifier before executing the authentication procedure. There is also a requirement that $\beta \geq \alpha$.

Figure 8.9 depicts the protocol that we introduced in Section 7.6.3. The message sent by the verifier in Step 3 must reach the prover before α units of time are counted, otherwise the prover will interrupt the protocol. If the response is delivered in time, the prover waits until β units of time are counted before sending the last message to the verifier. This strategy limits the possibility of nesting sessions by a group of cooperating malicious verifiers. We note that the timing assumptions are already present in many existing solutions [Beth & Desmedt 1991; Brands & Chaum 1993; Neuman & Ts'o 1994; Dwork *et al.* 2004].

On the one hand, in practical ZKP implementations, α and β should be high enough to ensure authentication even for slow browsers. On the other hand, the procedure should be fast enough to satisfy the response-time standards. Thus, we attempted to verify if authentication can be performed within one second.

We took into account results obtained for the parallel version and we set the number of challenges to 40. Since the authentication time is short, we also found it reasonable that time-outs (α) should be as high as possible. Therefore, we set $\beta = \alpha$. In the case of 40 challenges, Internet Explorer (IE) performed worst. Thus, we started our evaluation with this browser. In our tests, we sampled the authentication time 10 times. Initially we set β to 800 ms. In IE, all

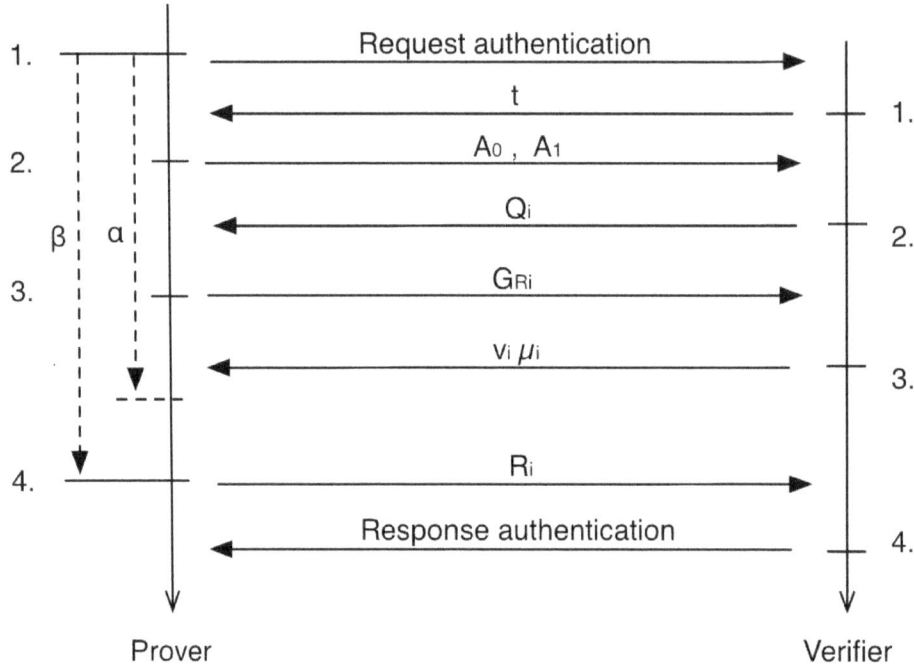

Figure 8.9: The proposed protocol

authentication times for this β value were considered as timeout by our script. Thus, we increased β to 900 ms. In this case 9 out of 10 samples were marked as timeouts. We increased β again to 1000 ms, and we noticed an improvement: only 2 out of 10 samples were considered as timeout. Finally, for β equal 1100 ms all the samples were approved within the specified time constraints.

With this setting we continued our evaluation and tested other browsers. Figure 8.10 shows our results. We did not notice any timeouts for these values of α and β for any browser. The longest authentication time was observed for Firefox and it was 1304 ms. The quickest authentication was observed for Opera and it was 1134 ms. The median values for Firefox, IE, Opera, and Safari were respectively 1177 ms, 1203 ms, 1165.5 ms, 1163 ms. Thus, the difference between the highest and the smallest median values is 40 ms. Such a difference is impossible to notice by the end users.

Therefore, the timing assumptions did not only provide the possibility of the concurrent composition, but they also made the users' perception of each browser almost exactly the same. We note that there is no need to perform the interrupted sessions attack for the concurrent composition as the results would be exactly the same as for the parallel version: the attacker will not respect the delay (β) value.

We present detailed data samples in Appendix C.

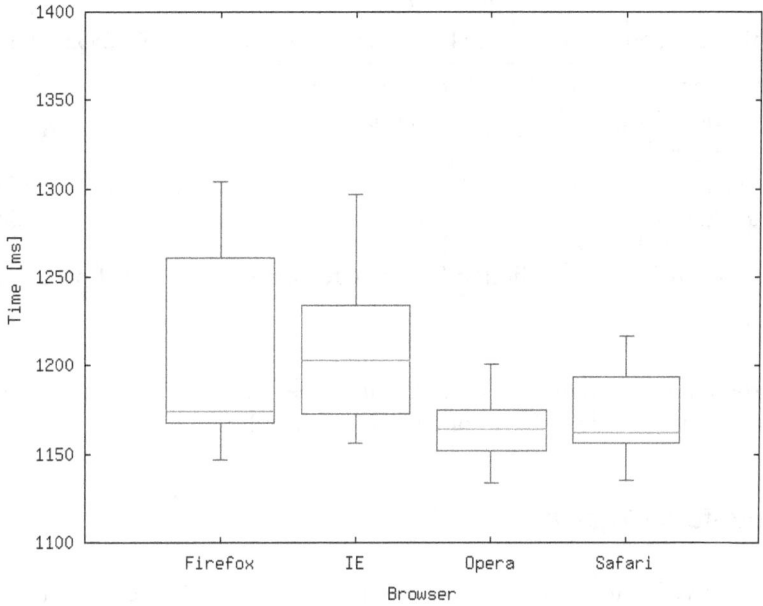

Figure 8.10: Results for the concurrent composition ($\beta = \alpha = 1100ms$).

8.5 Other Protocol Threats

In this section we consider typical attacks on the user's password verifier. Among them, the dictionary attacks that are often perceived as the main threat for password-based authentication protocols. Then, we consider brute-force attacks on the users' public keys. Finally, we consider a situation in which the attacker is not interested in the password, but instead is searching directly for the user's permutation π_{priv} that is the user's private key.

8.5.1 Dictionary Attacks

To test the resistance of the proposed ZKP protocol against dictionary attacks (see Section 3.1.3), we implemented an additional program to verify if a given password is in our password dictionary. In this scenario we assumed that the attacker has a pair of the public graphs G_1 and G_2 and attempts to calculate if a given password candidate satisfies the relation $G_1 = \pi_{candidate}(G_2)$, where $\pi_{candidate}$ is computed from the password candidate. Passwords dictionaries are different from language dictionaries. Therefore, we ran our tests using dictionaries specially created for this purpose[12]. For the configuration we had, we were able to verify approximately 220 passwords per second.

The efficiency of dictionary attacks is, however, questionable. On the one hand, according to [Florencio & Herley 2007], users tend to pick low quality passwords that are easy to guess. On the other hand, [Schneier 2006] claims that only 3.8 % of users' passwords can be found in

---

[1]http://www.openwall.com/passwords/wordlists/password.lst
[2]http://www.maxalbums.com/password_list.php

Password size	1	2	3	4	5	6
Possible passwords	62	3844	238328	14776336	916132832	56800235584
Time to check [s]	0.27	17				
Time to check [m]			17.57			
Time to check [h]				45.4		
Time to check [d]					7.7	478
Time to check [y]						1.35

Table 8.4: Time prediction for brute force attacks on short passwords

passwords dictionaries. Therefore, even if a single password can be verified with a dictionary in a reasonable time, the probability of success is really low.

8.5.2 Brute-force Attacks

To perform a naive brute force attack, we created a program that enumerates and tests passwords of a given length. We limited the number of characters to the keyboard accessible characters only. The speed of such an attack was comparable to the one obtained for dictionary attacks; and by average we were able to generate and test 226 passwords per second. Table 8.4 contains a simple time prediction for brute-force attacks assuming that the obtained password verification speed. We note that on the computer used for evaluation testing a password of size 6 or more was infeasible due to long computation time.

8.5.3 Brute-force Attacks on Graph Isomorphism

In two previous attacks we assumed that the attacker wanted to obtain the user's password and thus followed the protocol's steps. Here, we also consider the possibility of attacking the permutation directly. Instead of selecting a password candidate; then calculating the hash of the password; and finally calculating the permutation, we performed an attack in which the attacker generates sequentially all possible permutations. In such a scenario, the disadvantage is that the password is not obtained. However, the permutation alone would be sufficient to perform a successful authentication. This approach enabled testing 6750 permutations per second on the computer used for evaluation. For a graph of 41 nodes there are 41! possible permutations. The time necessary for checking all of them with the obtained speed would be around $1.57 * 10^{38}$ years.

8.6 Open Questions of Graph Isomorphism

In Section 6.2.4, we noted that the graph isomorphism problem can be solved for a number of graphs of restricted types such as planar graphs, graphs of bounded genus, trees, strongly regular graphs and several others. There are tools such as Nauty[3] that analyses patterns of

---

[3]http://cs.anu.edu.au/~bdm/nauty/

the graphs to find the isomorphism. Therefore, one of the challenges for the protocol is the selection of the optimal graphs. In our case we select graphs randomly; thus, an attacker cannot assume any of those restricted types. Hence, the only one feasible approach for the attacker would be to use a probabilistic method, for example [Czajka & Pandurangan 2008]. However, it would not guarantee the success and also the complexity cost would be higher. Another open question is the optimal number of vertices for the graphs used in the protocol. [Ayeh & Namuduri 2009] suggest that the number should be in the range of hundreds. However, they do not justify their choice and propose a slightly different protocol that is tested with Nauty. We note that the size of the graphs in our protocol can be changed, if a different hash function is applied; and also the complexity of the algorithm is linear. Therefore, even much higher computational requirements could be compensated for through some hardware adjustments.

8.7 Summary and Conclusion

In this section we have evaluated the proposed password-based interactive Zero Knowledge Protocol. Firstly, we analyzed its stability showing that it behaves stable on a wide range of contemporary web browsers.

Then, we showed that it satisfies one set of empirical response-time standards without compromising authentication security. Our evaluation demonstrated that the response-times are highly predictable. Thus, we were able to calculate a linear regression for each tested browser with a high confidence (over 98%).

The obtained models were used to determine the minimal and maximal possible number of challenges that would provide secure authentication while still satisfying the usability standards. In addition we estimated how much data is necessary to perform authentication with a given confidence level. Our considerations were helpful in deriving a formula for a successful attack on parallel ZKP protocols. We present a model of attacks on such protocols taking into account the number of challenges and the attacker's confidence level.

We compared three versions of the proposed protocol: sequential, parallel, and concurrent. We demonstrated that the concurrent composition not only increases security, but also makes the protocol to behave similarly and predictable on a number of browsers. Then, we analyzed other threats for the proposed protocol and demonstrated its resilience to each of these; finally it was determined that a secure version would require an adequate level of conventional password security to eliminate possibility of matching using a password dictionary. In conclusion it was demonstrated that 40 challenge-response cycles are more than adequate to satisfy both security and response-time standards for transactions involving "real money" (RMT). For information-only transactions 20-30 challenges will still provide quite robust security with better user-response times.

Figure 8.11 depicts the conducted tests. We note that the bracket of the acceptable number of challenges has been determined by both security and usability.

We demonstrated that in the case of sequential composition, to perform secure authentication on the web, the number of challenges must be high enough; and we also concluded in Section 8.3.5 that the system latency also determines the minimal amount of challenges.

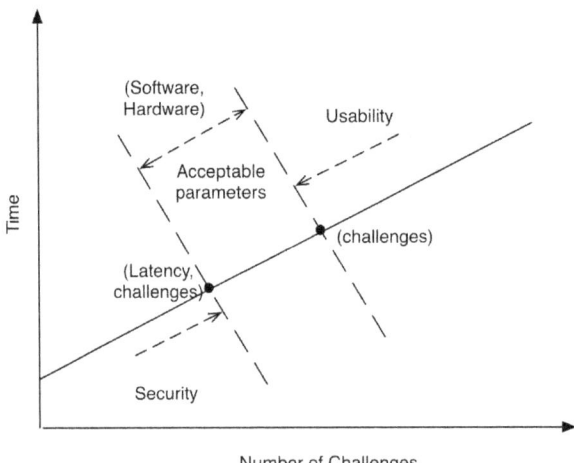

Figure 8.11: Time measurements conclusion

However, the number of challenges cannot be too high because that would cause long waiting times for the users; and thus, such an implementation would not satisfy usability requirements. The size of the acceptable configuration bracket is determined by a combination of software and hardware parameters.

Part IV

Conclusions

"It is not knowledge, but the act of learning, not possession,
but the act of getting there which generates
the greatest satisfaction."

— Carl Friedrich Gauss

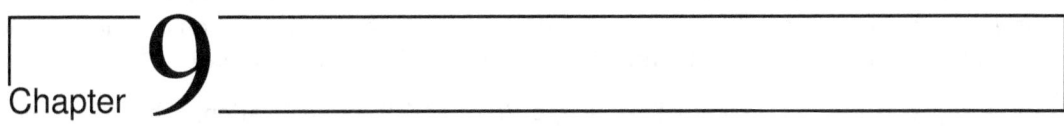

Chapter 9

Summary and Future Work

In this chapter we summarize the previous chapters and the thesis contribution. We also discuss our future work and plans.

9.1 Summary

This thesis began with an observation that access control models have evolved and have become an important part of todays' online economies.

In Chapter 2 we described the state of the art of access control approaches and their most notable historical developments: Role-Based Access Control (RBAC), Trust Management, Digital Rights Management (DRM), and usage control models. We also discussed DRM-related technologies such as Rights Expression Languages (RELs), digital watermarking and trusted computing because these are parts of the conceptual model for access control. Finally, we mentioned fair use and demonstrated the implications for the existing content usage control solutions.

In Chapter 3 we presented a number of vulnerabilities of authentication protocols. We also presented the best known solutions in use today, including generic HTTP techniques, SSL, TTP-based protocols, plugins and PAKE.

In Chapter 4 we introduced online Social Networks [Barnes 1954] that we use to represent relationships between people. Our presentation includes both practical examples and and theoretical definitions. Then, we presented the Friend-of-a-Friend (FOAF) vocabulary that enabled exchange of social data on the web. We specifically focused on its applicability for trust management and authentication.

In Chapter 5, we identified several problems of existing Usage Control and DRM solutions. Specifically, the need for a more flexible usage control model that keeps the usage workflow secure. We also noted that there is a need for trust management adopted to meet the needs of social networks. When combined, these techniques would provide a basis for a secure and convenient means of authentication in a distributed Web environment. One of our goals is to enable a more open environment for the exchange of digital content. Here we emphasize the need for mechanisms to integrate licensing metadata with content in a way that prevents its removal. We also observe that the existing solutions cause interoperability problems and raise issues relating to fair use rights of consumers. Fair Rights Management (FRM) is proposed as a mean to deal with such issues. We demonstrated how FRM differs from existing UCON solutions. Then, we described how the authentication decision is made. Finally, we defined conceptual foundations for the FRM implementation.

Chapter 6 introduced Zero Knowledge Proof (ZKP) authentication, which is a secure method of proving identity. We also presented a generic ZKP protocol and the main mathematical problems that could be used to create such a protocol. We specifically focused on graph isomorphism describing various approaches to attack it. We also discussed usability issues for a web deployment of ZKP.

In Chapter 7 we described how the conceptual model introduced in Chapter 5 had been implemented. We specifically focus on its main components: (i) trust management and access control; (ii) applied rights expression model; (iii) digital content watermarking; and (iv) the proposed authentication service. This authentication service is evaluated in Chapter 8. To demonstrate how these components works together we also present a use case scenario and we describe how FRM approaches the fair use situations that we identified.

In Chapter 8, we demonstrated and evaluated, a practical realization of password-based Zero Knowledge Proof (ZKP) protocol. We analyzed three protocol compositions: sequential in Section 8.2; parallel in Section 8.3; and finally, concurrent in Section 8.4. We used the obtained results to verify if existing browsers are fast enough to perform a secure authentication that is still transparent for the users. Our evaluation demonstrated that the response-time is predictable and its linear regression could be calculated for each browser we tested with a high level of confidence (over 98%). The resulting models were used to determine the minimal and maximal number of challenges to provide secure authentication while still satisfying usability standards. An estimate is provided of how much data is required to perform authentication within a given confidence level.

A model of the attack vulnerability of the ZKP protocol was presented. This takes into account the number of challenges and the confidence level of the attacker. It was shown how to estimate a sufficient number of challenges to satisfy both security and response-time standards for a given user's hardware configuration. We presented a model of attacks on such protocols taking into account the number of challenges and the attacker's confidence level.

9.2 Conclusions and Contributions

Although the foundation of authentication and authorization are solid, the Web poses new challenges. In this thesis we addressed these challenges and we proposed a number of improvements in the area of authorization, authentication, usage control, and trust. Specifically, we answered the following research questions:

- **How to create a more user-friendly DRM that offers a similar level of security as existing solutions?** We proposed extensions for the existing DRM/UCON solutions.

Our proposal included using social networks and creative commons licenses to enforce fair use. We demonstrated through application scenarios how this works and we also presented necessary security enhancements to provide reliable access control solution.

- **What is necessary to enable better privacy in existing DRM/UCON solutions?** To address the privacy gap in the existing solutions, we proposed using zero-knowledge proof protocols. These protocols let the users to keep their credentials away from the servers and are never transmitted during the authentication procedure. Thus, this solution is much more secure against many impersonation attempts. We also proposed a DRM model that takes advantage of social networks for access control. So the users have new ways of controlling their content.

- **How Semantic Web technologies can be used to improve security of web applications?** We showed that semantic web vocabularies such as FOAF can be used for trust, authentication, and authorization purposes. We also shown that the semantic version of the creative commons vocabulary can be used to create a rights expression language. We combined these vocabularies with some new classes and properties to create a new rights expression language (REL). We showed that the new REL provided interoperability with existing solutions. Since it is based on creative commons licenses, its semantic descriptions have a legal value.

- **What is necessary to enable authentication protocols using Zero-Knowledge proofs on the web?** Our evaluation results showed that existing infrastructure elements, including web servers and browsers, are sufficient for enabling zero-knowledge proof authentication on the web. To verify that, we implemented the proposed protocol and we evaluated its performance using a number of different settings.

- **What is necessary to enable more secure authentication protocols that does not involve digital certificates?** We proposed using public key-based cryptography while the users keep using their passwords. In this approach each user's private key is computed on-the-fly by the user browser. This is necessary because the browsers do not have access to the underlaying file systems to store private keys in a secure way. We showed, however, that this is not a computational limitation for today's personal computers.

Addressing these research questions we made a number of contributions, among which the major are:

- **A novel usage control model.** It was proposed to adapt to suit the needs of social networks. It is more friendly for the users and it attempts to introduce fair use rights to the digital world. It was also shown that users' policies specified in this approach are enforced by law in many jurisdictions. This approach is unique in comparison with existing REL languages and it makes this approach promising. It was demonstrated that this solution introduces better privacy protection than the existing UCON solutions.

- **Authentication service using an efficient Zero-Knowledge Proof (ZKP) protocol.** Such a service was proposed and implemented. This is the first successful work using this approach in the web environment.

- **A methodology to determine the required number of challenge-response rounds.** This is crucial to make a ZKP implementation secure. This methodology is generic and can be applicable also for other ZKP-based solutions.

- **A set of challenges for secure and usable authentication.** We presented a list of desirable security properties. We also classified existing authentication solutions taking into account their web-applicability.

9.3 Future Work

The continuation of this work was started in the SEcure DIgital CredentIals (SeDiCi) project (grant REI 1005). The project was also invited to the business partners programme organized by Enterprise Ireland to further investigate its commercial possibilities. Thus, there will be a possibility of licensing its libraries for other applications.

In terms of future project work, we would like to verify possibilities of using the protocol with different settings such as larger graphs, alternative hash functions or to apply alternative NP problems. The most important research question for this thesis is whether there is a polynomial algorithm for finding graph isomorphism of two given graphs. There were many attempts to find such a polynomial algorithm, but so far all of these efforts have failed. Thus, this challenge remains open to be solved.

We also note that we still have not observed any relevant non-interactive ZKP protocol using graph algorithms. Most of existing solutions rely on the difficulty of the integer factorization or discrete logarithm. It would be very interesting to experiment with alternative approaches deployed in serious commercial applications.

Taking a medium to long term perspective, to widely adopt work presented in this thesis, there is a need for semantic technologies to become more widely adopted by computer users. Specifically, there is a need for verified sources of trust that could be extracted from existing social networks. For the ZKP protocol part, it would be very helpful if such solutions could be directly incorporated into web-browsers as plugins or as a part of the underlaying specification of browser architecture.

Part V

Appendices

*"Everything should be made
as simple as possible,
but not simpler."*

— Albert Einstein

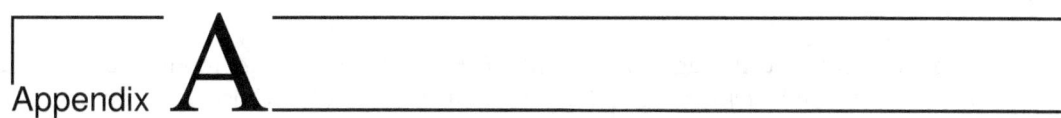

Appendix A

FRM Implementation Design

This section demonstrates the most essential procedures of FRM, such as Object discovery, Object download, listing member's Objects, borrow Objects and buy Objects.

A.1 Object Discovery

Algorithm 3 Object Discovery

Require: $userQuery \neq null$
Ensure: $search_{results} \in \{resultTable\}$
  $query_{exp} \Leftarrow semanticQueryExpansion$
  $resultTable \Leftarrow browseIndex(query_{exp})$
  for $elem \in resultTable$ **do**
    retrieve object details
    find lowest price
    if $auth_D = true$ **then**
      indicate if can borrow $elem[result]$
    end if
  end for
  return $resultTable$

The Object Discovery procedure (see Algorithm 3) is used by the *Content Distribution & Catalogues* module. It is executed each time a member decides to search for an object. A member's query is semantically expanded using WordNet and Wikipedia Forward page. Hence, if a member search for a term *government*, the platform also searches the index for its synonyms and related terms, for example: *authorities, regime, political science, administration*. For each relevant result the platform finds its details. For example, if the object is accessible at more than one provider or on many different terms, the lowest price is determined and displayed. Then the system computes if there is a possibility of borrowing the object for the member who issued the query. Browsing the complete social network would be very computationally expensive. Therefore to lower the complexity of this operation, only the direct friends are checked.

A.2 Object Download

Objects are downloaded through the *Content Distribution & Catalogues* module, but they are also processed by the *Watermarking* and *Content Manager* modules. Object Download invokes also the watermarking procedure (see Algorithm 8) to ensure that members never obtains the Objects in their plain form uploaded by the content provider. To download the watermarked file the member must be authenticated and authorized directly or though his/her social network. The downloaded Objects can be different for each member. If a member downloads a file that is borrowed through a friend. The file is watermarked with the Id of the owner of the file. The watermarking algorithm is content dependent; and thus its implementation is different for each different digital media component (see Section A.6).

Algorithm 4 Object download

Require: $auth_D \neq false$ and $memberA \neq null$ and $Object \neq null$
Ensure: $Object \neq Object2$
  if $authorization(memberA, Object) = false$ **then**
    $Object2 \Leftarrow null$
  else
    $Object2 \Leftarrow watermark(Object)$
  end if
  return $Object2$

A.3 Member Item

Procedure 5 enables *memberA* to display and navigate over the purchased and borrowed Objects. The platform evaluates, if the given Object was bought on terms that permit sharing and indicate this possibility. If *memberA* is not the owner of the Object, the platform evaluates sharing possibilities in a recursive way; in the social network digraph, trust between *memberA* and the owner of the Object is examined and validated if all constraints set by the intermediate social network members are satisfied. Hence, this structure is dynamic and it may return different results for each member's requests.

A.4 Borrow Object

In FRM, *memberA* can borrow an object $Object2 \in memberB_{Objects}$ from *memberB*, if there is a direct or derived trust relationship between them. In addition *memberB* must enable and set the minimal trust level that permits sharing. If *memberA* satisfy the distance and the trust level requirements, the sharing operation is permitted and the Object can be downloaded (see

---

Algorithm 5 Member's Objects

Require: $auth_D \neq false$ and $memberA \neq null$
Ensure: $Objects_{results} \in \{ObjectsTable\}$
  $objectsTable \Leftarrow purchasedObject(memberA)$
  $objectsTable2 \Leftarrow borrowedObjects(memberA)$
  for $elem \in objectsTable$ **do**
    if $elem.License.Permission.Distribution = true$ **then**
      $elem.canBorrow = true$
    end if
  end for
  for $elem \in objectsTable2$ **do**
    if $elem.License.Permission.Distribution = true$ and $maxItemSharingDistance >$
    $currentItenSharingDistance$ **then**
      $elem.canBorrow = true$
    end if
  end for
  $objectsTable \Leftarrow objectsTable \cup objectsTable2$
  return $objectsTable$

Section A.2). As a result of this operation, *memberA* is given a watermarked copy of the *Object* that was requested.

Algorithm 6 Borrow Object

Require: $auth_D \neq false$ and $memberA \neq null$ and $memberB \neq null$ and $Object \in memberB_{Objects}$
Ensure: $Object2 \in memberB_{Objects} \cup null$
  $role \Leftarrow isInRole(memberA, memberB, Object)$
  if $role = true$ **then**
    $Object2 = objectDownload(auth_D, memberA, Object)$
  else
    $Object2 = null$
  end if
  return $Object2$

A.5 Buy Object

In order to buy an Object, a member must successfully perform a financial transaction. The member is given with a personalized version of the purchased Object on the terms that were agreed during the transaction and are expressed in the license. The terms and the member *id* are attached to each download request that can be sent by the member or his/her friends. To download the Object, a member authenticates in a zero-knowledge proof way (see Section 7.6).

Algorithm 7 Buy Object

Require: $auth_D \neq false$ and $memberA \neq null$ and $Object \neq null$ and $License \neq null$
Ensure: $Object \in Objects$ and $License \in Object_{Licenses}$
    $result \Leftarrow financialTransaction(memberA, Object, License)$
    if $result = true$ **then**
        $memberA_{Objects} \Leftarrow memberA_{Objects} \cup Object$
    end if
    return $result$

A.6 Digital Watermarking

The main operation performed by this module is to produce an *FRM Object* (see Definition 5.3) that is compatible with the Object uploaded by the content uploader but it additionally has extra information embedded. The FRM platform stores Objects in their plain form. However, the members are always given personalized files that enables tracking copyright infringement and also performing authorization. The part of information related to authorization and authentication is readable for content players and it is signed by the FRM platform. The part that enables tracing copyright infringement is hidden from the players and requires knowledge about a password used at the watermarking procedure. This procedure is crucial from the perspective of the Object security. The watermarking procedure (see Figure 8) is dependent on the Object media type.

Algorithm 8 Watermark

Require: $auth_D \neq false$ and $memberA \neq null$ and $Object \neq null$ and $watermark \neq null$ and
    $password \neq null$
Ensure: $memberA has role uploader$
    $Object2 \Leftarrow watermark(Object, password, watermark)$
    return $Object2$

A.7 Content Player

The players can play the purchased Objects. They also can determine if any copyright infringement had place, but they are unable to check who is the offender. Therefore, such an Object is reported to the system in which the content uploader can find out the offender's id.

The FRM player is a user interface level application that enables using subjects' objects. The members must prove their identities by passing the authentication procedure. They also have to satisfy the authorization requirements. The authorization process depends on the member' social network which is a dynamic structure. Therefore, it can generate different results at different points in time. Right after the *Rights Validation* process, the decision is made if the given Object is permitted to be played or not.

Algorithm 9 Play Object

Require: $auth_D \neq false$ and $memberA \neq null$ and $Object2 \neq null$
Ensure: $Object2 is not corrupted$
  if $Object2 is corrupted$ **then**
    $reportIllegalContent(Object2, memberA)$
  end if
  $result \Leftarrow hasRole(Object2, memberA)$
  if $result = true$ **then**
    $play(Object2)$
  else
    $exit$
  end if

RDF Examples of FRM Data Samples

This appendix contains sample RDF data to fulfill the examples presented in Chapter 7.

```
<rdf:Description rdf:about="http://drmlab.org/Bob">
        <rdf:type rdf:resource="http://xmlns.com/foaf/0.1/Person"/>
        <foaf:name>Bob</foaf:name>
        <dc:creator rdf:resource="http://drmlab.org/Dave/Resource/spanishCourse"/>
</rdf:Description>
<rdf:Description rdf:about="http://drmlab.org/Dave/Resource/spanishCourse">
        <rdf:type rdf:resource="http://web.resource.org/cc/Work"/>
        <dc:description>An online Spanish course for beginners.
        </dc:description>
        <dc:rights rdf:resource="http://drmlab.org/Dave/Resource/spanishCourse/license1"/>
        <dc:rights rdf:resource="http://drmlab.org/Dave/Resource/spanishCourse/license2"/>
        <dc:subject>Spanish</dc:subject>
        <dc:subject>eLearning</dc:subject>
</rdf:Description>
<rdf:Description rdf:about="http://drmlab.org/Dave/Resource/spanishCourse/license1">
        <rdf:type rdf:resource="http://web.resource.org/cc/License"/>
        <cc:permits rdf:resource="http://web.resource.org/cc/Distribution"/>
        <cc:permits rdf:resource="http://web.resource.org/cc/Reproduction"/>
        <frm:price>200</frm:price>
</rdf:Description>
<rdf:Description rdf:about="http://drmlab.org/Dave/Resource/spanishCourse/license2">
        <rdf:type rdf:resource="http://web.resource.org/cc/License"/>
        <cc:prohibits rdf:resource="http://web.resource.org/cc/CommercialUse"/>
        <frm:price>100</frm:price>
</rdf:Description>
```

Listing B.1: Resource description example

```
<rdf:Description rdf:about="http://drmlab.org/Alice">
        <foaf:knows rdf:resource="http://drmlab.org/Dave"/>
        <rdf:type rdf:resource="http://xmlns.com/foaf/0.1/Person">
        <frm:purchase rdf:resource="http://drmlab.org/Alice/Purchase/spanishCourse"/>
        <foaf:name>Alice</foaf:name>
</rdf:Description>
<rdf:Description rdf:about="http://drmlab.org/Dave">
        <rdf:type rdf:resource="http://xmlns.com/foaf/0.1/Person">
        <foaf:name>Dave</foaf:name>
</rdf:Description>
<rdf:Description rdf:about="http://drmlab.org/Alice/Purchase/spanishCourse">
        <s3b:accessibleTo>F[mailto:alice@frm.drmlab.org]2.7</s3b:accessibleTo>
        <dc:references rdf:resource="http://drmlab.org/Dave/Resource/spanishCourse"/>
        <dc:license rdf:resource="http://drmlab.org/Alice/Purchase/spanishCourse/license1"/>
        <rdf:type rdf:resource="http://s3b.corrib.org/sscf/0.1/WebResource">
</rdf:Description>
<rdf:Description rdf:about="http://drmlab.org/Alice/Purchase/spanishCourse/license1">
        <rdf:type rdf:resource="http://web.resource.org/cc/License"/>
        <cc:permits rdf:resource="http://web.resource.org/cc/Distribution"/>
        <cc:permits rdf:resource="http://web.resource.org/cc/Reproduction"/>
        <frm:price>200</frm:price>
</rdf:Description>
<rdf:Description rdf:nodeID="blankNode1">
        <rdf:type rdf:resource="http://www.w3.org/1999/02/22-rdf-syntax-ns#Statement"/>
        <rdf:subject rdf:resource="http://drmlab.org/Alice"/>
        <rdf:predicate rdf:resource="http://xmlns.com/foaf/0.1/knows"/>
        <rdf:object rdf:resource="http://drmlab.org/Dave"/>
        <fr:friendshipLevel>0.75</fr:friendshipLevel>
</rdf:Description>
<rdf:Description rdf:nodeID="blankNode2">
        <rdf:type rdf:resource="http://www.w3.org/1999/02/22-rdf-syntax-ns#Statement"/>
        <rdf:subject rdf:resource="http://drmlab.org/Alice/Purchase/spanishCourse"/>
        <rdf:predicate rdf:resource="http://purl.org/dc/elements/1.1/license"/>
        <rdf:object rdf:resource="http://drmlab.org/Alice/Purchase/spanishCourse/license1"/>
        <frm:signature>aef76d8fa8bf</frm:signature>
</rdf:Description>
```

Listing B.2: An example Alice's profile

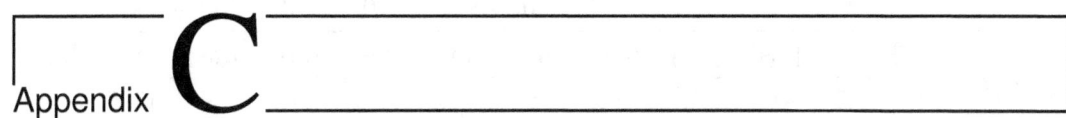

Appendix **C**

Sampled Data

This appendix contains data samples that we used in our evaluation in Chapter 8

C.1 Parallel composition

Tables C.1 – C.4 presents data samples obtained for Firefox, Internet Explorer, Opera and Safari browsers. These results are used for calculations in Chapter 8.

C.2 Concurrent composition

This section contains results that were obtained for the concurrent protocol composition (see Section 8.4). Table C.5 presents results for the Internet Explorer browser for β value between 800 and 1000 ms. Table C.6 contains values for all the browsers for $\beta = \alpha = 1100$.

		Challenges										
		0	10	20	30	40	50	60	70	80	90	100
		[ms]	[ms]	[ms]	[ms]	[ms]	[ms]	[ms]	[ms]	[ms]	[ms]	[ms]
Sample number [%]	1	445	417	441	565	655	649	668	712	735	1275	968
	2	502	943	720	532	885	895	1023	865	1156	942	2511
	3	310	399	422	815	587	596	689	834	835	1093	1059
	4	553	329	308	720	559	555	784	781	802	1108	1000
	5	379	427	347	552	515	2468	2134	940	938	927	1027
	6	315	368	351	538	2178	581	1184	712	778	867	949
	7	342	423	611	570	761	577	759	2052	762	884	1436
	8	425	285	403	533	573	679	672	805	1363	928	1687
	9	2621	340	695	568	482	661	817	876	1006	1466	1002
	10	359	2269	3126	602	1960	698	692	912	1874	1012	1251

Table C.1: Sampled authentication time for Firefox

		Challenges										
		0	10	20	30	40	50	60	70	80	90	100
		[ms]	[ms]	[ms]	[ms]	[ms]	[ms]	[ms]	[ms]	[ms]	[ms]	[ms]
Sample number [%]	1	187	407	625	891	1375	1469	1844	2922	2760	3141	3594
	2	187	375	625	984	1328	1406	1656	2656	2719	3078	3188
	3	219	391	657	938	1109	1359	1766	2610	2891	3000	3828
	4	187	391	609	875	1172	1406	1828	2484	2750	3094	3437
	5	188	437	593	921	1157	1500	1719	1953	2750	2922	3391
	6	171	422	672	953	1125	1469	1766	2110	2703	3109	3125
	7	3172	406	641	938	1234	1531	1812	1859	2875	2937	3266
	8	188	375	625	922	1172	1485	1813	2016	2812	3047	3297
	9	172	391	734	953	1109	1563	1812	2703	2828	3266	3453
	10	218	391	657	937	1235	1531	1719	1890	2641	3125	3250

Table C.2: Sampled authentication time for Internet Explorer

		Challenges										
		0	10	20	30	40	50	60	70	80	90	100
		[ms]	[ms]	[ms]	[ms]	[ms]	[ms]	[ms]	[ms]	[ms]	[ms]	[ms]
Sample number [%]	1	124	317	455	658	1041	1176	1315	1521	1861	2013	2235
	2	100	244	441	669	907	1215	1425	1566	1740	1881	2070
	3	94	289	465	646	986	1154	1435	1546	1737	1992	2082
	4	88	300	455	677	890	1096	1437	1536	1843	2146	2255
	5	160	258	507	705	898	1160	1356	2114	1802	1877	2156
	6	119	308	449	719	998	1206	1485	1484	2110	1920	2232
	7	115	294	448	692	917	1128	1434	1796	1651	1993	2150
	8	148	282	461	657	988	1212	1454	1591	1759	1954	2198
	9	104	301	459	635	896	1210	1454	1710	1879	1947	2251
	10	117	252	478	771	928	1252	1455	1529	1745	2094	2471

Table C.3: Sampled authentication time for Opera

		Challenges										
		0	10	20	30	40	50	60	70	80	90	100
		[ms]	[ms]	[ms]	[ms]	[ms]	[ms]	[ms]	[ms]	[ms]	[ms]	[ms]
Sample number [%]	1	405	466	869	767	930	1090	1338	1595	1783	2108	2204
	2	387	384	584	731	877	1232	1328	1574	1809	2126	2165
	3	637	388	518	763	895	1049	1573	1546	2252	2099	2483
	4	316	580	737	747	914	1098	1493	1594	1851	2276	2458
	5	272	435	659	734	827	1128	1728	1765	2018	2169	2095
	6	477	337	482	730	900	1161	1361	1520	1825	2120	2155
	7	411	482	490	699	926	1094	1609	1766	1876	2147	2508
	8	482	413	600	681	908	1101	1368	2377	1723	2114	2214
	9	396	450	699	723	896	1185	1373	1606	2425	2444	2585
	10	513	840	697	657	1011	1139	1436	1565	1794	2089	2212

Table C.4: Sampled authentication time for Safari

		Sample Number									
		1	2	3	4	5	6	7	8	9	10
	β	[ms]	[ms]	[ms]	[ms]	[ms]	[ms]	[ms]	[ms]	[ms]	[ms]
IE	800	1110*	1094*	1032*	1141*	1094*	1141*	1110*	1079*	1078*	1016*
	900	1032	984*	1032*	1031*	1032*	1032*	1094*	1000*	1000*	1016*
	1000	1079	1047	1109	1093*	1047	1110	1094	1032	1063	1125*

Table C.5: Sampled data for Internet Explorer for various β values (* these samples were not approved because of timeout)

| | | Sample Number | | | | | | | | | |
		1	2	3	4	5	6	7	8	9	10
		[ms]	[ms]	[ms]	[ms]	[ms]	[ms]	[ms]	[ms]	[ms]	[ms]
Browser	Firefox	1261	1147	1168	1174	1162	1180	1271	1304	1214	1172
	Internet Explorer	1297	1203	1172	1250	1156	1173	1234	1188	1204	1203
	Opera	1175	1171	1201	1164	1143	1167	1134	1152	1183	1156
	Safari	1135	1170	1217	1162	1164	1213	1146	1162	1156	1194

Table C.6: Sampled authentication times for concurrent protocol composition for various browsers for $\beta = 1100$

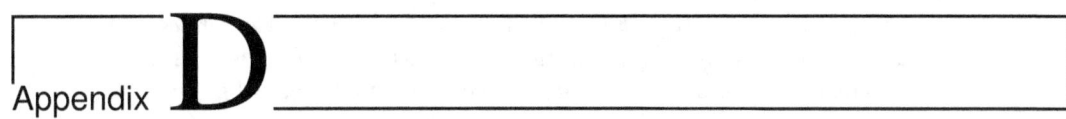

Appendix D

Academic Contributions

This appendix contains a list of peer-reviewed publications and other contributions made during Ph.D studies.

D.1 Principle Academic Contributions

During Ph.D studies more than 20 academic paper were published. The core chapters of this thesis have been published in several international journals, conferences, workshops and also book chapters. These are listed below with a short summary of each to place it within the context of this thesis:

- Journals

  - [Grzonkowski *et al.* 2009]: Sławomir Grzonkowski, Adam Gzella, Sebastian Ryszard Kruk, John G. Breslin, Tomasz Woroniecki and Jarosław Dobrzanski. Sharing information across community portals with FOAFRealm. Int. J. Web Based Communities, vol. 5, no. 3, pages 351-370, 2009.

    Community portals such as blogs, wikis and photo-sharing sites have become the new channels for information dissemination on the web. They contain a huge amount of valuable information that is often voluntarily delivered by experts. The most useful results of searching the web very often come from some sort of a community site. We present a method of sharing information across multiple community portals through a Social Semantic Collaborative Filtering (SSCF) system. It utilises FOAFRealm, a user profile management system which extends the popular Friend of a Friend' (FOAF) metadata and enables users to share the bookmarks and community documents that they create. Moreover, the proposed solution allows both a seamless connection of different portals and the easy identification of contributors. We describe the required infrastructure, including the components that enable content sharing and browsing. Finally, we demonstrate a verification of our idea.

- Conference papers

– [Grzonkowski & Corcoran 2009]: Sławomir Grzonkowski and Peter M. Corcoran. A Secure and Efficient Micropayment Solution for Online Gaming. In Proceedings of the International IEEE Consumer Electronics Society's Games Innovations Conference 2009 (ICE-GIC 09), 2009.

   An innovative micropayment solution is proposed which incorporates both distributed security and social networking features. This has significant potential to impact on both the provision of new services and community features in online multiplayer gaming worlds.

– [Grzonkowski & McDaniel 2008]: Sławomir Grzonkowski and Bill McDaniel. FRM: Towards a Semantic Platform for Fair Content Distribution. In AXMEDIS'08: Proceedings of the Fourth International Conference on Automated Production of Cross Media Content for Multi-Channel Distribution. IEEE Computer Society, November 2008.

   Fair use policy allows legal owners to share products they bought with their acquaintance; it is based on the assumptions that the owners pass an original product and they cannot use it at the same time.
   In the digital world, we can hardly apply those assumptions since they are based on a physical availability. Furthermore, digital content providers want to have control over the distribution of their products; thus, Digital Rights Management (DRM) systems do not assist and even forbid sharing.
   We present Fair Rights Management (FRM) that is our work towards fair use in the digital world. We propose taking advantage of social networks and terms negotiations. We illustrate our approach by extending existing solutions with semantic descriptions. We describe how to apply and implement the proposed improvements in the standard DRM model. Finally, we evaluate our proposition with the most common fair use scenarios.

– [Grzonkowski *et al.* 2008b]: Sławomir Grzonkowski, Wojciech Zaremba, Maciej Zaremba and Bill McDaniel. Extending Web Applications with a Lightweight Zero Knowledge Proof Authentication. In CSTST'08: Proceedings of the 5th international conference on Soft computing as transdisciplinary science and technology, pages 65-70, New York, NY, USA, 2008. ACM.

   User authentication is a crucial requirement for secure transactions and access to the sensitive resources on the Web. We propose, implement and evaluate a Zero-Knowledge Proof Authentication (ZKP) algorithm based on isomorphic graphs. The proposed mechanism allows for authentication with varying confidence and security levels.
   We suggest that most of the computations should be carried out by the user's web browser without revealing password or login at any point in time; instead generated random isomorphic graphs and permutation functions based on the user login/password can be exchanged.
   Our experimental evaluation shows that by combining the asynchronous web with ZKP protocols, it is feasible to satisfy existing usability standards on the web.

– [Grzonkowski *et al.* 2007]: Sławomir Grzonkowski, Brian D. Ensor, Sebastian Ryszard Kruk, Adam Gzella, Stefan Decker and Bill McDaniel. A DRM Solution Based on Social Networks and Enabling the Idea of Fair Use. In Procedings of Media in Transition 5, April 2007.

*Fair use policy allows legal owners to share products they bought with their ac-
quaintance; it is based on the assumptions that the owners pass an original product and
they cannot use it at the same time. In the digital world, we can hardly apply those
assumptions since they are based on a physical availability. Furthermore, digital content
providers want to have control over the distribution of their products; thus, Digital
Rights Management (DRM) systems do not assist and even forbid sharing. In this paper,
we describe a DRM system that takes advantage of a social network. We will describe
how a model of an existing on-line social network, which includes users' roles and trust
relationships can be applied. We will present that roles and trust metrics, maintained by
the users can be coupled with sharing policies controlled by the content providers. Our
solution gives flexibility to the users; it still also leaves, enough control over the content
distribution to the content providers. We will show how to extend an existing Digital
Rights Language (DRL) to support properties defined in social networks metadata and
compare it with other approaches. Finally, we will discuss if our solution introduces the
fair use policy to the digital world.*

- [Breslin *et al.* 2007]: John G. Breslin, Sławomir Grzonkowski, Adam Gzella,
  Sebastian Ryszard Kruk and Tomasz Woroniecki. Sharing Information Across
  Community Portals with FOAFRealm. In Proceedings of the 4th IADIS Interna-
  tional Conference on Web-Based Communities (WBC 2007), February 2007.

*Community portals such as blogs, wikis and photo sharing sites have become the
new channels for information dissemination on the Web. When searching for information,
many results end up in some type of community site. However, one cannot make use
of the wealth of information that is available through the preferences of one's thematic
social network, or through bookmarks or other documents, only those accessible through a
social network. Also, due to multiple accounts being registered on a variety of community
portals, there is a lack of semantics regarding the information that a particular user has
created or bookmarked across this set of portals. This paper presents a method for sharing
information across multiple community portals through a social semantic collaborative
filtering system; this collaborative filtering extends a popular "Friend Of A Friend"
(FOAF) network; it enables users to share the bookmarks and community documents that
they create.*

- [Kruk *et al.* 2006b]: Sebastian Ryszard Kruk, Sławomir Grzonkowski, Adam
  Gzella, Tomasz Woroniecki and Choi Hee-Chul. D-FOAF: Distributed Identity
  Management with Access Rights Delegation. In Procedings of Asian Semantic
  Web Conference 2006, September 2006.

*Todays WWW consists of more than just information. The WWW provides a large
number of services, which often require identification of it's users. This has lead to the fact
that today users have to maintain a large number of different credentials for different websites - distributed or shared identification systems are not widely deployed. Furthermore,
current authorisation systems require strict centralisation of the authorisation procedure
- users themselves are usually not enabled to authorise their trusted friends to access
services, although often this would be beneficial for services and businesses on the Web.
In this article we present D-FOAF, a distributed identity management system which
deploys social networks. We show how information inherent in social networks can be*

utilised to provide community driven access rights delegation and we analyse algorithms for managing distributed identity, authorisation and access rights checking. Finally we show how the social networking information can be protected in a distributed environment.

- [Grzonkowski *et al.* 2005]: Sławomir Grzonkowski, Adam Gzella, Henryk Krawczyk, Sebastian Ryszard Kruk, Francisco J. Martin-Recuerda Moyano and Tomasz Woroniecki. D-FOAF - Security Aspects in Distributed User Management System. In Proceedings of IEEE International Conference of Technologies for Homeland Security and Safety. (TEHOSS 2005), 2005.

The contemporary Internet offers various services ranging from electronic newspapers to online social networks. To authorize themselves, users have to register to on-line services. However, most of the authentication and user management systems are incompatible with each other. Therefore the registration process must be repeated each time from the beginning, requiring multiple login-password-site triples with adequate security constraints. Very often, user management systems do not allow user to view or manipulate their profile information, and so users cannot determine the actual information gathered about them after registration. To overcome the problem with multiple registrations and sign-ons, a number of solutions like Microsoft Passport have been proposed. In this article we elaborate on potential security risks concerning single registration, single sign-on and access to profile data. We present how required security levels in a user management system can be provided without losing the accessibility of the service. We define how the potential user can benefit from this user management system based on open standards and open architectures. Finally, we present the D-FOAF, a distributed user management system based on FOAF metadata and a P2P architecture that implements presented solutions for secure distributed user management system.

- Book chapters

  - [Grzonkowski *et al.* 2010]: Sławomir Grzonkowski, Brian D. Ensor and Bill Mc-Daniel. Applied Cryptography in Electronic Commerce. In Hamid R. Nemati and Li Yang, editors, Applied Cryptography for Cyber Security and Defense: Information Encryption and Cyphering, pages 125147. IGI Global, 2010. (to appear).

Electronic commerce has grown into a vital segment of the economy of many nations. It is a global phenomenon providing markets and commercialization opportunities world-wide with a significantly reduced barrier to entry as compared to global marketing in the 20th century. Providing protocols to secure such commerce is critical and continues to be an area for both scientific and engineering study. Falsification, fraud, identity theft, and disinformation campaigns or other attacks could damage the credibility and value of electronic commerce if left unchecked. Consequently, cryptographic methods have emerged to combat any such efforts, be they the occasional random attempt at theft or highly organized criminal or political activities. This chapter covers the use of cryptographic methods and emerging standards in this area to provide the necessary protection. That protection, as is common for web-based protocols, evolves over time to deal with more and more sophisticated attacks. At the same time, the provision of security in a manner convenient enough to not deter electronic commerce has driven research efforts to find easier to use and simpler protocols to implement even as the strength of the cryptographic methods has increased. This chapter covers current standards, looking at several facets of the secure commercialization problem from authentication to intrusion detection and identity and reputation management. Vulnerabilities are discussed as well as capabilities.

– [Grzonkowski *et al.* 2008a]: Sławomir Grzonkowski, Sebastian Ryszard Kruk, Adam Gzella, Jakub Demczuk and Bill McDaniel. Community-aware Ontologies. In Sebastian Ryszard Kruk and Bill McDaniel, editors, Semantic Digital Libraries, pages 125-139. Springer, 2008. ISBN: 978-3-540-85433-3.

There is something more than just semantic web that the DLs need to adopt in order to keep up with the current changes on the Internet. There is a huge potential in the notion of online communities, which can be used to fill in the gap that was created when human librarian was moved out of the scope in digital libraries. We are going to describe how community-aware ontologies, such as FOAF, can be implemented in the vision of Semantic Digital Libraries.

– [Choi *et al.* 2008]: Hee-Chul Choi, Sebastian Ryszard Kruk, Sławomir Grzonkowski, Katarzyna Stankiewicz, Brian Davis and John Breslin. Trust Models for Community-Aware Identity Management. In Ravu Jumar Jain B, editor, Trust Management in Virtual Environment, pages 95-122. The ICFAI University Press, 2008. ISBN 81-314-1254-1.

In this article, we begin by detailing how trust can be modeled within online communities. We present methods for constructing community-aware identity management systems and for computing trust levels between users of a social network, using a novel trust model that takes advantage of both the capabilities of the Semantic Web and of a distributed topology. We also describe how the trust of a particular person relies on the separate social networks that they are members of. Finally, we evaluate our research against current studies in the psychology domain.

• Workshops

– [Choi *et al.* 2006]: Hee-Chul Choi, Sebastian Ryszard Kruk, Sławomir Grzonkowski, Katarzyna Stankiewicz, Brian Davids and John G. Breslin. Trust Models for Community-Aware Identity Management. In IRW2006/WWW2006 Workshop, May 2006.

The contemporary Web is heading towards its next stage of evolution. From a clump of unorganised information spaces, the Web is becoming more focused on the meaning of information (the Semantic Web) and on community awareness (Web 2.0). One of the key concepts in this new Web is that of social networking, where both sophisticated trust modelling and personal identity/reputation management are required for the creation of social networks and for the exchange of information in these networks. The Web has many instances of sites and services where reputation management and trust form the basis of social and commercial interaction between members of those sites. However, there are few systems that enable users to share their credentials among many websites. It is also important that systems should provide strong security and protect user identities, but all of these features should also be transparent from a user's perspective.
In this article we begin by detailing how trust can be modelled within online communities. We present methods for constructing community-aware identity management systems and

for computing trust levels between users of a social network, using a novel trust model that takes advantage of both the capabilities of the Semantic Web and of a distributed topology. We also describe how the trust of a particular person relies on the separate social networks that they are members of. Finally, we evaluate our research against current studies in the psychology domain.

– [Kruk *et al.* 2006a]: Sebastian Ryszard Kruk, Sławomir Grzonkowski, Adam Gzella and Mariusz Cygan. DigiMe - Ubiquitous Search and Browsing for Digital Libraries. In MDM'06: Proceedings of the 7th International Conference on Mobile Data Management, page 84, Washington, DC, USA, 2006. IEEE Computer Society.

Vast sources of information, such as the Internet are difficult to browse and/or search through. Existing tools can be sometimes frustrating for many people. So far a number of techniques have been proposed to deliver user-oriented solutions. The problem re-surfaces however within a ubiquitous computing paradigm. Aside from a possible delay in response time, their are additional drawbacks with respect to mobile devices such as: Bandwidth size, storage(what type of costs do you mean) and performance costs and client UI size. In this paper we introduce three search and browsing features: fulltext search, collaborative filtering and multifaceted browsing, all of which can be enriched with semantic and community information. We present two of the aforementioned techniques implemented in our interface for digital libraries - DigiMe.

• Posters and Demos

– [Grzonkowski 2010]: Sławomir Grzonkowski. SeDiCi: An Authentication Service Taking Advantage of Zero-Knowledge Proofs. In Financial Cryptography. Springer, 2010.

Transmission of users' profiles over insecure communication means is a crucial task of today's ecommerce applications. In addition, the users have to create many profiles and remember many credentials. Thus they retype the same information over and over again. Each time the users type their credentials, they expose them to phishing or eavesdropping attempts.These problems could be solved by using Single Sign-on (SSO). The idea of SSO is that the users keep using the same set of credentials when visiting different websites. For web-aplications, OpenID[1] is the most prominent solution that partially impelemtns SSO. However, OpenID is prone to phishing attempts and it does not preserve users' privacy [Adida 2007a].
To address phishing and eavesdropping, we developed SeDiCi, a secure SSO. This technology takes advantage of Zero-Knowledge Proof (ZKP) authentication that is based on our previous work [Grzonkowski et al. 2008b]. The technology also supports REST-based API that enables taking advantage of the service by mobile phones, web-applications and other client applications. To provide interoperability with other systems, SeDiCi stores data using semantic web standards such as FOAF. Thus, the users are able to use their profiles and social networks from other services.

– Slawomir Grzonkowski, SeDiCi - SEcure DIgital CredentIals: A Novel Authentication Method for the Web. In Proceedings of the Semantic Technology Conference (poster session) 2009.

---

[1]OpenID 2.0 spec: http://openid.net/specs/openid-authentication-2_0.html

SeDiCi is a new online unique authentication service. This technology allows authenticating users in such a way that a password never leaves the user's browser and the verifier is unable to impersonate the user.

For commercial software, including banking and on-line shopping, credentials are not stored on the servers in their plain text form and asymmetric cryptography communication protocols are used, for instance, HTTPS. However, the credentials are given to the servers in a readable form during the authentication procedure. It gives servers the unlimited control over the user identity. This is a serious privacy problem.

Phishing and identity fraud was not the only one goal of the project. SeDiCi was developed with semantic technologies in mind. It uses FOAF, XFN to provide social aspects of users' collaboration and interactions.

– Slawomir Grzonkowski, FRM: Fair Rights Management. In Proceedings of the Semantic Technology Conference (poster session) 2009.

Fair Rights Management (FRM) is our work towards fair use in the digital world. We propose taking advantage of social networks and terms negotiations. FRM is also a semantic fair content distribution platform. The platform provides a reliable identity management system using FOAF, machine-readable digital licenses using Creative Commons RDF Vocabulary, and protection means for the content that is distributed.

It supports the fully automated extension of diverse license offers to customers. The social method of sharing content is sophisticated but legal as well as the propagation and revocation of user rights across networks of providers, distributors, and consumers. Security and privacy are maintained by our architecture while maximizing the flexibility needed by the next generation of content consumers.

– [Grzonkowski & Kruk 2006]: Sławomir Grzonkowski and Sebastian Ryszard Kruk. HyperCuP Lightweight Implementation: A Universal Solution for Making Application Distributed. In 3rd European Semantic Web Conference (ESWC 2006), 2006.

Contemporary applications need an efficient solution for communication to implement robust information retrieval mechanisms and fault tolerant networks. Apart from implementing an robust, scalable communication protocol the solution should be accessible with easy to use API that would not require too much of an effort to use it. In this article we present HyperCuP Lightweight Implementation (HLI) which delivers an alternative P2P architecture based on web services. This implementation has already been deployed with diverse systems like JeromeDL, a semantic digital library and FOAFRealm, a distributed identity management system based on social networking. We describe an architecture of the HyperCuP Lightweight Implementation. We show how to deploy it with one's own application and how to take advantage of the established hypercube topology.

– [Kruk et al. 2006c]: Sebastian Ryszard Kruk, Adam Gzella and Sławomir Grzonkowski. D-FOAF: Distributed Identity Management based on Social Networks. In 3rd European Semantic Web Conference (ESWC 2006) - Demos and Posters, 2006.

Contemporary Web consists of more than just information, it provides a large number of services, which often require identification of it's users. Since distributed or shared identification systems are not yet widely adopted many users have to maintain a large number of different credentials for different services. Furhermore current authorisation systems require strict centralisation of the authorisation procedure. Although the feature of enabling user's friends or good friends of a friends to access user resources would be benefical for services and business on the Web, it is not usually offered by existing systems. In this article we present D-FOAF, a distributed identity management system that utilizes social networks. We show how information inherent in social networks can be utilised to provide community driven access rights delegation and distributed authorisation.

The main outcome of this thesis: the ZKP protocol has been protected with a patent application(*A method and apparatus for authenticating a user*. Patent Pending, January 2008. Patent App. S2008/0001) [Grzonkowski & Zaremba 2008]. The protocol also became the main topic of an Enterprise Ireland Proof of Concept commercialization grant (REI 1005): *SeDiCi: SEcure DIgital CredentIals*. Sławomir Grzonkowski was a Principal Investigator (PI) of the project. *SeDiCi* was further invited to the *business partner* programme organized by Enterprise Ireland to further investigate commercial possibilities.

D.2 Supplemental Publications and Academic Contributions

There are also several publications that are not directly related with the main hypothesis:

- [Nasirifard *et al.* 2008]: Peyman Nasirifard, Sławomir Grzonkowski and Vassilios Peristeras. OntoPair: Towards a Collaborative Game for Building OWL-Based Ontologies. In Proceedings of the CISWeb Workshop, located at the 5th European Semantic Web Conference ESWC 2008, June 2008.

- [Jeong *et al.* 2007]: Senator Jeong, Sławomir Grzonkowski, Sungin Lee and Hong-Gee Kim. Semantically Enhanced Event Description. In 5th Annual Conference on Teaching and Learning: Learning Technologies, June 2007.

- [O'Nuallain & Grzonkowski 2006]: Caoimhin O'Nuallain and Sławomir Grzonkowski. Collaboration. In Proceedings of the IADIS International Conference WWW/INTERNET 2006, October 2006.

- [O'Nuallain *et al.* 2006]: Caoimhin O'Nuallain, Brian Davis, Krystian Samp, Bill McDaniel, Sławomir Grzonkowski and Sebastian Ryszard Kruk. Search Interface Based on Natural Language Query Templates. In Proceedings of the IADIS International Conference WWW/INTERNET 2006, October 2006.

D.3 Volunteer Work & Contributions

During Ph.D studies, there was also professional volunteer work conducted in terms of participating in TPC of conferences and reviewing other scholars papers, viz:

- 29th International Conference on Consumer Electronics (ICCE 2011)

- 3rd International Conference on Internet Technologies and Applications (ITA 09)

- 2nd International Conference on Internet Technologies and Applications (ITA 07)

and also reviewing publications after receiving other TPC members or editors invitations, viz:

- Book: Applied Cryptography for Cyber Security and Defense: Information Encryption and Cyphering (2 chapters)

- Journal of Organizational Computing and Electronic Commerce, 2009

- Peer-to-peer Networking and Applications, Journal, Springer 2009

- World Wide Web (WWW) 2008

- International Semantic Web Conference, ISWC 2008

- International Semantic Web Conference + Asian Semantic Web Conference, ISWC+ASWC 2007

- International Conference on Scalable Information Systems 2007

- Business Information Systems, BIS 2007

- Knowledge Engineering and Knowledge Management Managing Knowledge in a World of Networks, EKAW 2006

Moreover, two workshops that are not directly related with the main hypothesis were co-organized:

- 2nd Workshop on Emerging e-Learning Web Technologies (EeLT 2009) in conjunction with 12th International Conference on Business Information Systems (BIS 2009)

- 1st Workshop on e-learning for Business needs in conjunction with 12th International Conference on Business Information Systems (BIS 2008)

Finally, the responsibility of the DRM lab and SeDiCi project leadership were taken and performed during the time of my PhD studies.

Bibliography

[Abelson *et al.* 2008] Hal Abelson, Ben Adida, Mike Linksvayer and Nathan Yergler. *ccREL: The Creative Commons Rights Expression Language*, March 2008.

[Adelsbach *et al.* 2005] André Adelsbach, Markus Rohe and Ahmad-Reza Sadeghi. *Towards multilateral secure digital rights distribution infrastructures*. In DRM '05: Proceedings of the 5th ACM workshop on Digital rights management, pages 45–54, New York, NY, USA, 2005. ACM.

[Adida 2007a] Ben Adida. *Beamauth: two-factor web authentication with a bookmark*. In CCS '07: Proceedings of the 14th ACM conference on Computer and communications security, pages 48–57, New York, NY, USA, 2007. ACM.

[Adida 2007b] Ben Adida. *The Browser as a Secure Platform for Loosely Coupled Private-Data Mashups*. In W2SP 2007, Proceedings of the First Workshop on Web 2.0 Security and Privacy, Oakland, CA, USA, 2007.

[Ahn & Sandhu 2000] Gail-Joon Ahn and Ravi S. Sandhu. *Role-based authorization constraints specification*. ACM Trans. Inf. Syst. Secur., vol. 3, no. 4, pages 207–226, 2000.

[Aho *et al.* 1974] Alfred V. Aho, John E. Hopcroft and Jeffrey D. Ullman. The design and analysis of computer algorithms. Addison-Wesley, 1974.

[Ambainis 2004] Andris Ambainis. *Quantum algorithms a decade after shor*. In STOC '04: Proceedings of the thirty-sixth annual ACM symposium on Theory of computing, pages 111–111, New York, NY, USA, 2004. ACM Press.

[Arnab & Hutchison 2005] Alapan Arnab and Andrew Hutchison. *Fairer usage contracts for DRM*. In DRM '05: Proceedings of the 5th ACM workshop on Digital rights management, pages 1–7, New York, NY, USA, 2005. ACM.

[Arnab & Hutchison 2007] Alapan Arnab and Andrew Hutchison. *Persistent access control: a formal model for drm*. In DRM '07: Proceedings of the 2007 ACM workshop on Digital Rights Management, pages 41–53, New York, NY, USA, 2007. ACM.

[Arrow 1972] Kenneth J. Arrow. *Gifts and exchanges*. Philosophy and Public Affairs, vol. 1, no. 4, pages 343–362, 1972.

[Ayeh & Namuduri 2009] Eric Ayeh and Kamesh Namuduri. *ZERO-KNOWLEDGE PROOF BASED NODE AUTHENTICATION*. Technical report, University of North Texas, May 2009.

[Babai & Kucera 1979] L. Babai and L. Kucera. *Canonical Labelling of Graphs in Linear Average Time*. In Proc. of the 20-th Annual Symp. Foundations of Computer Science. IEEE Computer Society, 1979.

[Babai *et al.* 1980] László Babai, Paul Erdos and Stanley M. Selkow. *Random Graph Isomorphism*. SIAM Journal on Computing, vol. 9, no. 3, pages 628–635, 1980.

[Barabasi 2003] Albert-Laszlo Barabasi. Linked: How everything is connected to everything else and what it means. Plume, April 2003.

[Barker *et al.* 2007] Elaine Barker, William Barker, William Burr, William Polk and Miles Smid. *Recommendation for Key Management - Part 1: General (Revised)*. Technical report, National Institute of Standards and Technology (NIST), March 2007.

[Barlas 2006] Chris Barlas. *Digital Rights Expression Languages (DRELs) (TSW0603)*. Technical report, London: JISC, 2006.

[Barnes 1954] J. A. Barnes. *"Class and Committees in a Norwegian Island Parish"*. volume 7, pages 39–58. "Human Relations", 1954.

[Baudet 2005] Mathieu Baudet. *Deciding security of protocols against off-line guessing attacks*. In CCS '05: Proceedings of the 12th ACM conference on Computer and communications security, pages 16–25, New York, NY, USA, 2005. ACM.

[Bell & Lapadula 1973] David E. Bell and Leonard J. Lapadula. *Secure Computer Systems: Volume I – Mathematical Foundations, Volume II – A Mathematical Model, Volume III – A Refinement of the Mathematical Model*. Technical Report MTR-2547, The MITRE Corporation, Bedford, Massachusetts, 1973.

[Bellare *et al.* 1990] Mihir Bellare, Silvio Micali and Rafail M Ostrovsky. *Perfect zero-knowledge in constant rounds*. In STOC '90: Proceedings of the twenty-second annual ACM symposium on Theory of computing, pages 482–493, New York, NY, USA, 1990. ACM.

[Bellovin & Merritt 1990] Steven M. Bellovin and Michael Merritt. *Limitations of the Kerberos authentication system*. SIGCOMM Comput. Commun. Rev., vol. 20, no. 5, pages 119–132, 1990.

[Bellovin & Merritt 1992] Steven M. Bellovin and Michael Merritt. *Encrypted Key Exchange: Password-Based Protocols SecureAgainst Dictionary Attacks*. In SP '92: Proceedings of the 1992 IEEE Symposium on Security and Privacy, page 72, Washington, DC, USA, 1992. IEEE Computer Society.

[Bem 1972] Daryl J. Bem. *Self-perception theory*. In L. Berkowitz, editor, Advances in Experimental Social Psychology, volume 6, pages 1–62. Academic Press, New York, 1972.

[Berners-Lee & Fischetti 1999] Tim Berners-Lee and Mark Fischetti. Weaving the web: The original design and ultimate destiny of the world wide web by its inventor. Harper San Francisco, 1999. Foreword By-Michael L. Dertouzos.

[Berners-Lee *et al.* 1996] T. Berners-Lee, R. Fielding and H. Frystyk. *Hypertext Transfer Protocol – HTTP/1.0 (RFC 1945)*, 1996.

[Bertino *et al.* 2001] Elisa Bertino, Barbara Catania and Roberta Gori. *Enhancing the expressive power of the U-Datalog language.* Theory Pract. Log. Program., vol. 1, no. 1, pages 105–122, 2001.

[Beth & Desmedt 1991] Thomas Beth and Yvo Desmedt. *Identification Tokens - or: Solving the Chess Grandmaster Problem.* In CRYPTO '90: Proceedings of the 10th Annual International Cryptology Conference on Advances in Cryptology, pages 169–177, London, UK, 1991. Springer-Verlag.

[Blake *et al.* 1999] Ian F. Blake, G. Seroussi and N. P. Smart. *Elliptic curves in cryptography.* Cambridge University Press, New York, NY, USA, 1999.

[Blaze *et al.* 1996] Matt Blaze, Joan Feigenbaum and Jack Lacy. *Decentralized Trust Management.* In IEEE Symposium on Security and Privacy, pages 164–173, 1996.

[Blum *et al.* 1988] Manuel Blum, Paul Feldman and Silvio Micali. *Non-Interactive Zero-Knowledge and Its Applications (Extended Abstract).* In STOC, pages 103–112, 1988.

[Bouch & Sasse 1999] A. Bouch and M.A. Sasse. *It ain't what you charge, it's the way that you do it: a user perspective of network QoS and pricing.* pages 639 –654, 1999.

[Bouch *et al.* 2000] Anna Bouch, Allan Kuchinsky and Nina Bhatti. *Quality is in the eye of the beholder: meeting users' requirements for Internet quality of service.* In CHI '00: Proceedings of the SIGCHI conference on Human factors in computing systems, pages 297–304, New York, NY, USA, 2000. ACM Press.

[Boyd 2004] Danah Michele Boyd. *Friendster and Publicly Articulated Social Networking.* In Conference on Human Factors and Computing Systems (CHI 2004), http://www.danah.org/papers/CHI2004Friendster.pdf, 2004.

[Brainard *et al.* 2006] John Brainard, Ari Juels, Ronald L. Rivest, Michael Szydlo and Moti Yung. *Fourth-factor authentication: somebody you know.* In CCS '06: Proceedings of the 13th ACM conference on Computer and communications security, pages 168–178, New York, NY, USA, 2006. ACM.

[Brands & Chaum 1993] Stefan Brands and David Chaum. *Distance-Bounding Protocols (Extended Abstract).* In EUROCRYPT, pages 344–359, 1993.

[Brassil *et al.* 1999] J.T. Brassil, S. Low and N.F. Maxemchuk. *Copyright protection for the electronic distribution of text documents.* Proceedings of the IEEE, vol. 87, no. 7, pages 1181–1196, Jul 1999.

[Breslin *et al.* 2007] John G. Breslin, Sławomir Grzonkowski, Adam Gzella, Sebastian Ryszard Kruk and Tomasz Woroniecki. *Sharing Information Across Community Portals with FOAFRealm.* In Proceedings of the 4th IADIS International Conference on Web-Based Communities (WBC 2007), February 2007.

[Callas *et al.* 2007] J. Callas, L. Donnerhacke, H. Finney, D. Shaw and R. Thayer. *OpenPGP Message Format.* RFC 4880 (Proposed Standard), November 2007.

[Canetti *et al.* 2000] Ran Canetti, Oded Goldreich, Shafi Goldwasser and Silvio Micali. *Reset-table zero-knowledge (extended abstract)*. In STOC '00: Proceedings of the thirty-second annual ACM symposium on Theory of computing, pages 235–244, New York, NY, USA, 2000. ACM.

[Carney 1975] James Carney. *The Invention of the Ogam Cipher*. Ériu, no. 26, pages 53–65, 1975.

[Cederquist *et al.* 2007] J. G. Cederquist, Ricardo Corin, M. A. C. Dekker, Sandro Etalle, J. I. den Hartog and Gabriele Lenzini. *Audit-based compliance control*. Int. J. Inf. Sec., vol. 6, no. 2-3, pages 133–151, 2007.

[Chapin *et al.* 2008] Peter C. Chapin, Christian Skalka and X. Sean Wang. *Authorization in trust management: Features and foundations*. ACM Comput. Surv., vol. 40, no. 3, pages 1–48, 2008.

[Chiariglione 2006] Leonardo Chiariglione. *Digital Rights Management, Interoperability and MPEG-21*, September 2006. IBC News.

[Choi *et al.* 2006] Hee-Chul Choi, Sebastian Ryszard Kruk, Sławomir Grzonkowski, Katarzyna Stankiewicz, Brian Davids and John G. Breslin. *Trust Models for Community-Aware Identity Management*. In IRW2006/WWW2006 Workshop, May 2006.

[Choi *et al.* 2008] Hee-Chul Choi, Sebastian Ryszard Kruk, Sławomir Grzonkowski, Katarzyna Stankiewicz, Brian Davis and John G. Breslin. *Trust Models for Community-Aware Identity Management*. In Ravu Jumar Jain B, editor, Trust Management in Virtual Environment, pages 95–122. The ICFAI University Press, 2008. ISBN 81-314-1254-1.

[Cialdini 2001] Robert B Cialdini. Influence : science and practice. Allyn and Bacon, Boston, MA, 2001.

[Cohen 2003] Julie E. Cohen. *DRM and privacy*. Commun. ACM, vol. 46, no. 4, pages 46–49, 2003.

[Corcoran & Cucos 2005] Peter Corcoran and Alex Cucos. *Techniques for securing multimedia content in consumer electronic appliances using biometric signatures*. Consumer Electronics, IEEE Transactions on, vol. 51, no. 2, pages 545–551, May 2005.

[Corneil & Gotlieb 1970] D. G. Corneil and C. C. Gotlieb. *An Efficient Algorithm for Graph Isomorphism*. J. ACM, vol. 17, no. 1, pages 51–64, 1970.

[Covington *et al.* 2001] Michael J. Covington, Wende Long, Srividhya Srinivasan, Anind K. Dev, Mustaque Ahamad and Gregory D. Abowd. *Securing context-aware applications using environment roles*. In SACMAT '01: Proceedings of the sixth ACM symposium on Access control models and technologies, pages 10–20, New York, NY, USA, 2001. ACM.

[Cox *et al.* 1997] Ingemar Cox, Joe Kilian, Tom Leighton and Talal Shamoon. *Secure spread spectrum watermarking for multimedia*. IEEE Transactions on Image Processing, vol. 6, no. 12, pages 1673–1687, Dec 1997.

[Cox *et al.* 2002a] Ingemar Cox, Matthew L. Miller and Jeffery A. Bloom. Digital watermarking. Morgan Kaufmann Publishers Inc., San Francisco, CA, USA, 2002.

[Cox *et al.* 2002b] Ingemar Cox, Matthew L. Miller, Jeffery A. Bloom and Chris Honsinger. *Digital Watermarking*. Journal of Electronic Imaging, vol. 11, no. 3, pages 414–414, 2002.

[Csányi & Szendrői 2004] Gábor Csányi and Balázs Szendrői. *Structure of a large social network*. Phys. Rev. E, vol. 69, no. 3, page 036131, Mar 2004.

[Czajka & Pandurangan 2008] Tomek Czajka and Gopal Pandurangan. *Improved random graph isomorphism*. J. Discrete Algorithms, vol. 6, no. 1, pages 85–92, 2008.

[Czerwinski 2007] Reiner Czerwinski. *A Polynomial Time Algorithm for Graph Isomorphism*. CoRR, vol. abs/0711.2010, 2007.

[Daemen & Rijmen 1999] J. Daemen and V. Rijmen. *AES Proposal: Rijndael*, 1999.

[Damgard 1999] Ivan Damgard. *Concurrent Zero-Knowledge is Easy in Practice*, 1999. Appeared in the THEORY OF CRYPTOGRAPHY LIBRARY and has been included in the ePrint Archive. ivan@daimi.aau.dk 10500 received June 16th, 1999. Revised July 28th, 1999.

[Dan Brickley and Libby Miller 2005] Dan Brickley and Libby Miller. *FOAF Vocabulary Specification*, 2005.

[Dang 2009] Quynh Dang. *Recommendation for Applications Using Approved Hash Algorithms*. Technical report, National Institute of Standards and Technology, February 2009. NIST Special Publication 800-107.

[Davis & Vitiello 2005] Ian Davis and Jr Eric Vitiello. *RELATIONSHIP: A vocabulary for describing relationships between people*, August 2005.

[Delgado *et al.* 2005] Jaime Delgado, Jose Prados and Eva Rodriguez. *Profiles for Interoperability between MPEG-21 REL and OMA DRM*. In CEC '05: Proceedings of the Seventh IEEE International Conference on E-Commerce Technology, pages 518–521, Washington, DC, USA, 2005. IEEE Computer Society.

[DeMartini *et al.* 2003] T. DeMartini, X. Wang and B. Wragg. *MPEG-21 Working Documents - Part 5 and Part 6, MPEG-21 Rights Expression Language*, March 2003.

[Denning & Sacco 1981] Dorothy E. Denning and Giovanni Maria Sacco. *Timestamps in key distribution protocols*. Commun. ACM, vol. 24, no. 8, pages 533–536, 1981.

[Dierks & Allen 1999] T. Dierks and C. Allen. *The TLS Protocol Version 1.0 (RFC 2246)*, 1999.

[Dijkstra 1959] E. W. Dijkstra. *A note on two problems in connexion with graphs*. Numerische Mathematik, vol. 1, pages 269–271, 1959.

[DMCA 1998] DMCA. *Text of the DMCA http://thomas.loc.gov/cgi-bin/query/z?c105:H.R.2281:*, 1998.

[DMM 2003] DMM. *THE DIGITAL MEDIA MANIFESTO: http://www.chiariglione.org/manifesto/major_actions.htm*, 2003.

[Duda 2008] Jarek Duda. *Polynomial algorithm for graph isomorphism problem*. CoRR, vol. abs/0804.3615, 2008.

[Dwork & Sahai 1998] Cynthia Dwork and Amit Sahai. *Concurrent Zero-Knowledge: Reducing the Need for Timing Constraints*. In CRYPTO '98: Proceedings of the 18th Annual International Cryptology Conference on Advances in Cryptology, pages 442–457, London, UK, 1998. Springer-Verlag.

[Dwork *et al.* 1998] Cynthia Dwork, Moni Naor and Amit Sahai. *Concurrent Zero-Knowledge*. In STOC, pages 409–418, 1998.

[Dwork *et al.* 2004] Cynthia Dwork, Moni Naor and Amit Sahai. *Concurrent zero-knowledge*. J. ACM, vol. 51, no. 6, pages 851–898, 2004.

[Eagly & Chaiken 1993] Alice Hendrickson Eagly and Shelly Chaiken. The psychology of attitudes. Fort Worth, TX : Harcourt Brace Jovanovich College Publishers, 1993.

[Eastlake & Jones 2001] D. Eastlake 3rd and P. Jones. *US Secure Hash Algorithm 1 (SHA1) (RFC 3174)*, 2001.

[ElGamal 1985] Taher ElGamal. *A public key cryptosystem and a signature scheme based on discrete logarithms*. In Proceedings of CRYPTO 84 on Advances in cryptology, pages 10–18, New York, NY, USA, 1985. Springer-Verlag New York, Inc.

[Erickson 2003] John S. Erickson. *Fair use, DRM, and trusted computing*. Commun. ACM, vol. 46, no. 4, pages 34–39, 2003.

[European Parliament and Council 2001] European Parliament and Council. *Directive on the harmonisation of certain aspects of copyright and related rights in the information society*. Official Journal L 167 , 22/06/2001 P. 0010 - 0019, 2001.

[Feige *et al.* 1988] Uriel Feige, Amos Fiat and Adi Shamir. *Zero-Knowledge Proofs of Identity*. J. Cryptology, vol. 1, no. 2, pages 77–94, 1988.

[Feige *et al.* 1990] Uriel Feige, Dror Lapidot and Adi Shamir. *Multiple Non-Interactive Zero Knowledge Proofs Based on a Single Random String (Extended Abstract)*. In FOCS, pages 308–317, 1990.

[Felten 2003] Edward W. Felten. *A skeptical view of DRM and fair use*. Commun. ACM, vol. 46, no. 4, pages 56–59, 2003.

[Ferraiolo & Kuhn 1992] David Ferraiolo and Richard Kuhn. *Role-based access controls*. In In Proceedings of 15th NIST-NCSC National Computer Security Conference, pages 554–563, 1992.

[Ferraiolo *et al.* 2001] David Ferraiolo, Ravi Sandhu, Serban Gavrila, Richard Kuhn and Ramaswamy Chandramouli. *Proposed NIST standard for role-based access control*. ACM Trans. Inf. Syst. Secur., vol. 4, no. 3, pages 224–274, 2001.

[Festinger 1957] L. Festinger. A theory of cognitive dissonance. Stanford University Press, 1957.

[Fielding *et al.* 1999] R. Fielding, J. Gettys, J. Mogul, H. Frystyk, L. Masinter, P. Leach and T. Berners-Lee. *Hypertext Transfer Protocol – HTTP/1.1 (RFC 2616)*, 1999.

[Filotti & Mayer 1980] I. S. Filotti and Jack N. Mayer. *A polynomial-time algorithm for determining the isomorphism of graphs of fixed genus*. In STOC '80: Proceedings of the twelfth annual ACM symposium on Theory of computing, pages 236–243, New York, NY, USA, 1980. ACM Press.

[Fitzpatrick 2005] Brad Fitzpatrick. *Distributed Identity: Yadis.* LiveJournal. http://community.livejournal.com/lj_dev/683939.html, May 2005. Retrieved 2010-06-30.

[Florencio & Herley 2007] Dinei Florencio and Cormac Herley. *A large-scale study of web password habits*. In WWW '07: Proceedings of the 16th international conference on World Wide Web, pages 657–666, New York, NY, USA, 2007. ACM Press.

[Ford & Kaliski 2000] Warwick Ford and Jr. Burton S. Kaliski. *Server-Assisted Generation of a Strong Secret from a Password*. In WETICE '00: Proceedings of the 9th IEEE International Workshops on Enabling Technologies, pages 176–180, Washington, DC, USA, 2000. IEEE Computer Society.

[Franks *et al.* 1997] J. Franks, P. Hallam-Baker, J. Hostetler, P. Leach, A. Luotonen, E. Sink and L. Stewart. *An Extension to HTTP : Digest Access Authentication (RFC 2069)*, 1997.

[Franks *et al.* 1999] J. Franks, P. Hallam-Baker, J. Hostetler, S. Lawrence, P. Leach, A. Luotonen and L. Stewart. *HTTP Authentication: Basic and Digest Access Authentication (RFC 2617)*, 1999.

[Fukuyama 1995] Francis Fukuyama. Trust: The social virtues and the creation of prosperity. Free Press, New York, NY, USA, 1995.

[Gambetta 1988] Diego Gambetta. *Can we trust trust*. In Trust: Making and Breaking Cooperative Relations, pages 213–237. Basil Blackwell, 1988.

[García & Tummarello 2006] Roberto García and Giovanni Tummarello. *Semantic Digital Rights Management for Controlled P2P RDF Metadata Diffusion*. In 2nd International Semantic Web Policy Workshop (SWPW'06), November 2006.

[García *et al.* 2007] Roberto García, Rosa Gil and Jaime Delgado. *A web ontologies framework for digital rights management*. Artif. Intell. Law, vol. 15, no. 2, pages 137–154, 2007.

[García 2006] Roberto García. *A Semantic Web Approach to Digital Rights Management*. PhD thesis, Computer Science and Digital Communication Department of Technology, Universitat Pompeu Fabra, 2006.

[Garfinkel & Spafford 2001] Simson Garfinkel and Gene Spafford. Web security, privacy and commerce. O'Reilly & Associates, Inc., Sebastopol, CA, USA, 2001.

[Garfinkel 2004] Simson Garfinkel. *Fingerprinting Your Files. MIT Technology Review*. Technical report, August 2004.

[Gefen 2000] David Gefen. *E-commerce: the role of familiarity and trust*. Omega, vol. 28, no. 6, pages 725 – 737, 2000.

[Genov 2007] Eugene P. Genov. *Digital watermarking of bitmap images*. In CompSysTech '07: Proceedings of the 2007 international conference on Computer systems and technologies, pages 1–6, New York, NY, USA, 2007. ACM.

[Gentry *et al.* 2005] Craig Gentry, Philip Mackenzie and Zulfikar Ramzan. *Password authenticated key exchange using hidden smooth subgroups.* In CCS '05: Proceedings of the 12th ACM conference on Computer and communications security, pages 299–309, New York, NY, USA, 2005. ACM.

[Gentry *et al.* 2006] Craig Gentry, Philip MacKenzie and Zulfikar Ramzan. *A Method for Making Password-Based Key Exchange Resilient to Server Compromise.* In CRYPTO, pages 142–159, 2006.

[Gerck 2000] Ed Gerck. *Overview of Certification Systems: X.509, PKIX, CA, PGP and SKIP.* The Bell, 1(3):8, july 2000.

[Gil & Zibin 2005] Joseph Gil and Yoav Zibin. *Efficient algorithms for isomorphisms of simple types.* Mathematical. Structures in Comp. Sci., vol. 15, no. 5, pages 917–957, 2005.

[Golbeck & Hendler 2006] Jennifer Golbeck and James Hendler. *Filmtrust: Movie recommendations using trust in web-based social networks.* In Proceedings of the Consumer Communications and Networking Conference, 2006.

[Golbeck *et al.* 2003] Jennifer Golbeck, Bijan Parsia and James Hendler. *Trust Management for the Semantic Web.* In Proceedings of Cooperative Intelligent Agents, http://www.mindswap.org/papers/CIA03.pdf, 2003.

[Golbeck 2005] Jennifer Golbeck. *Computing and Applying Trust in Web-based Social Networks.* PhD thesis, University of Maryland, 2005.

[Goldreich & Krawczyk 1990] Oded Goldreich and Hugo Krawczyk. *On the composition of zero-knowledge proof systems.* In Proceedings of the seventeenth international colloquium on Automata, languages and programming, pages 268–282, New York, NY, USA, 1990. Springer-Verlag New York, Inc.

[Goldreich & Krawczyk 1996] Oded Goldreich and Hugo Krawczyk. *On the Composition of Zero-Knowledge Proof Systems.* SIAM J. Comput., vol. 25, no. 1, pages 169–192, 1996.

[Goldreich *et al.* 1988] Oded Goldreich, Silvio Micali and Avi Wigderson. *Proofs that Yield Nothing but their Validity.* Technical report, Technion, 1988. Technical Report #498, preliminary version in FOCS 86.

[Goldreich 2002] Oded Goldreich. *Concurrent zero-knowledge with timing, revisited.* In STOC, pages 332–340, 2002.

[Goldwasser *et al.* 1985] Shafi Goldwasser, Silvio Micali and Charles Rackoff. *The knowledge complexity of interactive proof-systems.* In STOC '85: Proceedings of the seventeenth annual ACM symposium on Theory of computing, pages 291–304, New York, NY, USA, 1985. ACM Press.

[Gong *et al.* 1993] L. Gong, M. A. Lomas, R. M. Needham and J. H. Saltzer. *Protecting Poorly Chosen Secrets from Guessing Attacks.* IEEE Journal on Selected Areas in Communications, vol. 11, no. 5, pages 648–656, 1993.

[Grzonkowski & Corcoran 2009] Sławomir Grzonkowski and Peter M. Corcoran. *A Secure and Efficient Micropayment Solution for Online Gaming.* In Proceedings of the International IEEE Consumer Electronics Society's Games Innovations Conference 2009 (ICE-GIC 09), 2009.

[Grzonkowski & Kruk 2006] Sławomir Grzonkowski and Sebastian Ryszard Kruk. *HyperCuP Lightweight Implementation: A Universal Solution for Making Application Distributed*. In 3rd European Semantic Web Conference (ESWC 2006), 2006.

[Grzonkowski & Kruk 2007] Sławomir Grzonkowski and Sebastian Ryszard Kruk. *FOAF-Realm Ontology Description*. Technical report, DERI, January 2007.

[Grzonkowski & McDaniel 2008] Sławomir Grzonkowski and Bill McDaniel. *FRM: Towards a Semantic Platform for Fair Content Distribution*. In AXMEDIS '08: Proceedings of the Fourth International Conference on Automated Production of Cross Media Content for Multi-Channel Distribution. IEEE Computer Society, November 2008.

[Grzonkowski & Zaremba 2008] Sławomir Grzonkowski and Wojciech Zaremba. *A method and apparatus for authenticating a user*. Patent Pending, January 2008. Patent App. S2008/0001.

[Grzonkowski *et al.* 2005] Sławomir Grzonkowski, Adam Gzella, Henryk Krawczyk, Sebastian Ryszard Kruk, Francisco J. Martin-Recuerda Moyano and Tomasz Woroniecki. *D-FOAF - Security Aspects in Distributed User Management System*. In Proceedings of IEEE International Conference of Technologies for Homeland Security and Safety. (TEHOSS 2005), 2005.

[Grzonkowski *et al.* 2007] Sławomir Grzonkowski, Brian D. Ensor, Sebastian Ryszard Kruk, Adam Gzella, Stefan Decker and Bill McDaniel. *A DRM Solution Based on Social Networks and Enabling the Idea of Fair Use*. In Procedings of Media in Transition 5, April 2007.

[Grzonkowski *et al.* 2008a] Sławomir Grzonkowski, Sebastian Ryszard Kruk, Adam Gzella, Jakub Demczuk and Bill McDaniel. *Community-aware Ontologies*. In Sebastian Ryszard Kruk and Bill McDaniel, editors, Semantic Digital Libraries, pages 125–139. Springer, 2008. ISBN: 978-3-540-85433-3.

[Grzonkowski *et al.* 2008b] Sławomir Grzonkowski, Wojciech Zaremba, Maciej Zaremba and Bill McDaniel. *Extending Web Applications with a Lightweight Zero Knowledge Proof Authentication*. In CSTST '08: Proceedings of the 5th international conference on Soft computing as transdisciplinary science and technology, pages 65–70, New York, NY, USA, 2008. ACM.

[Grzonkowski *et al.* 2009] Sławomir Grzonkowski, Adam Gzella, Sebastian Ryszard Kruk, John G. Breslin, Tomasz Woroniecki and Jarosław Dobrzanski. *Sharing information across community portals with FOAFRealm*. Int. J. Web Based Communities, vol. 5, no. 3, pages 351–370, 2009.

[Grzonkowski *et al.* 2010] Sławomir Grzonkowski, Brian D. Ensor and Bill McDaniel. *Applied Cryptography in Electronic Commerce*. In Hamid R. Nemati and Li Yang, editors, Applied Cryptography for Cyber Security and Defense: Information Encryption and Cyphering, pages 125–147. IGI Global, 2010. (to appear).

[Grzonkowski 2010] Sławomir Grzonkowski. *SeDiCi: An Authentication Service Taking Advantage of Zero-Knowledge Proofs*. In Financial Cryptography. Springer, 2010.

[Guillou & Quisquater 1988] L. C. Guillou and J.-J. Quisquater. *A practical zero-knowledge protocol fitted to security microprocessor minimizing both transmission and memory*. In Lecture Notes in Computer Science on Advances in Cryptology-EUROCRYPT'88, pages 123–128, New York, NY, USA, 1988. Springer-Verlag New York, Inc.

[Halderman *et al.* 2005] J. Alex Halderman, Brent Waters and Edward W. Felten. *A convenient method for securely managing passwords*. In WWW '05: Proceedings of the 14th international conference on World Wide Web, pages 471–479, New York, NY, USA, 2005. ACM Press.

[Halevi & Krawczyk 1999] Shai Halevi and Hugo Krawczyk. *Public-Key Cryptography and Password Protocols*. ACM Transactions on Information and System Security, vol. 2, no. 3, pages 25–60, 1999.

[Hardt 2004] Dick Hardt. *Personal Digital Identity Management*. In FOAF Workshop proceedings, 2004.

[Hilty *et al.* 2007] Manuel Hilty, Alexander Pretschner, David A. Basin, Christian Schaefer and Thomas Walter. *A Policy Language for Distributed Usage Control*. In ESORICS, pages 531–546, 2007.

[Hogg 2009] Tad Hogg. *Security challenges for reputation mechanisms using online social networks*. In AISec '09: Proceedings of the 2nd ACM workshop on Security and artificial intelligence, pages 31–34, New York, NY, USA, 2009. ACM.

[Hua-jun *et al.* 2007] Huang Hua-jun, Sun Xing-ming, Sun Guang and Huang Jun-wei. *Detection of steganographic information in tags of webpage*. In InfoScale '07: Proceedings of the 2nd international conference on Scalable information systems, pages 1–2. ICST (Institute for Computer Sciences, Social-Informatics and Telecommunications Engineering), 2007.

[Hwang *et al.* 2003] Yong Ho Hwang, Dae Hyun Yum and Pil Joong Lee. *EPA: An Efficient Password-Based Protocoal for Authenticated Key Exchange*. In Reihaneh Safavi-Naini and Jennifer Seberry, editors, ACISP, volume 2727 of *Lecture Notes in Computer Science*, pages 452–463. Springer, 2003.

[Iannella 2002] Renato Iannella. *Open Digital Rights Language Specification v1.1*. Technical report, IPR Systems, Ltd., Sydney, 2002. http://www.w3.org/TR/odrl/.

[Iannella 2005] Renato Iannella. *ODRL Creative Commons Profile*. Technical report, ODRL Initiative, July 2005. http://odrl.net/Profiles/CC/SPEC.html.

[Jablon 1996] David P. Jablon. *Strong password-only authenticated key exchange*. SIGCOMM Comput. Commun. Rev., vol. 26, no. 5, pages 5–26, 1996.

[Jackson *et al.* 2005] Margaret Jackson, Supriya Singh, Jenine Beekhuyzen and Jenny Waycott. *DRMs, fair use and users' experience of sharing music*. In DRM '05: Proceedings of the 5th ACM workshop on Digital rights management, pages 8–16, New York, NY, USA, 2005. ACM Press.

[Jagatic *et al.* 2007] Tom N. Jagatic, Nathaniel A. Johnson, Markus Jakobsson and Filippo Menczer. *Social phishing*. Commun. ACM, vol. 50, no. 10, pages 94–100, 2007.

[Jajodia *et al.* 2001] Sushil Jajodia, Pierangela Samarati, Maria Luisa Sapino and V. S. Subrahmanian. *Flexible support for multiple access control policies.* ACM Trans. Database Syst., vol. 26, no. 2, pages 214–260, 2001.

[Jeong *et al.* 2007] Senator Jeong, Sławomir Grzonkowski, Sungin Lee and Hong-Gee Kim. *Semantically Enhanced Event Description.* In 5th Annual Conference on Teaching and Learning: Learning Technologies, June 2007.

[Jobs 2007] Steve Jobs. *Thoughts on Music,* February 2007.

[John Leyden 2002] John Leyden. *Alan Cox attacks the European DMCA. The Register, UK.,* 2002.

[Jonansen 1999] Jon Jonansen. *The Truth about DVD CSS cracking,* Nov 1999.

[Jøsang 1999] Audun Jøsang. *An Algebra for Assessing Trust in Certification Chains.* In NDSS, 1999.

[Jung *et al.* 2004] Han-Seung Jung, Young-Yoon Lee and Sang Uk Lee. *RST-resilient video watermarking using scene-based feature extraction.* EURASIP J. Appl. Signal Process., vol. 2004, no. 1, pages 2113–2131, 2004.

[Kamvar *et al.* 2003] Sepandar D. Kamvar, Mario T. Schlosser and Hector Garcia-Molina. *The Eigentrust algorithm for reputation management in P2P networks.* In WWW, pages 640–651, 2003.

[Kaye 2004] Robert Kaye. *Next-Generation File Sharing with Social Networks.* http://www.openp2p.com/pub/a/p2p/2004/03/05/file_share.html, 2004.

[Klein 1983] Melville H. Klein. *Trusted Computer System Evaluation Criteria.* Technical report, The MITRE Corporation, August 1983.

[Kleinberg 2001] J. Kleinberg. *Small-world phenomena and the dynamics of information,* 2001.

[Klensin *et al.* 1997] J. Klensin, R. Catoe and P. Krumviede. *IMAP/POP AUTHorize Extension for Simple Challenge/Response (RFC 2195),* 1997.

[Knuth 1997] Donald E. Knuth. Seminumerical algorithms, volume 2 of *The Art of Computer Programming.* Addison-Wesley, third édition, 1997.

[Koblitz 1987] Neal Koblitz. *Elliptic Curve Cryptosystems.* "j-MATH-COMPUT", vol. 48, no. 177, pages 203–209, January 1987.

[Koenen *et al.* 2004] R.H. Koenen, J. Lacy, M. Mackay and S. Mitchell. *The long march to interoperable digital rights management.* Proceedings of the IEEE, vol. 92, no. 6, pages 883–897, June 2004.

[Kruk *et al.* 2006a] Sebastian Ryszard Kruk, Slawomir Grzonkowski, Adam Gzella and Mariusz Cygan. *DigiMe - Ubiquitous Search and Browsing for Digital Libraries.* In MDM '06: Proceedings of the 7th International Conference on Mobile Data Management, page 84, Washington, DC, USA, 2006. IEEE Computer Society.

[Kruk *et al.* 2006b] Sebastian Ryszard Kruk, Sławomir Grzonkowski, Adam Gzella, Tomasz Woroniecki and Hee-Chul Choi. *D-FOAF: Distributed Identity Management with Access Rights Delegation.* In Procedings of Asian Semantic Web Conference 2006, September 2006.

[Kruk *et al.* 2006c] Sebastian Ryszard Kruk, Adam Gzella and Sławomir Grzonkowski. *D-FOAF: Distributed Identity Management based on Social Networks*. In 3rd European Semantic Web Conference (ESWC 2006) - Demos and Posters, 2006.

[Kruk 2004] Sebastian R. Kruk. *FOAF-Realm - control your friends' access to the resource*. In FOAF Workshop proceedings, 2004.

[Kwon 2000] Taekyoung Kwon. *Authentication and Key Agreement via Memorable Password*. Technical Report 2000/26, 2000.

[LaMacchia 2002] Brian A. LaMacchia. *Key Challenges in DRM: An Industry Perspective*. In Digital Rights Management Workshop, pages 51–60, 2002.

[Lampson 1971] Butler W. Lampson. *Protection*. In Proceedings of the 5th Princeton Conference on Information Sciences and Systems, pages 437–443. Reprinted in ACM Operat. Syst. Rev. 8, 1, 18-24, 1974, 1971.

[Lampson 1974] Butler W. Lampson. *Protection*. SIGOPS Oper. Syst. Rev., vol. 8, no. 1, pages 18–24, 1974.

[Lessig 2004] Lawrence Lessig. *The Creative Commons*. Montana Law Review, no. winter, pages 1–13, 2004.

[Liu *et al.* 2003] Qiong Liu, Reihaneh Safavi-Naini and Nicholas Paul Sheppard. *Digital rights management for content distribution*. In ACSW Frontiers '03: Proceedings of the Australasian information security workshop conference on ACSW frontiers 2003, pages 49–58, Darlinghurst, Australia, Australia, 2003. Australian Computer Society, Inc.

[MacKenzie *et al.* 2002] P. MacKenzie, T. Shrimpton and M. Jakobsson. *Threshold password-authenticated key exchange*, 2002.

[MacNeill 1929] Eoin MacNeill. *Archaisms in the Ogham Inscriptions*. Proceedings of the Royal Irish Academy. Section C: Archaeology, Celtic Studies, History, Linguistics, Literature, vol. 39, pages pp. 33–53, 1929.

[McCoy 2007] Bill McCoy. *Steve Jobs: "Eliminate Music DRM!": So, What About eBooks?* http://blogs.adobe.com/billmccoy/2007/02/steve_jobs_elim.html, February 2007.

[McKinley 2004] Holly Lynne McKinley. *Digital Rights Management & XML Protocols: Head-to-Head or Hand-in-Hand*. In Annual Computer Security Applications Conference, 2004.

[Medvinsky & Hur 1999] A. Medvinsky and M. Hur. *Addition of Kerberos Cipher Suites to Transport Layer Security (TLS) (RFC 2712)*, 1999.

[Memon & Wong 1998] Nasir Memon and Ping Wah Wong. *Protecting digital media content*. Commun. ACM, vol. 41, no. 7, pages 35–43, 1998.

[Menezes *et al.* 1996] Alfred J. Menezes, Scott A. Vanstone and Paul C. Van Oorschot. Handbook of applied cryptography. CRC Press, Inc., Boca Raton, FL, USA, 1996.

[Michiels *et al.* 2005] Sam Michiels, Kristof Verslype, Wouter Joosen and Bart De Decker. *Towards a software architecture for DRM*. In DRM '05: Proceedings of the 5th ACM workshop on Digital rights management, pages 65–74, New York, NY, USA, 2005. ACM.

[Microsoft Corporation 2004] Microsoft Corporation. *Architecture of Windows Media Rights Manager*, 2004.

[Milgram 1967] Stanley Milgram. *The Small World Problem*. Psychology Today, pages 60–67, May 1967.

[Miller 1968] Robert B. Miller. *Response Time in Man-Computer Conversational Transactions*. In Proc. AFIPS Fall Joint Computer Conference Vol. 33, pages 267–277, San Francisco, Calif, 1968.

[Miller 1986] Victor S Miller. *Use of elliptic curves in cryptography*. In Lecture notes in computer sciences; 218 on Advances in cryptology—CRYPTO 85, pages 417–426, New York, NY, USA, 1986. Springer-Verlag New York, Inc.

[Mitnick & Simon 2002] Kevin Mitnick and William L. Simon. The Art of Deception. 2002.

[Morris & Thompson 1979] Robert Morris and Ken Thompson. *Password Security: A Case History*. Communications of the ACM, vol. 22, pages 594–597, 1979.

[Mourad *et al.* 2005] Magda Mourad, Gerard L. Hanley, Barbra Bied Sperling and Jack K. Gunther. *Toward an Electronic Marketplace for Higher Education*. IEEE Computer 38(6), pages 66–75, 2005.

[Musser & O'Reilly 2006] John Musser and Tim O'Reilly. Web 2.0 principles and best practices. O'Reilly, 2006. ISBN 0-596-52769-1.

[Narayanan & Shmatikov 2005] Arvind Narayanan and Vitaly Shmatikov. *Fast dictionary attacks on passwords using time-space tradeoff*. In CCS '05: Proceedings of the 12th ACM conference on Computer and communications security, pages 364–372, New York, NY, USA, 2005. ACM.

[Nasirifard *et al.* 2008] Peyman Nasirifard, Sławomir Grzonkowski and Vassilios Peristeras. *OntoPair: Towards a Collaborative Game for Building OWL-Based Ontologies*. In Proceedings of the CISWeb Workshop, located at the 5th European Semantic Web Conference ESWC 2008, June 2008.

[Needham & Schroeder 1978] Roger M. Needham and Michael D. Schroeder. *Using encryption for authentication in large networks of computers*. Commun. ACM, vol. 21, no. 12, pages 993–999, 1978.

[Neuman & Ts'o 1994] B. Clifford Neuman and Theodore Ts'o. *Kerberos: An Authentication Service for Computer Networks*. In IEEE Communications, 32(9):33-38, September 1994.

[Neuman *et al.* 2005] Clifford Neuman, T. Yu, S. Hartman and K. Raeburn. *The Kerberos Network Authentication System (RFC4120)*, July 2005.

[Neumann & Strembeck 2003] Gustaf Neumann and Mark Strembeck. *An approach to engineer and enforce context constraints in an RBAC environment*. In SACMAT '03: Proceedings of the eighth ACM symposium on Access control models and technologies, pages 65–79, New York, NY, USA, 2003. ACM.

[Newman 2000] M. Newman. *Models of the Small World: A Review*, May 2000. Journal of Statistical Physics 101: 819-841.

[Nielsen 1999] Jakob Nielsen. Designing web usability: The practice of simplicity. New Riders Publishing, Thousand Oaks, CA, USA, 1999.

[Nitsche *et al.* 1998] U. Nitsche, R. Holbein, O. Morger and S. Teufel. *Realization of a Context-Dependent Access Control Mechanism on a Commercial Platform.* In In Proc. of the 14th International Information Security Conference (IFIP/SEC, pages 160–170, 1998.

[Oecd 2006] Oecd. *Future Digital Economy: Digital Content Creation, Distribution and Access - Conference conclusions.* OECD Digital Economy Papers 118, OECD Directorate for Science, Technology and Industry, May 2006.

[Oechslin 2003] Philippe Oechslin. *Making a Faster Cryptanalytic Time-Memory Trade-Off.* In The 23rd Annual International Cryptology Conference, CRYPTO '03, volume 2729 of *Lecture Notes in Computer Science*, pages 617–630, 2003.

[O'Nuallain & Grzonkowski 2006] Caoimhin O'Nuallain and Sławomir Grzonkowski. *Collaboration.* In Proceedings of the IADIS International Conference WWW/INTERNET 2006, October 2006.

[O'Nuallain *et al.* 2006] Caoimhin O'Nuallain, Brian Davis, Krystian Samp, Bill McDaniel, Sławomir Grzonkowski and Sebastian Ryszard Kruk. *Search Interface Based on Natural Language Query Templates.* In Proceedings of the IADIS International Conference WWW/INTERNET 2006, October 2006.

[O'Reilly 2005] O'Reilly. *O'Reilly Network: What Is Web 2.0.* 2005.

[Page *et al.* 1999] Lawrence Page, Sergey Brin, Rajeev Motwani and Terry Winograd. *The PageRank Citation Ranking: Bringing Order to the Web.* Technical Report SIDL-WP-1999-0120, Stanford University, November 1999.

[Park & Sandhu 2002] Jaehong Park and Ravi Sandhu. *Towards usage control models: beyond traditional access control.* In SACMAT '02: Proceedings of the seventh ACM symposium on Access control models and technologies, pages 57–64, New York, NY, USA, 2002. ACM.

[Park & Sandhu 2004] Jaehong Park and Ravi Sandhu. *The UCONABC usage control model.* ACM Transactions on Information and System Security, vol. 7, no. 1, pages 128–174, 2004.

[Parrott 2001] David Parrott. *Requirements for a rights data dictionary and rights expression language.* Technical report, Reuters Ltd., June 2001.

[Petty & Cacioppo 1986] R.E. Petty and J.T Cacioppo. The elaboration likelihood model of persuasion. New York: Academic Press, 1986.

[Pinkas & Sander 2002] Benny Pinkas and Tomas Sander. *Securing passwords against dictionary attacks.* In CCS '02: Proceedings of the 9th ACM conference on Computer and communications security, pages 161–170, New York, NY, USA, 2002. ACM.

[Podilchuk & Delp 2001] Christine I. Podilchuk and Edward J. Delp. *Digital watermarking: algorithms and applications.* Signal Processing Magazine, IEEE, vol. 18, no. 4, pages 33–46, Jul 2001.

[Popescu *et al.* 2004] Bogdan C. Popescu, Bruno Crispo, Andrew S. Tanenbaum and Frank L.A.J. Kamperman. *A DRM security architecture for home networks.* In DRM '04: Proceedings of the 4th ACM workshop on Digital rights management, pages 1–10, New York, NY, USA, 2004. ACM.

[Rabin 1979] Michael O. Rabin. *DIGITALIZED SIGNATURES AND PUBLIC-KEY FUNC-TIONS AS INTRACTABLE AS FACTORIZATION.* Technical report, Cambridge, MA, USA, 1979.

[Recordon & Reed 2006] David Recordon and Drummond Reed. *OpenID 2.0: a platform for user-centric identity management.* In DIM '06: Proceedings of the second ACM work-shop on Digital identity management, pages 11–16, New York, NY, USA, 2006. ACM Press.

[Rescorla 2000] E. Rescorla. *HTTP Over TLS (RFC 2818)*, 2000.

[Richardson & Kilian 1999] Ransom Richardson and Joe Kilian. *On the Concurrent Composition of Zero-Knowledge Proofs.* In EUROCRYPT, pages 415–431, 1999.

[Rivest *et al.* 1978] R. L. Rivest, A. Shamir and L. Adleman. *A method for obtaining digital sig-natures and public-key cryptosystems.* Commun. ACM, vol. 21, no. 2, pages 120–126, 1978.

[Rivest 1992] Ronald L. Rivest. *The MD5 Message-Digest Algorithm (RFC 1321)*, 1992.

[Rodriguez & Delgado 2006] Eva Rodriguez and Jaime Delgado. *Towards the Interoperability between MPEG-21 REL and Creative Commons Licenses.* In AXMEDIS '06: Proceedings of the Second International Conference on Automated Production of Cross Media Con-tent for Multi-Channel Distribution, pages 45–52, Washington, DC, USA, 2006. IEEE Computer Society.

[Rosenblatt & Dykstra 2003] By Bill Rosenblatt and Gail Dykstra. *Integrating content man-agement with digital rights management - imperatives and opportunities for digital content lifecycles.* 2003.

[Rosenblatt 2005] Bill Rosenblatt. *2005 Year in Review: DRM Technologies.* http://www.drmwatch.com/drmtech/article.php/3573381, December 2005.

[Rothman 2007] David Rothman. *Social DRM vs. traditional Mobipocket-style DRM: Time for a switch?* http://www.teleread.org/2007/08/24/social-drm-vs-traditional-mobipocket-style-drm-time-for-a-switch/, August 2007.

[Rowel 2006] Laurie Freeman Rowel. *The ballad of DVD Jon.* netWorker, vol. 10, no. 4, pages 28–34, 2006.

[Samuelson 2003] Pamela Samuelson. *DRM and, or, vs. the law.* Commun. ACM, vol. 46, no. 4, pages 41–45, 2003.

[Samwald & Adlassnig 2008] Matthias Samwald and Klaus-Peter Adlassnig. *The bio-zen plus ontology.* Applied Ontology, vol. 3, no. 4, pages 213–217, 2008.

[Sandhu *et al.* 1996] Ravi S. Sandhu, Edward J. Coyne, Hal L. Feinstein and Charles E. Youman. *Role-Based Access Control Models.* Computer, vol. 29, no. 2, pages 38–47, 1996.

[Sandhu *et al.* 2000] Ravi Sandhu, David Ferraiolo and Richard Kuhn. *The NIST model for role-based access control: towards a unified standard*. In RBAC '00: Proceedings of the fifth ACM workshop on Role-based access control, pages 47–63, New York, NY, USA, 2000. ACM.

[Schneier 2005] Bruce Schneier. *Two-factor authentication: too little, too late*. Commun. ACM, vol. 48, no. 4, page 136, 2005.

[Schneier 2006] Bruce Schneier. *MySpace Passwords Aren't So Dumb*. Technical report, 2006.

[Schneier 2008] Bruce Schneier. *Mitigating Identity Theft*. In Bruce Schneier, editor, Schneier on Security, pages 205–208. Wiley Publishing, Inc., 2008. ISBN: 978-0-470-39535-6.

[Schnorr 1989] Claus-Peter Schnorr. *Efficient Identification and Signatures for Smart Cards*. In CRYPTO, pages 239–252, 1989.

[Schöning 1987] Uwe Schöning. *Graph Isomorphism is in the Low Hierarchy*. In STACS '87: Proceedings of the 4th Annual Symposium on Theoretical Aspects of Computer Science, pages 114–124, London, UK, 1987. Springer-Verlag.

[Shen & Dewan 1992] HongHai Shen and Prasun Dewan. *Access Control for Collaborative Environments*. In Jon Turner and Robert Kraut, editors, Proc ACM Conf. Computer-Supported Cooperative Work, CSCW, pages 51–58. ACM Press, 1992.

[Sheppard & Safavi-Naini 2006] Nicholas Paul Sheppard and Reihaneh Safavi-Naini. *Sharing digital rights with domain licensing*. In MCPS '06: Proceedings of the 4th ACM international workshop on Contents protection and security, pages 3–12, New York, NY, USA, 2006. ACM Press.

[Shor 1997] Peter W. Shor. *Polynomial-time algorithms for prime factorization and discrete logarithms on a quantum computer*. SIAM Journal on Computing, vol. 26, pages 1484–1509, 1997.

[Simpson & Weiner 1971] John Simpson and Edmund Weiner. Oxford english dictionary, page 3423. Oxford: Oxford University Press, the compact édition, 1971.

[Spielman 1996] Daniel A. Spielman. *Faster isomorphism testing of strongly regular graphs*. In STOC '96: Proceedings of the twenty-eighth annual ACM symposium on Theory of computing, pages 576–584, New York, NY, USA, 1996. ACM Press.

[Staab *et al.* 2004] Steffen Staab, Bharat Bhargava, Leszek Lilien, Arnon Rosenthal, Marianne Winslett, Morris Sloman, Tharam S. Dillon, Elizabeth Chang, Farookh Khadeer Hussain, Wolfgang Nejdl, Daniel Olmedilla and Vipul Kashyap. *The Pudding of Trust*. IEEE Intelligent Systems, vol. 19, no. 5, pages 74–88, 2004.

[Story *et al.* 2009] Henry Story, Bruno Harbulot, Ian Jacobi and Mike Jones. *FOAF+TLS: RESTful Authentication for the Social Web*. In Trust and Privacy on the Social and Semantic Web-SPOT2009, 2009.

[Thompson *et al.* 2003] Mary R. Thompson, Abdelilah Essiari and Srilekha Mudumbai. *Certificate-based authorization policy in a PKI environment*. ACM Trans. Inf. Syst. Secur., vol. 6, no. 4, pages 566–588, 2003.

[Ullmann 1976] J. R. Ullmann. *An Algorithm for Subgraph Isomorphism.* J. ACM, vol. 23, no. 1, pages 31–42, 1976.

[Ureche *et al.* 2008] Oana Ureche, Giovanni Tummarello, Mark Leyden, Peter Corcoran and Bill McDaniel. *Amulet - An Implementation Of A Digital Rights Management Trusted System Applied To Scorm Compliant Content.* In Miguel Baptista Nunes and Maggie McPherson, editors, e-Learning, pages 317–324. IADIS, 2008.

[Ureche 2009] Oana-Elena Ureche. *Digital Rights Management applied to SCORM content. MSc thesis,* 2009.

[Wagner & Schneier 1996] David Wagner and Bruce Schneier. *Analysis of the SSL 3.0 protocol.* In In Proceedings of the Second UNIX Workshop on Electronic Commerce, pages 29–40. USENIX Association, 1996.

[Wang *et al.* 2008] Xiang-Yang Wang, Pan-Pan Niu and Wei Qi. *A new adaptive digital audio watermarking based on support vector machine.* J. Netw. Comput. Appl., vol. 31, no. 4, pages 735–749, 2008.

[Wang 2004] Xin Wang. *MPEG-21 Rights Expression Language: Enabling Interoperable Digital Rights Management.* IEEE MultiMedia, vol. 11, no. 4, pages 84–87, 2004.

[Watts *et al.* 2002] D. J. Watts, P. S. Dodds and M. E. J. Newman. *Identity and Search in Social Networks.* Science, vol. 296. no. 5571, pages 1302 – 1305, May 2002.

[Wegman & Carter 1981] Mark N. Wegman and Larry Carter. *New Hash Functions and Their Use in Authentication and Set Equality.* J. Comput. Syst. Sci., vol. 22, no. 3, pages 265–279, 1981.

[Weibel *et al.* 1998] S. Weibel, J. Kunze, C. Lagoze and M. Wolf. *Dublin Core Metadata for Resource Discovery,* 1998.

[Wen-Guey & Chi-Ming 1999] Tzeng Wen-Guey and Hu Chi-Ming. *Inter-protocol interleaving attacks on some authentication and key distribution protocols.* Information Processing Letters, vol. 69, no. 6, pages 297 – 302, 1999.

[Wolfgang *et al.* 1999] Raymond B. Wolfgang, Christine I. Podilchuk and Edward J. Delp. *Perceptual watermarks for digital images and video.* Proceedings of the IEEE, vol. 87, no. 7, pages 1108–1126, Jul 1999.

[Woo & Lam 1993] Thomas Y. C. Woo and Simon S. Lam. *A framework for distributed authorization.* In CCS '93: Proceedings of the 1st ACM conference on Computer and communications security, pages 112–118, New York, NY, USA, 1993. ACM Press.

[Wu 1998] Thomas Wu. *The Secure Remote Password Protocol.* In Proceedings of the 1998 Internet Society Network and Distributed System Security Symposium, pages 97–111, 1998.

[Wu 2000] T. Wu. *The SRP Authentication and Key Exchange System (RFC 2945),* 2000.

[Xia & Brustoloni 2005] Haidong Xia and José Carlos Brustoloni. *Hardening Web browsers against man-in-the-middle and eavesdropping attacks.* In WWW '05: Proceedings of the 14th international conference on World Wide Web, pages 489–498, New York, NY, USA, 2005. ACM Press.

[Xiong & Liu 2002] Li Xiong and Ling Liu. *Building Trust in Decentralized Peer-to-Peer Electronic Communities*. In Fifth International Conference on Electronic Commerce Research (ICECR-5), 2002.

[Yang *et al.* 2009] Yafei Yang, Yan Lindsay Sun, Steven Kay and Qing Yang. *Defending online reputation systems against collaborative unfair raters through signal modeling and trust*. In SAC '09: Proceedings of the 2009 ACM symposium on Applied Computing, pages 1308–1315, New York, NY, USA, 2009. ACM.

[Yen *et al.* 2005] John Yen, Robert Popp, George Cybenko, Latanya Sweeney, K.A. Taipale and Paul Rosenzweig. *Homeland Security*. IEEE Intelligent Systems, vol. 20, no. 5, pages 76–86, 2005.

[Yu *et al.* 2004] Tom Yu, Sam Hartman and Ken Raeburn. *The Perils of Unauthenticated Encryption: Kerberos Version 4*. In Proceedings of the Network and Distributed System Security Symposium. The Internet Society, 2004.

[Zhang *et al.* 2008] Xinwen Zhang, Masayuki Nakae, Michael J. Covington and Ravi Sandhu. *Toward a Usage-Based Security Framework for Collaborative Computing Systems*. ACM Transactions on Information and System Security, vol. 11, no. 1, pages 1–36, 2008.

[Zhang 2004] Muxiang Zhang. *Analysis of the SPEKE password-authenticated key exchange protocol*. Communications Letters, IEEE, vol. 8, no. 1, pages 63–65, Jan. 2004.

[Zimmermann 1995] Philip R. Zimmermann. The official pgp user's guide. MIT Press, Cambridge, MA, USA, 1995.

List of Figures

1.1 Thesis organization and relations between the chapters 10

2.1 An example of access matrix model 19

2.2 Role Based Access Control model [Sandhu *et al.* 1996] 19

2.3 A typical-DRM architecture 25

2.4 The entities of the ODRL model 26

2.5 A watermark insertion algorithm 28

2.6 A watermark extraction algorithm 29

2.7 Usage Control Model [Zhang *et al.* 2008] 30

2.8 UCON coverage [Park & Sandhu 2004] 31

3.1 Kerberos authentication protocol 44

3.2 OpenID authentication protocol 45

5.1 Conceptual scenario 64

5.2 FRM Usage Control Model 65

5.3 Structure of Authorization Decision 67

6.1 A generic zero-knowledge proof protocol 72

6.2 An example graph isomorphism for $G_2 = \pi(G_1)$. 75

7.1 The conceptual model of the FRM platform 80

7.2   The proposed mapping of Creative Commons licenses to Rights Expression Languages (REL)   86

7.3   Key classes and properties of integrated ontology for rights management   . . .   87

7.4   Applied file watermarking method   89

7.5   ZKP implementation on the Web   92

7.6   The process of conversion a password to permutation   93

7.7   An example of an initial Alice's profile   99

7.8   An example of a Bob's offer containing the sale offer accessible on two different terms and conditions   99

7.9   The Alice's profile after the transaction with Bob   100

8.1   Tests for Firefox   107

8.2   Tests for Safari   107

8.3   Tests for Opera   108

8.4   Tests for Internet Explorer   108

8.5   An alert box informing that a script works too long under Windows   110

8.6   Bytes sent from a browser to a server during an authentication request (Bytes sent 1) and responding to the challenge (Bytes sent 2)   111

8.7   Time necessary in Firefox to send graphs and receive challenge question (partial time prediction) and authentication time based on sampled data   113

8.8   Regression models of the expected number of challenges for various browsers during authentication   115

8.9   The proposed protocol   116

8.10 Results for the concurrent composition ($\beta = \alpha = 1100ms$).   117

8.11 Time measurements conclusion   120

List of Tables

3.1 The main vulnerabilities of authentication protocols based on [Menezes *et al.* 1996] 39

3.2 Various authentication protocols and their vulnerabilities. — stands for the lack of support of a given requirement or vulnerability. ✓stands for resistance to a given problem or requirement support 49

4.1 Classes and properties of FOAF grouped into categories (based on [Dan Brickley and Libby Miller 2005]) 55

7.1 Summary of the principle Creative Commons licenses 84

8.1 The approximate number of attempts to perform the interrupted sessions attack with a given confidence and the number of challenges 112

8.2 Obtained time results for requesting the challenge vector from the verifier using the firefox browser 113

8.3 Estimated time to perform a successful impersonation attempt using the nested sessions attack with a given success confidence 114

8.4 Time prediction for brute force attacks on short passwords 118

C.1 Sampled authentication time for Firefox 142

C.2 Sampled authentication time for Internet Explorer 142

C.3 Sampled authentication time for Opera 143

C.4 Sampled authentication time for Safari 143

C.5 Sampled data for Internet Explorer for various β values (* these samples were not approved because of timeout) 143

C.6 Sampled authentication times for concurrent protocol composition for various browsers for $\beta = 1100$ 144

Glossary

Access Control Access control is an important aspect of computer security. It allows to permit or deny the use of a particular resource by a particular entity. It also defines the ways in which users can access systems resources.

Creative Commons licenses Creative Commons licenses (CC) were proposed and released by Creative Commons, a non-profit organization founded by Lawrence Lessig. The licenses allow the content creators to indicate if they would like to waive any of the rights for the benefit of others.

D-FOAF This is a distributed version of FOAFRealm, in which servers exchange information about users' profiles.

DRM Digital Rights Management (DRM) extends the scope of access control to client-side devices. This has led to an evolution in the original concept of RBAC, as DRM is not only responsible for providing access control, but also for protecting the content after access is given to the user. Thus, to success, it has to provide access control regardless the data location.

E-commerce E-commerce at its most basic is commerce as usual but transacted using electronic communication methods such as the telephone or internet.

FOAF The Friend-of-a-Friend (FOAF) vocabulary was created to support the publication of machine readable user profile descriptions as well as describing users' online social networks. The vocabulary consists of semantic web vocabularies such as RDF, RDFS, OWL.

FOAFRealm It is an authentication and trust management system using FOAF and social networks.

MITM Man In The Middle (MITM) is an important authentication problem that is relevant for any authentication protocol using just one communication channel that does not exclude the possibility of the presence of intermediate parties.

Ontology An ontology is a formal specification of knowledge by a set of concepts within a domain and the relationships between those concepts.

OWL The Web Ontology Language defined by W3C. It is built on the foundations of RDF(S)and XML. It is extensively used in the Semantic Web. See also `http://www.w3.org/TR/owl-ref/`.

RBAC Role-based Access Control (RBAC) was that the permissions should no longer be directly assigned to subjects (users), but rather to roles which are assigned to the subjects.

REL Rights Expression Languages (REL) assist in the expression and understanding of authorized actions. RELs operate as a formal agreement between systems governing permitted activity which is generated by some defined authority and enforced by another.

RDF Resource Description Framework is a graph-based model for representing knowledge on the Web.

RDF Schema An RDF Schema defines RDF constraints.
See also `http://www.w3.org/TR/rdf-schema/`.

Semantic Web The extension of the current Web with (formal, machine processable) semantics using RDF(S), OWL, etc.

Social Network A structure that consists of nodes that represent individual people or organizations. Such a structure depicts the ways in which people are connected through diverse social familiarities like acquaintance, friendship or close familiar bonds.

Trust Management Trust management focuses on the control of access to server-side objects. This concept, however, relates authorization to a subject's capabilities and properties. Thus, in opposite to access control, trust management enables authorization of strangers.

UCON Usage Control Models (UCON) aim at creation of a distributed usage model that spans many disciplines such as authorization, trust management and DRM

W3C World Wide Web Consortium is an organization lead by Tim Berners-Lee to develop Web standards . See also `http://www.w3c.org/`

WWW World Wide Web (WWW) delivers a system for sharing interlinked hypertext documents that contains text, images and, eventually, other types of media files.

ZKP zero-knowledge proof (ZKP) describes a group of challenge-response authentication protocols, in which parties are required to provide the correctness of their secrets, without revealing these secrets. Such protocols exist for any NP-set, provided that one-way functions exist.

Index

A

Access control, 18, 20
Authentication protocols
    Dictionary attacks, 40, 117
    Vulnerabilities, 38
Authorization decision, 66

C

Creative Commons, 83
    Example, 84
    Licenses, 83
    Ontology, 83

D

D-FOAF, 82, 83
Digital Rights Management, *see* DRM
Digital watermarking, 28, 88
    Applications, 28
DMCA, 23, 28
DRM, 20, 23, 33, 63
    Architecture, 24
    Challenges, 24
    Semantic approach, 27

E

E-commerce, 5

F

Fair Rights Management, *see* FRM
Fair Use
    Definition, 32
    Four factors, 32
    Versus DRM, 33
Fair use, 31, 97
FairPlay, 33
FOAF, 54, 82, 87
    Authentication, 56

    Example, 54
    Trust management, 55
    Vocabulary, 54
FOAFRealm, 53, 82, 87
Friend-of-a-Friend Vocabulary, *see* FOAF
FRM, 64
    Data examples, 139
    Definitions, 67
    Implementation, 79
    Model, 64, 79
    Ontology, 86
    Procedures, 133

G

Graph isomorphism, 75
    Algorithms, 76
    Brute-force, 118

H

HTTPS, 43

K

Kerberos, 43

M

Man In The Middle, *see* MITM
Matrix Access Control, 18
MITM, 6, 39
MPEG REL, 33, 83

N

NEMO, 26

O

OAuth, 46
ODRL, 26, 33, 83, 87
OpenID, 45

P

PAKE, 46

R

RBAC, 19
    framework, 19
REL, 25, 83
Rights Expression Languages, *see* REL
Role-Based Access Control, *see* RBAC

S

S2W, *see* Social Semantic Web
SeDiCi, 90, 152
    Authentication, 91
    Performance, 104
    Protocol, 95
Semantic Web, 7
Six degrees of separation, 51
Social network, 51, 82
Social Semantic Web, 7
SSL, 43

T

Thesis
    Contribution, 128
    Goals, 7
    Motivation, 5
    Reader's guide, 9
Three authentication factors, 18
Trust, 5, 21
    Metrics, 23, 53
    Properties, 53
    Psychological aspects, 22
    Psychological model, 22
    Web of trust, 23
Trust management, 20, 22, 53, 55, 66, 82
    Using social networks, 53
Two-factor authentication, 18

U

UCON, 29
    Coverage, 31
    Model, 29
UCON ABC, 65
Usage Control Model, *see* UCON

W

Web 2.0, 7, 52
Web authentication, 41, 90

FOAF, 56
HTTP Basic, 41
HTTP Digest, 42
World Wide Web, *see* WWW
WWW, 6

X

XFOAF, 87
XrML, 27

Z

Zero Knowledge Proof, *see* ZKP
ZKP, 71
    Approaches, 73
    Compositions, 76
    Concurrent, 77
    Non-interactive, 73
    Number of challenges, 110
    Parallel, 77
    Resettable, 77
    Sequential, 77, 105
    Usability, 78